RURAL WOMEN WORKERS IN ASIA

RURAL WOMEN WORKERS IN ASIA

KN Chaudhary

MD PUBLICATIONS PVT LTD
NEW DELHI
www.mdppl.com

Published by:

MD Publications Pvt Ltd
"MD House", 11, Darya Ganj,
New Delhi - 110 002
Phone : +91-11-45355555
E-mail : contact@mdppl.com
website : www.mdppl.com

ISBN: 978-81-7533-309-3

Published and Printed by Mr. Pranav Gupta on behalf of **MD Publications Pvt Ltd** at JJ offset Printers, Delhi.

Preface

Rural women throughout Asia make critical contributions to household production and consequently to household and national food security. Although the specific nature of their contribution varies among the various Asian countries, clearly the majority of rural women take on an increasing share of household labour and their lives are characterized by mounting drudgery.

The lack of a systematic synthesis of the findings hinders' efforts to build a realistic scenario of rural women's roles in household food security. However, a general pattern of gender roles emerges from these studies indicating that both rural men and rural women in Asia contribute to farm and home production. Gender roles vary within and between countries determined by agro-ecological systems and crops grown, farming systems adopted, linkages with livestock and fish production and opportunities for off-farm occupations in the rural economy.

This analysis of rural women's situation in household production synthesizes information from diverse sources into a framework portraying the diversity and complexity of rural women's contributions. The framework presents linkages among gender specific contributions, drudgery and resource access constraints within the household and community setting. Rural women's role in household production is considered in terms of farm production, home production, off-farm production and community production. The foundations of rural women's contributions can be seen in terms of labour and managerial inputs, as well as local and traditional knowledge and expertise. Rural women's gender roles, the community and household factors that affect women's roles and responsibilities and that affect their access to food and resources.

Rural women throughout Asia work long hours and confront drudgery as a reality of their daily existence. Poor women pursue a number of survival strategies to earn enough cash to feed and maintain their families; one indisputable facet of these strategies is the frequent and inordinate extension of working hours inside and outside the home. A review of case studies provides evidence suggesting that poor access to basic services such as water and sanitation, coupled with the need to search for fuel and food supplements, extends and intensifies the typical day of a rural woman, while adding innumerable difficulties.

Women play important roles in agriculture and food security in rural areas. Any economic strategy for agriculture and rural employment linked to poverty alleviation and food security must, therefore, consider gender equity and women's contributions as central issues in productivity and access to resources. The urban informal sector is also dominated by women as food vendors and small commodity traders earning income for household food security. Moreover, women are the food buyers and those who create use value for food at household level. In all these roles women have a vested interest in the sustainability of ecological resources, the community resource base and local market systems.

I am very grateful to Mr. Pranav Gupta, Director of MD Publications Pvt Ltd, New Delhi, for his kind cooperation and support for this book.

KN Chaudhary

Contents

Contents

1

New Rural Worlds

On the face of it, and despite the industrial growth of the past decades, Southeast Asia remains a region of farmers. Excluding the city state of Singapore and the oil-rich sultanate of Brunei, between 19 per cent (Malaysia) and 78 per cent (Laos) of each country's population are classified as working in the agricultural sector, and between 42 per cent (Philippines) and 84 per cent (Cambodia) as living in rural areas. Weighted according to population, the combined figures for the region as a whole are 50 per cent and 63 per cent respectively. Such statistics lend credence to the belief that the countries of Southeast Asia, like those of most developing regions, are dominated by agriculture. This view has it that the Southeast Asian world is still primarily a rural world; that this rural world is essentially an agricultural world; and, for the truly unreconstructed, that this agricultural world is, or should be, a peasant world.

As McVey explains: 'save for the city-state of Singapore, Southeast Asia has long been imagined as quintessentially agrarian, its symbol the peasant toiling in his paddy-field, and plantations the only real representatives of the modern economic sector'. But 'rural', like 'urban', has become a metaphor for much more than open spaces and green trees: it also implies a way of life, a set of values, and a shared commitment to a certain livelihood. Loaded words like 'community', 'self-reliance', 'indigenous technologies', and 'self sufficiency' are irrevocably associated, in the eyes and minds of many scholars and rural development workers, with the lives and livelihoods of rural people.

From the early 1960s, studies of rural Southeast Asia have made the point that the village economy is undergoing fundamental structural change as the forces of modernization impinge on formerly isolated, inward-looking, self sufficient and agriculturally based communities. Howard Kaufman's community study of Bangkhuad in Bangkapi (in the Central Plains region of Thailand, but now a suburb of Bangkok) concludes that 'Bangkhuad, like most of Thailand, is in the throes of extensive socio-economic change…from a simple, minimum subsistence economy to one of a complex export economy geared to enlarged production'. Kaufman's field research was conducted in 1954 and his book first published in 1960. Many of the characteristics of the 'New Rice Economy' that he identifies are also issues with which this section of the book is concerned: the growing importance of non-farming activities, migration, mechanization and the shift into alternative crops, for example.

Indeed, Kaufman was sufficiently prescient to identify a 'non-farming, urban - salaried - future' for the village. Michael Moerman's research for his community study in Northern Thailand was conducted between 1959 and 1960. Unlike Bangkhuad, Ban Ping was truly isolated - at least in the sense that getting there was not easy. Even so, extra-village links were important in defining the village itself and Moerman identifies a pattern of change not dissimilar from that of Kaufman's study. On his return to Ban Ping in 1965, the degree of 'progress' surprised the author, although he maintained that peasant life, at its core, remained redoubtable:

It is tempting to exaggerate these changes, to suggest that Ban Ping has progressed from insularity to dependence, from status to contract, from Gemeinschaft to Gesellschaft…. Although Ban Ping has indeed progressed towards increasing participation in the nation and in the world market, it is still a peasant village. This chapter is also about change, but focused on economic change. The perturbations in society, culture and politics, though important and profound, are not the main concerns here and will be discussed only in so far as they impinge and relate to economic change. Simply put, the chapter will present the evidence for fundamental and profound change in the economies of rural Southeast Asia.

Like Moerman, it will be argued that this change is, in a strict sense, one of degree rather than kind. The roots of commercialization are bedded deeply in the history of the region. Production for the market, payment in cash, the renting and sale of land, and human mobility all, for example, predate modernization. In this sense, it would be wrong to write that communities have moved from subsistence to market orientation; from family to wage labour; and from autonomy to dependence. Such dichotomies ignore the fact that there have always been market interactions and dependencies and a flourishing non-farm economy. But it might be argued that as degree augments degree, almost imperceptibly, a change of kind occurs.

The observation that rural Southeast Asia is changing is nothing new, but rarely is the breadth and depth of change in 'farming' communities in the developing world clearly set out. Nor, for that matter, are the implications of such changes sufficiently addressed. As a result perhaps, the enduring image of the village is one where a community of farmers gains a livelihood from working the land. Perhaps it is for these reasons that Angeles-Reyes finds that she is able to write that the 'Philippine economy remains predominantly rural.... No fundamental structural transformation has taken place in the economy since the later 1960s' (1994:134), while Chris Dixon in his review of the Thai economy published in 1999 is also able to state that 'the country remains an essentially agricultural one' where the agricultural sector 'remains the principal source of livelihood for some 60 per cent of the population'.

However, it does not take a very deep incision to cut through these layers of image and imagination to reveal the truth that the rural world has quietly but profoundly become a 'new' rural world. This requires a rethinking of the rural economy and rural life, a reappraisal of policy initiatives and planning strategies, and a reformulation of theories of agricultural and rural development. It also, it should be added, emphasizes the point that the modernization ethic has become part of the Southeast Asian landscape, both mental and physical.

VILLAGE IDENTITY AND IDENTIFICATION

Until quite recently, most studies of Southeast Asia assumed that the basic unit of rural life in the region was the village. The village represented the essential unit of identity and organization within which agricultural and other activities occurred. This view was not just restricted to Southeast Asia; Eric Wolf's designation of the village as a 'closed, corporate community' gained wide currency across the developing world (1967). However, from the early 1980s, studies that re-examined the historical evidence began to question whether the village, at least as it exists today, was not, in fact, a creation of the colonial period and our understanding of its structure and function a product of those whose minds were firmly rooted in European conceptions of rural life.

From the end of the nineteenth century, colonial authorities, and in the case of Siam the national authorities, found it necessary to control people and space more closely. To achieve this, a series of administrative reforms were introduced of which the creation of the administrative village (to distinguish it from the traditional village) was one. In Siam, for example, the brilliant and influential prince Damrong Rajanubhab, half-brother of King *Chulailongkorn* (Rama V) and Minister of the Interior, reformed village administration in the early 1890s. Bunnag describes the process as it was implemented near Bang Pa-In in the province of Ayutthaya, north of Bangkok:

Luang Thesachitwichan asked the heads of ten households, whose houses were situated near one another, to elect a village elder phu yai ban. He then asked the elected elders of villages, the number of which was governed by the natural features of the locality, to choose one of themselves as commune tambon elder kamnan.... Phraya Sisuriyaratchawaranuwat...began to persuade the heads of five to twenty households to elect a village elder... and then asked approximately ten village elders to choose a commune elder.

The picture is clearly one where people were manipulated in the interests of state control. The same appears to have been true in Java where the village has been described as a 'harnessed construction' and in Bali where villages became 'rationalized' into administrative communities (desa perbekelan). 'People found themselves', as Vickers puts it, 'in new villages to which they previously never had any connection'. In a similar vein, Shamsul, writing on Malaysia, explains that the village was 'created, recreated, sub-divided, rejoined and sometimes imagined to exist in the name of development'. Space, in short, was bureaucratized to put people in their place. As Scott writes, the intention was 'to enhance the legibility of a society to its rulers'.

This process is important in so far as it has laid the foundations for the impression that Southeast Asia remains a region of farmers. Ironically perhaps, the administrative reforms described above were so successful that a very real sense of villageness was, over time, created. Vital statistics are collected by village heads, cooperatives operate on the basis of the village unit, schools are arranged with catchment areas centred on villages or groups of villages, health centers are located within villages, funds are dispersed to village development committees, and so on. Villages, whether they are Indonesian desa, Malaysian kampung, Thai or Lao bân, Philippine barrios or barangays, Cambodian phum, Vietnamese thôn, or Burmese myo define for most people their place in the world.

The process described above has led to two important distortions in perception regarding the nature of the rural 'world'. First, it has meant that households tend to be recorded as living in villages even when individual household members may spend a greater proportion of their time in urban areas. In Thailand, the intricacies of the household registration system mean that there is a strong disincentive to register a change of residence. When migrants expect to work only temporarily in the city, few can be bothered to go through the rigmarole of changing their residency. And those few who do take the decision to try to re-register often find that it is impossible because the owners of the buildings where they happen to live, perhaps with hundreds of short-term tenants and wishing to avoid the bureaucratic hassle, refuse to enrol them - a requirement for re-registration.

The second distortion in perception is that it has led to the assumption that because the countryside is largely rural and because the word 'rural' is synonymous with 'agriculture', then these people are, virtually by definition, farmers. It should be added that this is not just a case of the state imposing its own notion of people's identities on rural inhabitants. Urban residents from rural areas themselves will often say they live in a village - even that they are farmers - when they live and work in the city. To some extent, village-ness has become a measure or badge of identity that people take with them to urban areas. They do not leave it behind with their paddy fields and ploughs - they wear it as a statement, as a distinguishing marker that sets them apart from other urban residents.

There may be a semantic problem here, compounded by complexities associated with different ways of 'knowing' and of categorization. To ask someone the apparently simple question 'Where do you live?' may be interpreted not so much as 'Where do you live your life?', but rather 'Where are your roots?' or 'What is home?' Many migrants in Southeast Asian towns and cities do not expect to live their entire lives in those places. The intention, often, is to return 'home' to the countryside and they often view themselves as sojourners in the city. The fact that they left that countryside 15 or 20 years previously may not alter this belief, and indeed many 'rural' people die in urban areas as old men or women, still anticipating, on their death beds, the day when they might return to their village roots.

It is also worth asking whether Eurocentric conceptions of a single 'home' can be applied cross-culturally. Chapman, in his 'autobiographies' of Pacific islanders, quotes one Melanesian,

John Waiko, who explains: 'We Melanesians are all engaged in a tapestry of life, where the threads of movement hold everything together'. Chapman goes on to hazard:

Consequently the essence and meaning of a people's mobility becomes far more comprehensible when conceived as an active dialog between different places, some urban, some rural, some both and some neither, as incorporating a range of times simultaneously ancient and modern, and as the most visible manifestation of a dialectic between people, communities, and institutions.

In other words, 'home' and 'place' are ambiguous and shifting notions, where multiple identities - both 'rural' and 'urban' - can be simultaneously embodied. As if this did not make things complicated enough, there is the added problem of categorizing people and households with diverse and multiple occupations within a simple, binary classification. How is someone who works as a farmer for six months and a textile worker for the other half of the year to be classified? It seems that often researchers (and government agencies) are only too ready to apply their own designations and determinants of membership, often based on overly rigid classifications rooted in conceptual exercises that may make perfect sense in an arid academic context, but which in the context of the village are patently inapplicable.

Alternatively, the researcher may adopt an emic approach, asking villagers themselves to decide the composition of their households. As such emic classifications are usually more nuanced and dynamic than researchers would like, it leaves the 'household' not as a unit with a clear-cut membership, but as a shifting entity whose membership is not just blurred at the edges but which may also change shape through the course of the year and between years. Not very helpful, in short, for scholars who wish to know the answer to apparently simple questions like, 'What proportion of household income is derived from non-farm sources?'

There has been much discussion - at the methodological, theoretical/ conceptual and practical levels - as to where a 'household', as a unit of analysis and identification, begins and ends. Given evolving rural-urban and farm-non-farm interactions, a spatial determination of 'household' (i.e. the co-residential dwelling unit or domicile) has become increasingly difficult to sustain. At a functional level, there is a strong argument that all those people who actively participate in the reproduction of the household should be included as members. Part of the reason for the differences of opinion is that the household is, at one and the same time, a conceptual construct, a functioning system, and a methodological unit of analysis. The demands of each tend to lead scholars to arrive at different definitions of the 'household'.

A broader, related, challenge lies in the question of whether the household is a useful or relevant unit of study at all. The study of household economy has tended to view all members as equal members, subsumed within and driven by one household-determined, welfare-maximizing ethic, and bound together by necessity and by kinship in a largely, at least from the analytical point of view, undifferentiated mass. This is most clearly linked with Gary Becker's New Household Economics. Critics, however, suggest that treating the household 'as an individual by another name', disguises the conflicts and contradictions that lie at the heart of the operation of the household as a functioning social and economic entity.

Household members do not passively subscribe to a household 'strategy' but negotiate, contest and resist their roles and place in the household. The household is a dynamic site of social interaction and, in extreme cases; individuals may simply abandon the household altogether. As the region has developed so the household has become more fractious, fractured and fragmented.

It has become increasingly spatially disembedded (leading to the creation of 'shadow' households); the interests of household members have diverged leading to starker divisions between the genders and generations; and the household economy itself has become increasingly multi-stranded as pluriactivity spreads.

This is not to suggest that the household, as a unit of analysis, should be abandoned in favour of something else: it is, for Southeast Asia at least, the best we have and there is a good deal of life left in the household, notwithstanding the changes of recent decades. Most people, after all, belong to households and understanding individuals' actions can usually only be achieved by embedding those actions in the wider context of the household. Some scholars would cast the net still wider to the community, most significantly argued in Scott's work on rural communities as 'moral economies'. In short, the 'household remains a stage where cooperation and conflict, corporatism and individualism, mutuality and inequality, and consensus and discordance, co-exist.... paradoxically, the household is defined by dissonance'.

Notwithstanding the difficulties of identifying where the 'household' and the 'village' begin and end, recent studies of village economies consistently show that a rapidly increasing share of total household income is derived from non-farm, or off-farm, sources.

Moreover, for a significant number of house-holds, non-farm activities represent their major source of income. There are numerous studies indicating this shift, too many for it to be regarded as exceptional. Hayami and Kikuchi's longitudinal study of 'East Laguna Village' in the Philippines - one of the most carefully documented such studies from the region - reveals that the contribution of non-farm income to total income increased from 14 per cent to 64 per cent between 1974-6 and 1995/6 (2000:237).

Eder's study of San Jose on Palawan, also in the Philippines, reveals a similarly dramatic re-orientation in livelihoods. In 1971, fewer than 20 per cent of households relied only on non-agricultural incomes; by 1988 this had more than doubled to 45 per cent (1999:75). So, in terms of identity, identification and activity, there has been a divergence. On the one hand people continue to be identified, and often identify themselves, in village terms. And yet structural change in the economy, coupled with raising expectations and a radically improved transportation system, is leading people down a path that is taking them out of agriculture and, in some cases, out of rural areas. But for the time being at least, rather than a complete transformation from farm to non-farm, livelihoods are becoming increasingly hybrid and blurred as households occupy, or have representation, in both the rural and urban worlds and, more to the point, earn a living from both agricultural and non-farming activities.

It is sufficient to say at this point that agencies charged with the task of administering or analysing development, like the ILO, tend to treat rural and urban-based enterprises separately, in the process disguising the degrees of interaction and dependence binding the two. Partly as a result, there is the linked tendency to characterize non-farm economic activity in rural areas as supplementary and marginal to the 'key' agricultural endeavours.

In former times we were happy when we had enough to eat. We were happy when life was stable and peaceful. But today we need more. Now we know about the necessity of development, we know better what we really need and how we can get it. But to reach it we have to work hard, we need a higher output.

Modernization and development have encouraged people in Southeast Asia to expect more from life; their 'pressure of needs' is intensifying and expanding year by year. The observation that 'basic needs' are in fact 'relative needs' has been recognized for many years. Adam Smith argued as long ago as 1776 that 'By necessities I understand not only the commodities which are indispensably necessary for the support of life, but whatever the custom of the country renders it indecent for creditable people, even of the lowest order, to be without'.

The challenge is for standards of living to keep pace with escalating expectations. Alison Murray, in her detailed description of an urban kampung in Jakarta, writes that 'a vinyl three-piece suite, coffee table and lacquered buffet are considered essential symbols of social standing, and it was considered shameful that one of the RT rukun tetangga or neighbourhood leaders in RW rukun warga or community "B" had no lounge suite and had to entertain visitors at his father-in-law's house'.

Nor is the driving concern for consumer goods and prestige measured in terms of wealth, just a function of city life. Robert Hefner, in his study of the village of Tosari in the Tengger Highlands of East Java, quotes a farmer as he laments the loss of subsistence innocence:

It's not like before. In the old days people here in the highlands were different from those in the lowlands. They weren't interested in wearing fine clothes that drew attention to themselves, or in eating special foods like those you see today. Even though some people owned more and some less, people dressed and ate the same .... Now it's different. Those who are well off want to give orders and keep their hands and feet clean of earth. They keep track of everything they give and everything they get in return. It's just like the lowlands. Everything is counted up and owned.

The rapidity of the transformation from the frugal lives of the past to livelihoods defined by modern consumption practices is sometimes startlingly quick. In a study of the village of Klong Ban Pho in Chachoengsao province in Central Thailand, Chantana Banpasirichote notes that the pick-up truck made the transformation from 'status symbol' to 'necessity' in the space of just five years. Even in the least developed of Southeast Asian countries like the Lao PDR consumer goods such as televisions and even motorcycles have become de rigueur for most households in many areas.

Closely allied with the drive to embrace modernity in the form of new consumption practices is the thirst for education. Primary-level education may now be virtually universal across Southeast Asia, but levels of secondary level enrolment are still low and uneven. One Northern Thai informant observed that while 'in the past, the parents' prime responsibility and concern was to feed their children, today... it is to educate their children'. It is remarkable the sacrifices that families are willing to endure to ensure their children get as good an education as possible. Families are divided, land sold or pawned, and other investments curtailed. The reasons for this reorientation of aspirations, reflected in the value accorded to education, are several. To begin with farming is increasingly regarded as a low status occupation.

The key requisite for any individual wishing to escape farming is the acquisition of an education - and the more the better. The low status of farming is partly driven by state-led initiatives to create populations of modern consumers, and this, in turn, is reinforced by the media and advertising. It is also true that economic realities are at work too. The decline in the returns to farming and the shrinking of the land resource (as the frontier in farmland expansion is reached) have emphasized too many young (and older) rural inhabitants that farming will not easily secure an adequate livelihood in the future.

With farming being squeezed, non-farm activities become the logical alternative livelihood route and education is recognized as the key ingredient in accessing that alternative route. This is reflected in the sectoral and spatial differentiation visible in villages as inhabitants embrace activities outside agriculture and, often, outside the local area. This impetus for change is reflected in the comments of a 41-year-old man in a village in Laos, newly exposed to commercial opportunities by the upgrading of route 13, west of Pakkading near the Mekong:

My dream is to buy a car, a pick-up. I am trying very hard to save money in the bank, for keeping cattle as capital is like hanging money in the tree. People see and steal it. You have to guard the cattle both day and night.

Last year I sold cattle to be able to buy a small tractor. Some villagers asked to borrow it. They pay me a small amount or buy benzoin or oil for me. Life has changed for the better during the last five years. Step-by-step we have bought cattle, a motorbike, tractor, shop and now we have a vehicle repair shop. People will soon need to have repairs done. I wait for them. Sooner or later they will come. (Hågankård)

The pace of change, and the degree to which new ideas, innovations and opportunities are entering villages and encroaching on rural inhabitants' minds, is reflected in the timeline of Ban Ang Noi in Sang Thong District around 55 kilometers upstream on the Mekong from Vientiane in the Lao PDR. While the village is relatively close to the capital, the road linking it with Vientiane is an unmade-up track for much of its length and reaching the capital takes 2½ to 3 hours by public transport during the dry season. In the wet season access is limited to four-wheel-drive vehicles.

THE TRANSPORT REVOLUTION

Aspirations are driven by changing needs, and needs by advancing vistas of knowledge and experience. Knowledge and experience, in their turn, are linked to expanding networks of contact and communication. A key element driving raising aspirations, and perhaps enabling those aspirations to be met, therefore, is the greater accessibility that has been afforded by road expansion and improvement, and the availability of cheap transport. In Indonesia, Dick and Forbes have termed this the 'quiet revolution' or the revolution colt. In most instances the transport revolution has involved interplay of government investment and private capital. Governments have built the roads, while private entrepreneurs have provided the means to galvanize a latent productive resource - roads - into an agent of rural development:

> At the outset of the New Order in Indonesia in 1968, walking was still the normal means out of the village, at least as far as the main road, if not all the way to the market town. During the 1970s this began to change...and by...the 1980s, at least in most parts of Java, Bali, and Lombok, transport between village and market town and between market town and city was quick, frequent, and cheap. (Dick and Forbes)

It is difficult today, in the countries of ASEAN, fully to appreciate the transport revolution that has occurred. Partly the problem was a simple lack of roads and consequent inaccessibility. But in some areas the state also limited mobility through decree and control. As is still the case in Myanmar and until quite recently in Vietnam, Laos and Cambodia, a mobile population was viewed as a potentially dangerous and destabilizing one. Villagers wishing to leave the local area needed to obtain a permission note from the authorities before they could board a bus. At the beginning of the 1960s, villagers in Gunung Kidal in the Special Region of Yogyakarta in Indonesia had to obtain an official letter of permission before they could take one of the few minibuses that made the journey between the city of Yogyakarta and Wonosari, just 35 kilometers to the southeast.

The authorities also often limited the number of licensed vehicles on the road, creating a situation where the demand for transport far exceeded supply. The motivation behind this lay in the desire to keep such licences rare and valuable commodities - a lucrative source of extra income for poorly paid regional officials. Even today in Thailand, villagers are required to have an ID card to travel beyond their province of residence, and in border areas the army routinely scrutinizes bus passengers' ID cards. Although this requirement is not a constraint on mobility for the majority of Thais, the hill minorities have sometimes found their mobility restricted by the regulation, and for most hill people the main advantage of having an official Thai ID card is the freedom to travel that goes with it.

Improved transport and communications do not just permit more efficient economic activity though; they act as a catalyst for increased and different economic activities. Booth, in the context of Indonesia, even suggests that improving transport links helps spread the ideology of economic development by permitting officials from local areas to travel to the centre (Jakarta) for briefings, courses and work-shops, returning to their home patches imbued and energized with new ideas. The role of government action in this revolution is critical. States have traditionally seen the control of space, through roads, as a central means of exerting their authority over remote and marginal regions and their populations.

Roads became a means to control people and space and an emblem of a state's virility. They also, for some, became emblems of oppression.

For Kundstandter roads permitted the Thai government to control people and enforce its policies in the highlands of the Kingdom; they allowed the state to deliver services; they were instrumental in encouraging the demise of subsistence shifting cultivation; they brought the market into the hills (and the people of the hills to the market); and they encouraged and permitted the move into cash cropping. 'Without roads', Kudstadter writes, 'many of these changes would have been impossible or economically impractical'. Roads, therefore, have both a geo-political/geo-strategic and an economic rationale. The effect, though, is perhaps most marked in social and cultural terms. As Dearden suggests, the development of Northern Thailand's road network 'has probably done more to change the landscape of the North and the mindscape of its inhabitants than any other single factor'.

The orthodox economic and developmental justification for road-building is reasonably clear: to integrate remote and isolated populations into the main-stream, thereby allowing them access to opportunities outside the local area while also permitting the institutions of the state (health, education, etc.) and private-sector initiatives (middlemen, input suppliers etc) an entrée into local areas. It is noted in numerous studies that poverty has a key spatial component and regional patterns of poverty are linked to geographical marginality and the high transaction costs that are associated with remoteness from administrative centers.

But the effects of road building, though they may be - in toto - poverty reducing can, at the same time, be inequality widening and poverty creating (for certain vulnerable groups). In other words, the market integration which is such an important outcome of improving communications creates winner and losers. While Windle and Cramb, writing of roads and rural development in Sarawak, may argue that roads 'have the potential to...provide benefits to all groups within a community...and do not inherently favour the rural elite', the outcome is usually not quite so benign. The opportunities that roads offer will be seized by some people to accumulate wealth while others will find their traditional livelihoods squeezed.

Moreover the 'winners' in the sequence of changes that accompany road building may be outsiders who gain access to new regions. Patterns of settlement by lowlanders in the highlands of Vietnam reveal that minorities are often marginalized by the very process of integration. De Koninck found in Lam Dong in the uplands of northern Vietnam that the Ko Ho minority were unable to exploit the new commercial opportunities (in particular, coffee cultivation) opened up by roads and instead 'were now reduced to working as labourers on the surrounding coffee plots cultivated by Kinh settlers'.

Another unintended consequence of road building is to cause off-road communities to become even less accessible and more remote. Businesses congregate by the roadside, traders refrain from travelling off-road to buy and sell goods expecting producers to come to the road to trade, and towns and villages with easy access to new or improved roads grow at the expense of communities with off-road locations. In other words, and paradoxically, the effort to improve road infrastructure, rather than making peripheral areas more accessible, may be serving to increase spatial inequalities within these peripheral areas.

RURAL LIFE

Pre-modern Southeast Asian life has tended to be characterized as essentially subsistence-based. As already noted, this emphasis on self-reliance and economic independence disguises the extent to which farmers produced for the market, and were tied into the market system (although often this was not capitalistic in the modern sense), even before the wholesale colonization of the region. None the less, the modern period has seen a significant increase in the commercialization and commoditization of the agricultural economy. Seven threads of change can be identified. While some build upon traditional activities, others are entirely new:

1. Subsistence crops: the application of increasing quantities of cash inputs like chemical fertilizers and pesticides, and the growing use of wage labour. The sale of an increasing proportion of production. Increasing mechanization of production.
2. Cash crops: the increase in the relative importance of cash crops, both in their contribution to the farm economy and in the relative area under cultivation. Their cultivation using increasing cash inputs and wage labour. Increasing mechanization of production.
3. Raising and sale of livestock: the raising of livestock for the market and the specialization by some households in livestock production, including fisheries.
4. Wage labouring, on-farm and local: a decline in reciprocal labour exchange and a shift to agricultural and farm-linked wage labouring.
5. Non-farming activities, on-farm: the expansion of on-farm, income-generating activities not linked to farming, such as cloth and mat production, and pottery and furniture-making. Some authors prefer to use the term off-field.
6. Non-farming activities, off-farm but local: the growing importance of part-time, seasonal and full-time non-farm employment in off-farm activities such as factory work, public sector jobs and activities within the informal sector. Workers usually return home to the village nightly.
7. Migration for employment: the increasing role of migration to employment beyond local areas. This may be to capital cities, regional urban centers, other rural areas or abroad. In each case, the migrant maintains a rural base.

Sometimes this process of economic change is presented not so much as one of economic differentiation (as here), but of proletarianization. In other words, from a position of self-employment on peasant farms, to wage labour in which individual control over resources is lost. Although proletarianization can, and does, occur within agriculture - for instance in the spread of estate agriculture and contract farming - more often proletarianization is part and parcel of economic differentiation, and not distinct from it.

The seven strategies listed above represent two approaches to increasing output. The first three represent intensification within agriculture; the latter three, intensifica-tion out of agriculture and the fourth strategy is an outcome of the first three. In the past there has been a tendency to see the sixth and seventh strategies listed above as being both spatially and economically distinct. Thus, employment in export-oriented garment and footwear factories would invariably entail migration beyond the local area; while those villagers who commute to work would be employed in small, local factories and in local service provision.

However, the location of large factory enterprises in rural areas, particularly in Java but also in the Central Plain and Northern regions of Thailand, Central Luzon in the Philippines, and in the Klang Valley around Kuala Lumpur in Malaysia, has opened up the possibility for factory employment while maintaining a home base. This expansion of the city into rural areas has been termed kotadesasi in the Asian context, and some studies talk of 'industrialized villages'. As the discussion below will show, diversification, and interpretations of the causes and effects of diversification, are themselves becoming more diverse. Generalizations and single-cause explanations for the changes affecting lives and livelihoods in rural areas of Southeast Asia cannot do justice to the multifarious processes underway.

The very terms used imply that such activities are subsidiary to farming and a residual product of essentially agrarian processes of change: 'non-farm', 'off-farm', 'off-field' and 'non-agricultural', for instance. This narrow, agriculture-centred mode of explanation is simply inadequate in the context of modern Southeast Asia. As the earlier discussion emphasized, village studies show that in increasing numbers of villages the majority of household income can be defined as non-farm and, in this sense, agriculture is becoming a side-line activity for many villagers.

Finally, it is necessary to emphasize the semantic problems connected with discussing 'non-farm' activities. Scholars like Evers (1991) and Cederroth (1995) have expended considerable scholastic energy trying to define their terms. Farm/non-farm and on/off-farm may refer to geographical criteria; they may highlight a sectoral distinction (agricultural/non-agricultural); they may distinguish between different types of households (those engaged in farming, those who are not, and those who do both); or they may refer to one, two or all three of these at the same time. It is tempting to get around this semantic morass by claiming, rather like the unicorn, that 'you will know it when you see it'.

The distinguishing categories used here are also ambiguous and there is a degree of blurring between them and the other categories. Notwithstanding these difficulties of classification the implications of rural economic differentiation are not affected. The following section, rather than outlining in general terms the processes underway in rural Southeast Asia will focus on a series of case studies from across the region, and use these to illuminate the broader issues at play. There is a strong case that a thorough understanding of the processes and tensions of rural change can only be achieved through the use of detailed case studies.

CASE STUDIES IN RURAL CHANGE FROM SOUTHEAST ASIA

When surveying villagers one cannot avoid being struck by the diversity in determination, energy, interest and entrepreneurship that the different individuals put into their activities and decisions.... It is striking, in particular, to observe that some individuals who inherited a similar area of land at the time they started working on their own account have sometimes prospered and sometimes declined...Such a mundane remark may be stating the obvious, but the relevance of the human factor is given little acknowledgement in the literature, which tends to see economic activities as predetermined by the resources on hand, by the constraints of the environments and by (lopsided) social or market relationships.

A striking example of fundamental rural change is Ban Lek in the Chiang Mai Valley, Northern Thailand. This village has been studied over almost two decades from 1974, first by Shigeharu Tanabe and later by Mark Ritchie. In 1974 when Tanabe first began work here it was an agricultural community, remote from the centre, where the livelihoods of nine in ten households were firmly based on farming. As Tanabe says, village activities were 'highly concentrated on agriculture' and he characterizes the community as a 'typical agricultural community based on rice cultivation'.

The construction of roads brought two-way access with regional centers. As a result, villagers gained access to markets and urban employment, while outsiders like traders, labour-recruitment agents, and land speculators gained access to the village. The granting of titles to land created a resource that could be bought and sold, and land began to become concentrated among an emerging group of more wealthy families. Young men and women from poorer households, unable to buy land now that it was scarce and expensive, moved into non-farm employment. In various material and non-material ways, and through direct and indirect policies, 'the Thai state facilitated the emergence of a hybrid rural class structure tightly articulated with urban areas'.

Over 20 years, Ban Lek became a mixed community of both agriculturalists and wage labourers. Ritchie observes that although the village may still be situated in a rural setting, 'the people and households who are involved in agriculture are now in a minority'. In 1974, only 7.5 per cent of all households in the village mixed farming and non-farm occupations; the figure in 1991 was over 30 per cent. By the 1990s, wage labour had become the dominant occupation in Ban Lek. Furthermore, while in 1974, 94 per cent of wage labour was agricultural labouring, by 1991 it was only 14.5 per cent.

Daily commuting to the city of Chiang Mai had become common, the largest single form of wage labouring being urban construction work (some 33 per cent of the total). What is striking, and challenging both from a policy perspective and in conceptual terms, is that 'while these transitional villages are physically placed within agrarian systems of production, the majority of individuals within the village are dependent on urban wage labour'. Ban Lek is not an example of urbanization, since the village is still rural. It represents the merging of the rural and urban worlds in a composite community.

In De Koninck's longitudinal study of two villages in the Muda Irrigation Scheme on Malaysia's Kedah Plain between 1975 and 1987, he identified the main cause of growth in non-farming employment as being the increase in women's participation. In turn, he interpreted this development as a 'consequence of the marginalization of their women's skills in the padi production process' stemming from the mechanization of rice production (1992:177-8). There were notable differences between the strategies employed by residents of the two villages in question. In the vicinity of Matang Pinang there were few local opportunities for off-farm employment. As a result, a comparatively much larger proportion of those involved in non-farm work migrated and took up employment beyond the locality. In Paya Keladi, a significantly greater role was played by employment in the immediate locality.

In analysing the results of the study, De Koninck notes that mobility is becoming so pronounced that 'it is difficult to identify a "family development" cycle regulating access to land' and postulates that 'an increasing number of the descendants of the peasants of Paya Keladi and Matang Pinang will need to break out of the community circle, if only to break out of agriculture'. Hart's longitudinal study of Sungai Gajah, also in the Muda irrigation area, revealed that in the decade between 1977 and 1987 the proportion of married men engaged primarily in non-agricultural activities rose from 5 per cent to 30 per cent.

A third case study comes from Luzon in the Philippines, where the village of East Laguna has been studied almost continuously since 1974 when Yujiro Hayami set out from the

International Rice Research Institute to look for a 'typical' rice village. As with the other villages noted here, when Hayami started work in the mid-1970s agriculture, in this case rice farming, was 'by far the most dominant enterprise' in East Laguna, concentrating the minds and bodies of 80 per cent of households. By the 1990s this figure has been eroded to just 6 per cent. But a particular feature was that the really significant structural changes in the village economy were driven by in-situ developments during the 1990s and, more particularly, by the introduction of village-based manufacturing activities such as metal-working enterprises.

Mirroring Ritchie's observation, Hayami and Kikuchi in their book A rice village saga wonder whether 'East Laguna Village can still be classified as an agrarian community'. For the authors, this profound shift from farm to non-farm, though it may have fundamentally re-worked the community they first encountered in the mid-1970s, has been without question to the overall benefit of the poor. During the period, income inequalities (already significant in 1974) have not widened, although land inequalities have and dramatically so. With the closing of the land frontier and rapid population growth only the proliferation of non-farm opportunities, both on and off-farm, has prevented the 'misery of the poor' being magnified still further.

Agriculture has become the livelihood of the minority while non-agricultural activities meet the income needs of the great rump of the inhabitants of East Laguna. In such a context, inequalities in land holdings, stark though they may be, offer only a very partial insight into the real divisions in village economy and society. Eder's longitudinal study of the village of San Jose on the Philippine island of Palawan spanning the years between 1971 and 1988 shows that the proportion of households engaged in agriculture declined from 80 per cent to 55 per cent, during a period in which the population of San Jose increased from 112 to 278 households. He writes:

Both self-employment and wage work are common. Frequent occupations of the self-employed include fishing, store-owning, market vending, charcoal making and tricycle driving.... Common forms of wage work included unskilled day labor, skilled labor (e.g., carpentry and masonry), salaried employment at private businesses in Puerto Princesa City, government employment (e.g., teaching, nursing, clerking), and contractual overseas employment.

Two key issues come through in Eder's case study that are of particular relevance to this discussion. First, there is considerable complementarity, in terms of labour availability, between agricultural and non-agricultural activities. In other words, households select activities so that they either reinforce or support established agriculture, or at least do not conflict with demands in established agriculture. And second, agriculture in San Jose is not experiencing a process of absolute decline; it remains dynamic and productive.

Eder is particularly concerned with processes of differentiation in San Jose, both sociological and materialist. The increasing role of non-agricultural incomes in the village is not, in his view, evidence of proletarianization or immiseration as landless and land-poor households are marginalized in non-farm activities. Those who sold land over the survey period, for the most part, did it out of choice and were not 'squeezed' into selling. Moreover, the incomes and livelihoods of those in non-farm work were on an upward trajectory over the period. So-styled 'offspring households', even those from poorer households, shared in the general improvement in incomes and livelihoods.

San Jose experienced twin, but partially intersecting, processes of agricultural intensification and economic diversification. Some households remained in farming and increased output (and returns) through the use of new technologies; some combined farming with non-farm pursuits and built inter-locking livelihoods; while other individuals and households based their livelihoods squarely on non-farm activities. While change had brought occasionally unwelcome tensions to San Jose, 'there is life ... after the frontier fills in and life after full time farming'.

Not all Southeast Asian villages, of course, are experiencing internal structural change at a rate, or to the degree, of those described above. Many settlements can still be characterized, essentially, as farming communities. A study conducted among 230 families in the Minahasa area of North Sulawesi in 1985, for example, showed that only 6 per cent of income came from off-farm employment, and more than 93 per cent from labour in agriculture and the work in the Lao PDR over the last few years also illustrates that livelihoods in many villages are determined, more than anything, by the vitality and productivity of agriculture. However, there is the nagging sense, which a glance at other regions of the world would seem to confirm, that the process of agrarian transition will inevitably take communities and most of their inhabitants down a path towards a (largely) non-farm future.

AGE AND GENDER IMPLICATIONS

The shifts within rural communities towards livelihood strategies that avoid agriculture by necessity (a shortage of land) or design (a wish not to be a farmer) tend to be generational. Thus, while among older cohorts, agriculture remains the dominant occupation, in younger cohorts it is, often, wage labouring. There are two possible explanations for this. The first is that it is a life-cycle shift, and when these young men and women enter middle age they not only marry and raise a family, but also settles back into farming. There is certainly some evidence to support the contention that off-farm wage labouring is a rite of passage in some rural areas of Southeast Asia.

The process of merantau among the Minangkabau of West Sumatra, of pai thiaw in Thailand, and of bejalai among the Iban of East Malaysia, is partially founded on the belief that migration is bound up in the process of attaining maturity. However, a more convincing argument in most rural areas is that the growing importance of non-farming pursuits among the young reflects a permanent change in the complexion of the rural economy linked to two broad issues.

First, a radical shift in resource availability and specifically in land but this should not necessarily be interpreted as neither displacement of young people into poorly paid non-farm activities or the marginalization of the old in stagnant agriculture (a point that Eder is at pains to make). It seems, and this is discussed below, that diversity has attractions in itself. Older people retain access to land, providing a source of stability, while younger household members search out and gain employment in non-farm work. The second issue concerns the equally profound shift in young people's aspirations.

For many young people farming is an occupation to be avoided and in such a context it is hard to believe that they will willingly return to it. In other words, both these factors suggest that the generational character of work in the farm and non-farm sectors may disguise a more fundamental shift in rural society and economy which just happens, for the time being, to be manifested in generational terms. Given time, the new character of the countryside will emerge.

A second characteristic of this change in the rural household economy is the growing importance of female employment. In Thailand, for example, a study conducted by the National Statistical Office (NSO) in 1986-8 revealed that 65 per cent of migrants in Bangkok were female - a significant change from the 1970s when most migrants were male. A slightly more recent NSO labour-force survey broadly confirmed these findings, revealing that between 1985 and 1990, 53 per cent of migrants to the capital were female. The raising female labour-force participation rate is a general trend, but is most pronounced in export-oriented activities such as the garment industry, electronics, and the footwear sector where 90 per cent or more of workers may be female.

There are a number of factors that lie behind this increase in female off-farm employment. Some may be viewed as 'enabling', others as 'determining'. From the village perspective, the social unacceptability of women engaging in off-farm work, which formerly deterred many from leaving the villages, has diminished. Coupled with such factors as declining fertility, delayed marriage, greater mobility and raising female education levels, this has created the conditions where women, for the first time, are in a position to work beyond the confines of the village.

But although this may be a general trend, there remain some areas where there are still strong cultural impediments to female participation. In West Java, for example, it seems that cultural constraints remain comparatively strong, and the same is true in the Muda area of Peninsular Malaysia, especially with regard to the newer labour markets. In Central Java, by contrast, the evidence indicates that such social sanctions are far weaker.

As well as this easing of previously powerful social barriers to female migration and off-farm employment (an enabling factor), developments in the agricultural economy may also be forcing - or perhaps permitting - women to take up off-farm employment. Some studies have argued that mechanization has selectively displaced women, thereby freeing them for, or displacing them into, other work. At the same time, a series of changes in the structure and nature of the industrial economy have encouraged and/or permitted an increase in female labour-force participation.

The lesson that underlies such studies is that rural people no longer see their future solely, or even mainly, in farming. Mike Parnwell writes of the Northeast of Thailand, for example: 'Thus we are faced with a situation whereby livelihoods for…a large and increasing number of people in the North-East region are becoming dependent upon the continued economic dynamism, and associated income-earning opportunities, which exist elsewhere i.e. in urban areas, and in particular in Bangkok'.

INCOME AND CLASS PERMUTATIONS

In addition to age and gender, it has long been assumed that variations in wealth are also a key factor determining patterns of non-farm employment. Although the picture is still sketchy, it seems that two groups within rural society are more likely to be involved in non-farm employment: the comparatively wealthy, and the poor. This distinction is often expressed in terms of land, defining the wealthy as the 'land-rich', and the poor as the 'landless' or the 'land-poor'. The problem with such a view is that it equates wealth in terms of agriculture, by using land ownership as a surrogate for income. It thus falls into the trap, noted above, of assuming that we can understand the rural world in agricultural terms.

Admittedly, in some case studies it seems that such an assumption about the close relationship between wealth, livelihood strategies and farm size does seem to hold true. However, elsewhere, and increasingly, it does not. For example, Rotgé notes in his village study on the Bantul Plain in Yogyakarta, Java that of the one in five households who gain no income from agriculture, most are relatively wealthy. Similarly, Eder writes of the village of San Jose in Palawan, the Philippines that 'relatively few of the land sales by core households between 1971 and 1988 reflected economic distress, and at least some reflected "strategies to prosper" '.

The loss of the status of land as a strategic resource is also reflected based on Hayami and Kikuchi's (2000) work in the village of East Laguna in the Philippines over a 30-year period. It shows that while land has become highly concentrated within the top quintile of the population, who control 99 per cent of the resource; inequalities in terms of income have remained stable over the period.

A key question is whether prior wealth enables villagers to engage in non-farm employment, or whether non-farm employment makes them wealthy. There are two particular difficulties here. First, longitudinal studies are comparatively rare, and so most accounts are forced to 'create' the past. And second, livelihoods show a good degree of dynamism and variability from season to season, from year to year, and as individuals and households progress through their life cycles.

In other words, even longitudinal studies conducted at two, three, four or more times over a period of 10 or 20 years may 'miss' critical episodes in community and individual livelihood dynamics. None the less, and putting aside these very real methodological challenges and shortcomings, work on migration and occupational diversification does appear to indicate that there are two, perhaps three, strategies underlying the process: migration as a strategy of further accumulation, for the already comparatively rich; migration as a strategy of survival, for the poor (so-called 'distress diversification'); and migration as a strategy of consolidation for middle income households.

This division is reflected in White and Wiradi's study of nine villages in Java. They note that while there is an inverse relationship between agricultural and non-farm incomes among the landless and very small landowning groups, for middle and large farmers the relationship is positive. In other words, they hazard, while for the members of the former group it is the 'inadequacy of agricultural sector incomes which propels them into non-farm activities as a survival strategy', for the latter group there is a 'dynamic strategy of accumulation, in which surpluses derived from one activity are used to gain access to the other'. They conclude that such non-farm activities not only allow middle and large landowners to accumulate wealth but at the same time allow smaller landowners, with 'sub-livelihood' holdings 'to achieve subsistence incomes without the distress sale of their plots'.

It is this latter point that helps to explain the striking persistence, in the face of modernization and commoditization, of farmers with small landholdings. The expectation that small-scale farmers would be elbowed out by land concentration driven by the forces of technological and economic change has not materialized. Cederroth, who anticipated that Green Revolution-induced change would marginalize large numbers of poorer farmers, explains this in terms of the 'unprecedented upswing in off-field employment' that not only compensated for the predicted decrease in farm productivity but allowed some of the poor to increase their standards of living.

Maurer's expectations were much the same when he studied four villages in Bantul Regency, Yogyakarta, between

1971 and 1987. Yet he found there was 'no real evidence of any strong land concentration or absolute impoverishment process' in the face of Green Revolution-driven agricultural modernization. As Maurer admits, he made the mistake of focusing on the agricultural economy, when it was the non-farm economy that was undergoing the greatest change. In large part, the emergence of occupational diversity has put off the displacement of the rural poor from their land and has, perversely, helped to sustain 'traditional' rural economies by allowing farm production to maintain an image of centrality.

While non-farm work may have sustained livelihoods for the rural poor and kept them 'on the farm' (and therefore prevented, for the time being at least, the distress sale of their land) this does not mean that returns have been sufficient to significantly raise their living standards. A key question, and one that has not been adequately addressed, is how far there is permanent movement across the poverty line (as opposed to oscillation around the line). There is no doubt that some individuals and households have been able to break the 'class envelope', but who these people are and how they have been able to escape their structurally determined place at the bottom of the economic pile are critically important questions about which we know far too little. But, and notwithstanding this shady (but important) group of 'achievers', there does seem to be a broad division of non-farm employment between petty trading, such as door-to-door hawking, for the poor and more capital intensive activities like operating taxi services or small-scale manufacturing enterprises for the rich. This is reflected in Effendi's work on Jatinom in Central Java.

The difficulty, however, with assigning particular responses to particular groups of people - usually labelled as representing different 'classes' and 'class interests' - is that these groups, though perhaps clear and distinguishable enough in conceptual terms, are often remarkably hard to identify on the ground. The fluidity and complexity of rural change, the overlapping and conflicting nature of class 'interests', and the lack of a class consciousness among the very people, who are supposed to be embroiled in class 'conflict', makes it questionable whether such notions have much utility. James Scott, for example, in his classic study of agrarian change in the Muda irrigation area of Kedah, West Malaysia, writes:

> It is all very well to identify a collection of individuals who all occupy a comparable position in relation to the means of production - a class-in-itself. But what if such objective, structural determinations find little echo in the consciousness and meaningful activity of those who are thus identified?

A further difficulty is that most local studies take the 'household' as the unit of study, while it is individuals who make up classes - not households. To place the members of entire households in one class or other makes little sense when those members may, individually, be best allotted to different classes. Laslett argues that a family represents a 'knot of individual interests', and observes that 'to make a clear and satisfactory analysis of the relationship between household production and membership in a wider collectivity it would be necessary to examine in detail the interest, roles, and above all the power of every class of member of households of every type and in every region or economy'.

As he admits, such an exercise is plainly impossible. Even so, it emphasizes the difficulties and dangers involved in teasing out generalizations from a system which is so complex and nuanced. So although we can, with relative certainty, argue that people engage in non-farm pursuits for very different reasons, to allot discrete groups into neat categories is probably impossible. We lack the longitudinal information required to undertake such a task at a cross-country scale; groups blur one into the next; rural residents themselves may have little conception of belonging to such groups or classes; and the usual unit of analysis - the household - does, itself, represent an amalgam of competing interests.

Finally, and this is the bane of so much 'empirical' work based on case-study material, it is uncertain how far such studies can be used to build global propositions about the nature of rural change. Are the poor displaced into low return non-farm work? Is technological change marginalizing the poor? Are richer classes able to capitalize on their position and create yet deeper intra-village inequalities? In all these, and many other key areas of debate, the evidence from village studies can be used to support any one of a range of positions, ideological or otherwise.

STRATEGIES OF NON-FARM EMPLOYMENT

The increasing diversity of the household economy described above is not always reflected in the local and regional economies. This is because while the household economy is, in essence, socially constructed, being based on a family, or extended-family unit, the local/regional economy is usually spatially designated.

As a result, while the former may include income from activities that occur far removed spatially (even remittances from abroad), the latter implies those activities and industries that are located within the spatial boundaries of a district, province/state or region.

Rotgé notes this tendency in his study of villages on the Bantul Plain in Yogyakarta, Java. For while a substantial share of the population work in non-farming activities, generating a considerable share of household income, 'the development of locally-based off-farm activities which are not retail trading, remains conspicuously low' (1992:19). Instead, villagers commute to urban areas for work. It is the movement to work outside the local area which is the basis, in many instances, for the diversification of the household economy and it is therefore non-local (or ex-situ) activities that sustain local consumption.

RURAL INDUSTRIALIZATION (AND DE-INDUSTRIALIZATION)

It is perhaps because of this disjuncture between the general unavailability of local non-farming employment on the one hand, and the need to satisfy a growing requirement for income on the other, that governments in the region are attempting to promote what has been termed 'rural industrialization':

> Rural industrialisation can be defined as a process involving the growth, development and modernisation of various forms of industrial production within the rural sector generally and rural villages specifically.

There appear to be several inter-related and overlapping reasons for this policy drive. First, governments and some scholars perceive rural industrialization as a means by which spatial inequalities can be narrowed, whether they are rural-urban or regional, or - most likely - both. Greater spatial equality is assumed to be a desirable aim for a variety of economic, political and social reasons, and rural industrialization can help in the achievement of this end. Second, urban-industrial development has failed, in many instances, to generate the necessary jobs to absorb surplus rural labour.

At the same time, the limits to agricultural growth have been reached. Taken together, the failure of the urban/ industrial and agricultural sectors to absorb surplus labour has encouraged policymakers to look elsewhere, and rural industrialization is an obvious avenue to explore. Third, rural industrialization may help to relieve congestion and the pressure on services in rapidly growing urban areas, reducing the environmental costs of growth and easing demand for housing and jobs and in this way, keeping farmers on the farm helps in urban management. The fourth attraction of rural industrialization is that it provides employment for rural people, generating income and raising living standards. In arguing for rural industrialization in Thailand, Parnwell states that 'as part of the strategy for alleviating the problems of rural areas and peripheral regions ... the case is not a difficult one to make' (1990:5), and he proceeds to list no less than thirteen positive attributes of rural industrialization.

But rural industrialization would not be a realistic policy option if there were not also some sound economic reasons for companies to base themselves in the countryside. Among the attractions of a rural location are generally lower wage rates, cheaper land and utilities, and fewer and less stringent environmental controls (notwithstanding some local opposition by environmental groups). Some companies also find that planning controls in urban areas inhibit their expansion plans.

There may even be local sources of some raw materials. To set against this, investors usually need to take into account, and contend with, higher transportation costs, the absence of a pool of skilled workers, difficulties in enticing managers to locate in comparatively remote and undesirable areas, and the inevitable dislocation from the key centre(s) of financial and bureaucratic decision-making (i.e. the capital city).

Broadly speaking there is a distinction between industries which are entirely new and alien to the rural setting, and those that build upon existing skills and activities. In poor areas of Thailand's Northern and Northeastern regions for example, T-Bird (Thai Business Initiative in Rural Development), an offshoot of C-Bird (Community-Based Integrated Rural Development), which, itself, is linked to the PDA (Population and Community Development Association), has encouraged a range of international and national firms to set up production bases in poor villages.

These include, for example, Bata, Nike, Adidas, Pierre Cardin, Van Heusen and Arrow and activities range from gem cutting and artificial flower making to ceramics and garment and footwear production. Ban Rong, one such village in the province of Buriram had 1,500 villagers employed in the scheme in 1998. The intention of the project is to allow villagers to tap into the modern economy without irrevocably undermining traditional rural livelihoods, by keeping people in the village, on the farm while also by permitting them to access work opportunities in the new economy.

During Thailand's economic downturn in 1997 and 1998, for example, the project actually encouraged villagers to concentrate their time more on agriculture in the light of prevailing economic conditions. T-Bird's work, and the logic that underpins it, is very much in the mould described by

Parnwell, above. By its promoters everyone is seen to be a winner: commercial firms can take advantage of cheaper production costs; villagers can gain access to jobs that pay considerably better than prevailing agricultural work; the national government benefits because it helps stem the drift of young people to urban areas with all the problems of urban management that this entails; local government benefits from increased tax revenues that can be ploughed back into improving local facilities and services; the agricultural economy remain resilient because of the complementarities that can be promoted between farm and non-farm work; and households are not divided as husbands, wives and children migrate to extra-local work.

But it should not be assumed that because industries are located in rural areas they necessarily employ, and benefit, rural people. This seems to be particularly the case in the vicinity of medium- and large-sized towns. Small companies may create workshops or factories in rural areas so that they can benefit from the advantages noted above, but then employ non-local settlers - so as to avoid some of the associated disadvantages. Therefore the emerging and growing interactions between rural and urban areas may not only bring rural people to the city, but also city dwellers to the countryside.

If this occurs - as Rotgé, for example, records in his study of employment in the vicinity of the Javanese city of Yogyakarta - then rural industrialization may not assist local rural people. Indeed, in both Thailand and Indonesia, researchers have noted the extent to which local people are 'displaced' from accessible rural areas to more remote places. Enticed by the raising value of their land, especially if it is located near a transit corridor, but unable to benefit from the process of rural industrialization that is occurring around them, they sell their land. The proceeds are then used either to buy a larger parcel of land in a more remote location, or 'squandered' on luxuries. If this process is widespread, then 'rural industrialization' should perhaps be reformulated as 'industrial extension and rural displacement'.

Many studies of rural industrialization stress the degree to which external agencies must support and intervene in the process. The apparent inability of rural people spontaneously to establish their own businesses is because they lack the management and technical skills, financial resources, collateral, contacts and marketing knowledge to make the leap from farmer to small businessman or woman. It is these gaps which NGOs and some government programme aim to fill. But although there may be an attractive logic in such efforts, successful examples of self-sustaining and profitable rural enterprises are hard to find.

As Udom Buasri of Khon Kaen University in the Northeast has been quoted as saying: 'Many NGOs have tried to teach people skills like traditional handicrafts so they'll stay at home. Mostly they fail. They're not able to keep people in the village'. This, perhaps, is because rural industries are being seen, in the policy context, as alternatives to migration and urban work, whereas for rural households they are viewed as an addition to existing strategies, helping to fill the 'expectation gap' between what people currently earn or produce and what they aspire to earn.

Although much recent policy prescription has emphasized the promotion of rural industrialization, there has always been an element of 'industry' in rural areas. And while governments may be pursuing one policy objective, the forces of economic restructuring and technological change may be encouraging just the reverse. This is especially true in those areas with a tradition of rural manufacturing. Hans Antlöv and Thommy Svensson's study of the traditional textile- producing area in the vicinity of the town of Majalaya, 35 kilometers southeast of the West Java city of Bandung, shows just such a shift as the locus of production moved, beginning in the early 1970s, from small workshops in the rural areas surrounding Majalaya to large textile factories in Majalaya town itself:

Today's urban-based textile industry was born in the countryside. Rural villages provide the reservoir of labour for the large-scale industrialization which is now taking place. But the villages also benefit economically from the textile workers who bring home and spend their factory incomes in the local setting. It is striking that most textile workers continue to live in the villages and commute daily to the town. On all the roads in Majalaya, at 6.30 a.m. and 5.00 p.m., innumerable mini-buses bring workers to and from the factories.

As Antlöv and Svensson describe, in some areas of Southeast Asia, for example in the Central Plains and Lower North of Thailand, the western seaboard of Peninsular Malaysia, the provinces surrounding Manila in the Philippines, and especially in Java, the close proximity of rural villages to centers of urban-industrial employment has allowed villagers to commute daily, maintaining their rural base but taking up formal and informal non-farm employment. At the same time, large export-oriented manufacturing enterprises have also found it desirable to locate in rural areas. In Java, Wolf describes ten large-scale 'modern' factories, driven by Western machinery and technology... squatting in the middle of the agricultural land of two villages that still have neither running water nor electricity ... Some ... nesting in rice fields, disrupting neat rows of rice shoots with metal fences and guards.

To some extent this evolution of highly integrated rural-urban economies links closely with the concept of the Extended Metropolitan Region (EMR). However, commuting to work in local towns is more widespread than the distribution of Southeast Asia's EMRs might suggest, and is becoming more so as transport links improve and the tendrils of public transport bring growing numbers of people within commuting distance of an urban centre. The agricultural and industrial elements of rural livelihoods are not in competition, but often fill complementary roles.

Income from urban employment is fed into agricultural investments, and as discussed above allows families working small, marginal and sub-marginal farms to continue to maintain a presence in the countryside. With cities spreading outwards, factories relocating in surrounding areas, and people moving faster and more frequently across a vital landscape of economic interaction, it is becoming increasingly hard to establish where urban ends and rural begins - certainly in functional terms, and often in physical terms too. Brookfied et al. talk of 'in-situ urbanization' to describe this process in the Klang Valley area around Kuala Lumpur (1991).

RURAL INDUSTRIALIZATION, EXPLOITATION AND ACCUMULATION

In the literature, rural industrialization is usually presented as a favourable alternative to urban employment. It keeps families together, reduces rural- urban migration, results in higher incomes in rural areas, and means that rural inhabitants can continue to enjoy the (assumed) better quality of life in the countryside. It may also be construed as a means of improving poor people's livelihoods without having to resort to politically sensitive and disruptive agrarian reforms such as land redistribution, making it highly attractive to embattled 'weak' states. However, there is also an argument that rural industrialization permits the hyper-exploitation of rural people.

As Wolpe famously argued with reference to the employment of rural migrants in South African industry:

Since in determining the level of wages necessary for the subsistence of the migrant worker and his family, account is taken of the fact that the family is supported, to some extent, from the product of agriculture in the Reserves, it becomes possible to fix wages at the level of subsistence of the individual worker.

Although Wolpe was focusing on the movement of people to work, the same argument could be applied to rural industrialization where the work moves to the people. Pleyte, in 1911, was highly dubious about the supposed advantages of small-scale rural industry in Java:

Small-industry propogandists, you know only the outward appearances and judge native industries by them. Go into the kampungs villages, visit the slums and hovels where the pieceworkers live and work, and see with your own eyes how the dispossessed in native society do their work and eke out their existence!

The contention that rural industrialization involves just the relocation of urban sweat shops to rural areas does receive some support in the contemporary literature. For example, in Ban Thung, a village in Thailand's central region, some households subsist entirely on the home-based piece-work production of ngop, or farmers' hats. The income this work generates though is so meagre that it does not allow any room for accumulation. As one villager explained, 'you can't do it quick enough to eat'.

In those instances where rural-based non-farm work does generate an adequate return it does not necessarily follow that it will narrow inequalities in the face of highly skewed patterns of land ownership. White notes that despite the fact that well over 50 per cent of rural incomes in Java in 1987 came from non-farm sources, those generating these additional returns tended also to be the larger landowners. In other words, and unlike such East Asian countries as Taiwan and South Korea, there was a positive relationship between levels of farm and non-farm income. Finally, there are ample examples of the conflicts and tensions that may arise between farm and non-farm activities as they compete for labour, time and capital.

THE NEW RURAL WORLD

Relatively few studies investigate, in detail, the non-farm (or non-agricultural) elements of the 'agrarian' economy. Yet, at the same time, almost all studies and the literature on agrarian change is truly voluminous emphasize that there is more to rural life than agriculture and that this 'more' is getting larger and more significant. This strange coincidence of recognition and then neglect is linked to the conceptual difficulties of dealing with farmers who might be industrial workers, and industrial workers who might be involved in farming. As this chapter has attempted to show, understanding how and why these interactions and linkages occur cuts across spatial, gender, class, age and temporal divisions. For example, at different times during the year a household may have its members involved in different activities.

The seasonality of agricultural production highlighted in the reference to the musim mati ('dead season') in Peninsular Malaysia, or musim lapar ('hungry season') in eastern Indonesia - illustrates the pronounced temporal fluctuations that occur in village production. The activities often built in and around these fluctuations, may involve daily movements of just a few kilometers, seasonal movements of hundreds of kilometers, or periodic movements of thousands of kilometers. Further, as each individual works through his or her life cycle, their economic roles may well change. Nor will households act - whether by accident or design - in the same fashion. Different 'classes' within the rural population will become involved in the economy in different ways. Conceptual bases for understanding rural change have, without exception, failed to deal effectively with these myriad and nuanced processes and interactions.

Although this chapter can hardly fill such a conceptual void, there are some tentative observations that can be offered. Most important, the processes of social and economic change sweeping through rural areas of Southeast Asia can rarely be understood in terms of just agricultural modernization. The forces of change have their roots, more likely than not, in the non-farm economy. Driven by raising needs, constrained in agriculture by a contracting resource base and unfavourable terms of trade, and infused by the belief that farming is a low-status occupation, rural inhabitants are turning to non-farm activities.

Researchers in different countries tend to use different terms - Grandstaff (1988) and Thomas (1988) in Thailand talk of a 'diverse portfolio of activities', White in Java (1976), of 'occupational multiplicity', Muijzenberg (1991) in Luzon, the Philippines of 'diversification for survival' but the underlying meaning of the terminology is the same. Households and individuals usually wish to maintain and develop both agricultural and non-farm activities.

The hybrid nature of the rural economy is usually explained in terms of risk-minimization. Giving up agriculture altogether is perceived to be a risky strategy for rural inhabitants inured over the generations into avoiding placing all their livelihood eggs in one basket. With a concern for consumption 'smoothing', rural people positively cultivate diversity. However, it is difficult to escape from the tyranny of the forces of economic structural transformation: that ultimately, most farmers will give up agriculture altogether. But for the present at least, most rural households have not reached this stage.

Instead, the demands of these non-farm activities rebound on agriculture, which adapts to the new production environment. At the same time, the presence of an army of rural workers willing and needing to take up industrial employment fuels the growth of manufacturing. It is perhaps sufficient to end this chapter by stating the obvious: that the Southeast Asian rural world(s) is (are) an unmistakably new rural world(s). The direction of change appears relatively clear - towards greater diversity, integration and commercialization. The effects of change, though, remain hazy.

2

Non-agricultural Employment for Rural Women

If they are to serve as authentic channels for social change, strategies for integrating women into the development process must be sensitive to differences in social and economic structures as well as in cultural values and beliefs. The strategy outlined in this chapter has a particular thrust in contending that one must begin with the creation of employment for rural women, and that this employment should produce income over which women have some controls. In addition, it should be located in small towns and villages; create jobs outside agriculture in small-scale, labor-intensive light industries; draw women out of their homes into a central workplace; organize production cooperatively; and offer additional services and incentives.

This particular combination of elements derives from observations of four countries (India, Pakistan, Bangladesh, and Nepal) that share certain characteristics such as their extreme poverty, relatively high rates of population growth, early and universal marriage patterns among women, and cultural systems valuing female seclusion. But structural and cultural conditions differ widely within these countries both by geographical region and by religion, caste, and class. Thus, the several parts of the model will have to be adapted to local situations, even in the South Asian context. The model is certainly not designed to be transplanted intact to other settings, although in some parts of Africa, Latin America, or elsewhere in Asia or the Middle East, conditions may resemble those described here more than one would initially suspect.

Before determining which projects are feasible, it is necessary to obtain information on the current productive activities of rural women. It is amazing how little we know, in general, about how rural women in most parts of the world spend their time.

A few valiant attempts have been made to compile comparative international data on women's access to schooling, employment in the formal and informal sectors, income, political power, and other resources, or to explore in diverse settings their decision-making roles in agriculture, small rural industries, marketing, community projects, and family care. Information from seven African and Latin American countries suggests certain similarities.

For example, even where women play an active role in agriculture as workers and decision makers, joining agricultural cooperatives or obtaining credit appears to be the prerogative of men. Thus, even in cultures setting few restrictions on women's mobility outside the home, programs may have to be aimed specifically at women-in order for them to benefit directly as active participants. In the sections that follow, I will explore the conditions under which it would be more appropriate to integrate women more fully into the agricultural sector rather than creating jobs for them in small industries, or to mingle the sexes in the workplace rather than restricting employment to women only, or to organize production more loosely or more rigidly rather than insisting on cooperatives.

Also, it may be more appropriate under some conditions to pay women workers partly or solely in kind rather than cash in order to avoid their having to turn over their earnings to the male household head, and to bypass inflationary increases in the cost of food staples. For most rural settings in Asia, Africa, Latin America, and the Middle East, it can be argued that upgrading women's domestic and subsistence activities to income-generating production is central to improving their status, promoting rural development, and altering reproductive aspirations and behavior.

THE IMPORTANCE OF EARNING MONEY

After months of discussions with women in her natal village in the Punjab, Syeda Abida Hussain decided ten years ago that the key to women's problems was their lack of control over money. She began, on a very small scale, to encourage an embroidery industry which now provides income for some two hundred Muslim girls and women in the village. Several of the original workers have saved enough money to buy their own homes. Many save for their own or their daughters' dowries. One girl loaned money to her father to start a vegetable shop. Parents are said to look on the birth of girls far more favorably now than was customary in the days when an unmarried daughter contributed nothing. The women themselves are proud of their skills and their ability to earn money.

It is remarkable how rarely people have come to this particular conclusion regarding the needs of rural women. Community development experts, in spite of the obvious and desperate financial need of many wives and widows, rarely suggest programs that would enable women to earn money. A 1975 seminar on Rural Women and Social Development, sponsored by the Family Planning Association of India, for example, drew up a plan for the Mahila Mandals (village women's associations). This plan, though promoting self-reliance, recommended merely (1) more awareness of community social problems, (2) more female participation in voluntary labor programs, and (3) more contraceptive centers with family-counseling services.

Yet it could be argued that the lack of money in poor households is the single most important factor retarding rural development, and that the lack of control over what money exists contributes to the low status of women and increases their motivation for frequent childbearing. The redistribution of income, land, wealth, and services may be essential to creating conditions favorable to socioeconomic development and fertility decline in developing countries. Income distribution within nations appears to explain the different fertility levels across countries more adequately than does per capita GNP.

At given levels of per capita GNP, those nations in which the poorest sector of the population receives a relatively higher percentage of the total income tend to have lower birthrates than those in which the poorest sector receives a smaller share. One direct method of raising the level of living for the poor is to reduce the ratio of dependents to workers by generating income-earning employment for women. This strategy is especially important where cultural restrictions limit women's mobility outside the home, or where women working outside the home receive little more than their midday meal in payment. Such conditions force male workers to support numerous dependents, including adult women, on impossibly small incomes.

Some economists have argued that, other things being equal, increasing household income is pronatalist because of its "pure income effect." In rural Pakistan at very low income levels, fertility tends to rise as income rises, although the net statistical effect of income on fertility overall is near zero. The pure income argument assumes that the fertility constraints induced by low incomes weaken as incomes rise and couples are able to afford more children. The question is whether the poor voluntarily limit childbearing or whether extreme destitution causes maternal malnutrition which, in turn, reduces fecundity and thus, involuntarily, fertility.

In any case, conditions are rarely as equal as the economists would wish. Incomes generally rise in the context of changing living conditions and altered tastes and aspirations, which simultaneously affect reproductive motivation and behavior. The effect of income on fertility also depends on which household member is earning and controlling the money. Income distribution between husband and wife or parent and child may be crucial to determining the power structure of the decision-making unit. A woman earning half the household income will likely have more bargaining power than the woman who earns none, even when total household earnings are the same. Whether the woman directs her power toward delaying marriage for herself or her daughter, or practicing birth control, would depend on the extent to which she is exposed to social rewards other than marriage and childbearing.

Earning money may help to delay the marriage of young girls by persuading their parents not to marry them off so early as long as they are contributing to household earnings, and by improving the young women's bargaining position over the timing of marriage and the choice of a mate. The strong preference for sons that is characteristic in so many parts of South Asia should also weaken if unmarried girls earn money, which would reduce fertility indirectly. Married women earning their money may exercise more choice about childbearing and feel less dependent on family members, particularly sons, for economic survival.

The emphasis of the Integrated Rural Development Program in Bangladesh on raising women's routine subsistence activities to the commercial level is premised on precisely this assumption: "The hypothesis is that a woman's income-earning capacity will of necessity give her an equal right to decide the largeness of her family, and provide her recognition for activities other than childbearing". In some situations, strong cultural values favoring male dominance may override the effects of women's economic independence on the decision-making power within the family. But patriarchal power relations within the rural family are not likely to be substantially altered if women do not earn and control some money.

Raising women's subsistence activities to the level of providing income is probably a highly unrealistic goal for some areas, especially for isolated communities far removed from sources of raw materials and from markets. The Bangladesh Rural Advancement Committee project, covering two hundred villages in the Sulla area near Sylhet, encourages self-sufficiency in agriculture and in basic household goods rather than promoting production aimed at a larger market. If women can grow vegetables for their own consumption or make baskets or fishnets for local use, then the cause of rural development will be served; households will be better off, even in the absence of women's earned incomes. Under other conditions, however, the generation of income for rural women is a viable possibility that can simultaneously create an effective demand for new goods and services within the village.

THE RURAL SITE

The rationale for locating income-generating employment in rural areas is simple. The vast majority of the South Asian population is rural: 81 per cent in India in 1971, 74 per cent in Pakistan, 93 per cent in Bangladesh, and 96 per cent in Nepal. Rural inhabitants experience more extreme poverty than do urban residents, in part because of the frequently high levels of both seasonal and permanent under and unemployment in the agricultural sector. In addition, rural women marry earlier and bear slightly more children on the average than do women in towns and cities. If national birth rates are to be substantially reduced, opportunities for rural women must be expanded beyond their current subsistence limits.

The decentralization of industrial development creates a diffusion effect by dispersing the sources of economic and social change throughout the country rather than concentrating them in urban centers. As a result of such dispersal, migration from the countryside to overcrowded cities will be slowed. But where should the new employment be located? Staley and Morse argue that villages are too small and too culturally conservative to serve as appropriate locations for most new rural industry, whereas intermediate-sized towns are more receptive to innovation and more easily linked with urban markets. It may be, however, that certain small-scale industries or agro-industries, such as fruit preservation or dairy processing, can be more efficiently sited close to the source of raw materials, that is, in villages rather than towns.

One could also question the assumption that villages are necessarily more culturally conservative than towns, especially in their attitudes about women's roles. One study of several Hindu Agarwal communities found that 50 per cent of rural women accepted without qualification the statement, "Women may work for money if they so choose," while only 37 per cent of women living in urban fringe areas and only 30 per cent living in Delhi agreed with the statement. (It should be noted that no men were in agreement with this idea.) Muslim families of the urban lower-middle class frequently adhere more strictly than do villagers to the observance of *purdah* in order to protect their tenuous social standing. Village women may consequently be more amenable to recruitment for income-generating employment outside the home than are women in towns.

NON-AGRICULTURAL EMPLOYMENT

In regions or among socioeconomic or ethnic groups in which women currently play an important role in agriculture-in the Himalayan regions, for example, or among the tribes and lower castes of India-the best strategy may well be to integrate women more fully into the agricultural process. Programs would aim at ensuring that women receive appropriate training in new methods of planting, cultivation, harvesting, storage, and processing, and in animal and poultry husbandry; that they have equal access with men to new technology, especially labor-saving methods and equipment; that they have equal access to membership in agricultural cooperatives, to land ownership and tenant status, to credit and marketing facilities; and that they receive equal wages for agricultural labor.

In many cases this would require that female agricultural extension workers be trained specifically to reach out to women clients. As a development strategy for India, Mazumdar proposes integrating-or, more accurately, rehabilitating-women in agriculture, on the grounds that agriculture is the most important productive sector of the economy, that women have acquired skills and an attachment to agricultural production by long tradition, and that the alternatives (rural industry, handicrafts, or the service sector) can employ a small minority only.

Recognizing that agricultural employment is frequently seasonal, unpredictable, and exploitative, Mazumdar argues that the answer is to ensure adequate wages, security of employment, and maternity benefits and child care for women workers, concluding that "agro-based industries and handicrafts are certainly needed to provide additional avenues of employment-but they should not be seen as alternatives to agricultural work. Food, after all, will always remain the most important productive function and even though the labour is hard the life it promises to women is more satisfactory than most other productive fields".

Mazumdar's emphasis on rehabilitation rests on the startling observation that the number of Indian women employed in agriculture has not grown since the early twentieth century (with the exception of 1961, when the census definition of labor-force participation was particularly liberal), while the female population has doubled in size during this period. Although changing definitions and undercounting throw some doubt on the reliability of the figures, apparently six million fewer women found employment in agriculture in 1971 than in 1911.

As the number of female cultivators shrank, the number of agricultural laborers grew; by 1971, half of the casual laborers, daily-wage workers, and contract and bonded laborers in agriculture were women, reflecting increasing landlessness and pauperization of the rural population in general. In some tribal areas of India (among the Garo, for example) new crops, new farming techniques, and the biases of extension workers were pushing women out of their traditional agricultural roles in the transition from shifting cultivation to orchards and terraces. I would argue that where women's role in agricultural production is declining or already low, an alternative strategy should be considered for generating rural employment.

To attempt to rehabilitate women workers in a sector in which there is little demand for their labor is to expose them to an especially vulnerable position. Where male unemployment and underemployment are high, women experience particular difficulty in finding work: the 1971 census of India defined 4.5 million unemployed rural women as compared with 3.2 million rural men, and national sample surveys counted more days of unemployment on the average for women than for men.

Similarly, where agricultural wages are low, women are paid less than men, even for the same work. Figures available from the Committee on the Status of Women in India for six Indian states show that legal minimum wages for male sowers, weeders, and reapers are approximately one-third higher than those for females, and even these wage minimums are notoriously difficult to enforce in rural areas where employment is geographically isolated and sporadic. Female agricultural workers are also far less likely than males to be paid for their work.

For example, in 1961 approximately 14 per cent of the rural male labor force in India consisted of unpaid family workers compared with 41 per cent of the rural female labor force; in Pakistan, the figures were 23 and 76 per cent, respectively. Even if they are paid, women may have no control over their earnings. Female cotton harvesters in Pakistan, for example, receive one sixteenth of the cotton they pick through the season, but the men take it to market. Women's agricultural labor in most developing countries has probably been consistently undercounted and undervalued. An economist in Pakistan remarked that men acknowledge the women's contribution "in their heart of hearts" but not in the sense that would permit female participation in institutions or decision making.

In Bangladesh "a farmer is valued on the basis of the rice he grows, but his wife's part in processing it is not considered an economic activity. Nor is her role in poultry raising, growing vegetables, fruits, making household clay utensils, mats, fans, and preservation of seeds, pickles, dry fish, dehydrated rice, etc. ever taken into account". Census definitions of economic activity usually exclude large numbers of women in agriculture, especially those who perform unpaid work in the family farm or who work seasonally or part-time. When talking to census takers, male household heads are likely to exaggerate their own efforts, while deflating the contributions of female family members. Women themselves undervalue their own work, frequently omitting any mention of their labor in the fields when they are asked whether they work outside the home.

Perhaps this should tell us something about the potential of most agricultural work for raising the status of women or promoting rural development. As Youssef concluded from an analysis of eight Muslim countries, "To promote women's inclusion into the agricultural sector will mean allowing women to continue dragging behind males; it will not add to the efficiency of labor productivity; it will only perpetuate the economic and psychological dependency of Muslim women on their men."

As for its effect on the birthrate, there is no reason to believe that female participation in agriculture should induce women to marry later or to want or to have fewer children. Alternatively, the creation of employment opportunities in small industries or organized services which can be monopolized by women could create an independent power base for women, provide a direct source of income, ensure more adequate scrutiny of earnings and working conditions, raise wages among women remaining in the agricultural sector, and, in the long run, create conditions favoring delayed marriage and controlled fertility among women workers.

SMALL-SCALE VILLAGE INDUSTRIES

India represents a classic example of displacement of women from agriculture without a concomitant absorption into the modern sector of the economy. Although female workers-even those in secondary and tertiary occupations-are likely to be undercounted in the census because of the scattered and unorganized nature of most of their employment, the absolute number of women in Non-agricultural jobs has dropped since 1911 in six of the seven employment categories. Particularly sharp declines appear in the economic activities traditionally employing large numbers of rural women-cottage industries, including spinning and weaving; paper making;

jute handicrafts; *bidi* (cigarette) making; rice processing and oil pressing; and trade and commerce.

Women in these occupations have been increasingly forced into competition with factory producers in the expanding industrial sector and with wholesalers and intermediaries in marketing. The control over income that many women had derived from marketing their own food or handicrafts has largely been lost. In 1971, women accounted for 28 per cent of rural workers engaged in household industries, for 14 per cent of workers in industries outside the household, but for only 8 per cent of those engaged in trade and commerce.

The number of women employed in mines and plantations (tea picking is traditionally defined as women's work) also dropped from 1.45 million in 1911 to under 1 million in 1971. Women construction workers declined in number, despite the growing utilization of female labor on public works projects. Although educated women have been entering clerical jobs, teaching, and the health professions in larger numbers, the general thrust of Indian development has also been to exclude more women from traditional service occupations than are absorbed into new tertiary jobs. Those displaced are disproportionately the illiterate and unskilled, as the demand for their labor shrinks and competition for scarce jobs intensifies.

In short, a small minority of middle-class women is able to take advantage of new opportunities for employment in the modern sector of the economy, but the majority of women living in rural areas and among low-income groups in the cities is pushed into marginal economic activities or out of the labor force entirely. Given this thrust, what are the possibilities for creating income-earning, Non-agricultural employment for rural women? Recruitment into construction projects, such as government rural works, is one possibility. Large numbers of tribal and scheduled caste women in India are currently employed in construction work, and Muslim women in Bangladesh-mostly destitute women widowed in the 1971 war or wives of unskilled workers-have begun to turn to the Food for Work program for rural employment.

However, construction work, even on government projects, is usually highly exploitative. Its critics point to failures of protective legislation covering wages, working conditions, and hours worked. Given the undernourished condition of the workers, the work tends to be exhausting. Women on construction projects are disproportionately concentrated in the lowest-skilled and lowest-paid jobs (generally, that of carrying earth or bricks) with no chance of learning new skills.

Employing women in the rural service sector is another possibility. With access to credit and with purchasing and marketing advice, some could be productively employed in personal service occupations or in trade and marketing. Again, this type of self-employment is economically vulnerable. Unorganized service workers are unlikely to acquire the capital and skills necessary to ensure sustaining economic returns. Villages require growing numbers of white-collar personnel as teachers, health workers, community development officers, agricultural extension agents, family-planning aides, and so on, but the extremely high levels of illiteracy among rural women in India, Bangladesh, Pakistan, and Nepal effectively preclude their participation in most of these occupations.

In some cases educational requirements could be lowered to recruit illiterate or semiliterate village workers for on-the-job training, an approach that would undoubtedly increase the representation of women in the service sector. On the whole, however, the main avenue of Non-agricultural employment for rural women would appear to be in small-scale industries and agro-industries. Even a brief investigation of foodstuffs and commodities available in rural markets in different seasons should suggest certain kinds of economic production that would promote self-sufficiency of the local community.

Ahmed suggests the decentralized manufacture of processed agricultural products, consumer goods, and light engineering goods, that is, commodities that are labor-intensive, based on local resources, and that require simple technology, small investment, and cheap or little fuel. Logical possibilities include preserved foods, cloth and ready-made clothing, soap, household and farm utensils, and small manufactured items such as transistor radios assembled from imported parts. In any case, if villages are strategically placed in a transportation and communications network, production can be aimed at supplying urban and export markets as well as (or instead of) filling local needs either directly or by substituting domestic for imported goods.

Women recruited into small-scale, rural industries could simultaneously create an effective demand for labor-saving goods and services in order to reduce their own domestic burdens, thereby generating new jobs catering to the needs of families of employed women. In their proposal for creating modern small industries in developing countries, Staley and Morse have created a typology of manufacturing based on the organization of work. Small industries range from those in which production is solely for family use to the small factory of, say, well under one hundred employees (fewer if production is highly mechanized). The family-use system consists of home-based production of commodities such as preserved food, clothing, pottery, and furniture for the household's own use, a type of production generally encouraged by community development programs.

The artisan system includes workers who are family members or, in the case of artisan workshops, apprentices in crafts such as weaving, tailoring, shoemaking, goldsmithing, and so forth. The putting-out or dispersed factory system involves a more complex division of labor, with the work being dispersed through middlemen, such as merchants, factory managers, or agents, who deliver raw materials to the home or shop and buy the entire output. Whereas industrial homework employs family members (usually paid on a piecework basis), the dependent or quasi-independent small shop relies primarily on hired labor that is paid either by piecework or on an hourly or daily wage.

Finally, the most centralized form of organization is the factory system, classified here into small, medium, and large factories on the basis of the number of employees and the power source used. Each of these organizational types may be located in either rural or urban areas, may be based on handwork or mechanization, and (with the exception of home consumption) may cater to either local or distant markets. What makes a small industry modern is its orientation to the needs of an emerging economy; its adaptability in the search for improved techniques, products, and design; its adoption of an appropriate physical technology and a more highly organized social technology; and a rationalized system of planning, budgeting, and marketing.

Small-scale production units are particularly well suited to the manufacture of many consumer goods required by a rapidly growing population and to labor-intensive employment which utilizes intermediate technology while reducing the need for high capital expenditures. Staley and Morse warn against taking the ideology of labor-intensiveness to extremes, for example, the employment of widows in India to make, by hand, matches that are far more efficiently (and less dangerously) made by machine. They argue, "Labor-intensiveness which achieves the saving of some scarcer productive factor, such as capital, is a virtue... but labor intensiveness without saving of other factors is pure waste". It then becomes an unproductive form of work relief rather than a genuine development effort.

THE CENTRAL WORKPLACE

Most government and private welfare programs aimed at raising the level of living of rural women and their families have concentrated on encouraging greater productivity in the home through training in child care and nutrition, cooking, vegetable and poultry raising, sewing, and other activities coming under the general rubric of home economics. If they have addressed the issue of income-earning activities for women at all, they have encouraged cottage industries such as weaving, basket making, or embroidery, with the products being marketed through intermediaries, local shops, or cooperatives. Frequently, programs are based on the desirability of raising consumption while leaving women's roles in the family and community basically unchanged.

Although home-based production for the family's own use or for sale undoubtedly improves the level of living of village women at least slightly, and although under some conditions home-based industries may be a necessary transitional stage to a higher form of economic organization, locating economic production in a central workplace carries a number of economic and social advantages. First, it permits closer supervision of workers, control over the quality of goods, and more adequate protection of working conditions and wages by regulating agencies. Second, it allows an economy of scale and division of labors that are impossible to achieve in a dispersed system and encourages specialization and diversification of tasks.

Third, it facilitates technological innovation and investment in capital equipment; and fourth, it draws women out of the isolation and conservatism of their domestic environments into social interaction with one another, capitalizing on their incentive to meet together. Fifth, it eases delivery of special training programs in vocational skills, literacy, nutrition, family planning, and other areas; and last, it encourages delayed marriage and fertility control by posing, among other contradictions, a degree of incompatibility between worker and family roles. Home-based industry, on the other hand, "... is almost always a barrier to improvements in production technology and managerial practices, is subject to grave abuses, and has psychological and social drawbacks that impinge on, among other things, the status of women and the control of population growth".

Removing women physically from the pervasive influence of the domestic environment for at least a few hours each day may be essential to altering their situation substantially. Ahmed argues, "To be recognized as a person in her own right, to become an acting individual, she must build a link with the world outside her family. The strongest link is economic, one of contributing skill and energy to the social whole and earning the material and psychological rewards of this contribution.

Individuality grows out of interaction." Removing production from the home can also ensure that women are paid for their economic activities directly rather than working as part of a labor unit in which the husband or father is the employer handling negotiations with the outside world, marketing the product, and controlling the household income. This situation is typical of female workers in the *khadi* (homespun) industry concentrated in Rajasthan, Punjab, Haryana, Jammu, Kashmir, and Himachal Pradesh. Women usually spin and, with their children, "help" with the weaving, but they are not paid directly.

Their productivity does not challenge the patriarchal structure of the village household. Similarly, women in a small village near Kathmandu spend all day squatting over a hot and smoky fire in the dark interior of their homes, making puffed rice which their husbands sell in the market. Their children play by the fire or in the dirt outside the door. If the women worked centrally, they could improve their equipment and techniques, save on expensive firewood, and take pleasure in one another's company.

Someone could watch all the children together, and a division of labor could be instituted in which some women are free to do the marketing while others boil, husk, dry, puff, and package the rice. The women themselves would decide on the selling price of their product and receive the direct benefits of their income.

Drawing women outside the home should also create conditions likely to lead to delayed marriage and birth control. The powerless, physically isolated woman, entirely dependent on her husband and children for social status and economic survival, is an unlikely candidate for family planning. Home-based industries tend to encourage childbearing because they so frequently employ young children to weave rugs or saris, wrap *bidis*, shell prawns, make baskets, or help in other tasks. Locating production in a central workplace should devalue the economic contribution of young children and deter their exploitation as a cheap labor force.

EMPLOYING IN THEIR EARLY REPRODUCTIVE YEARS

The proposal to create special employment for women is bound to stimulate controversy, for strong arguments can be made on both sides. Its proponents argue that work in an all-female setting fits with the cultural values limiting contact between the sexes, which is characteristic of much of South Asia. It also encourages the development of decision-making and technical skills among women who might otherwise withdraw from direct competition with men; and it can create strong bonds of solidarity, cutting across family and caste boundaries, to provide an alternative social and economic power base in the community. Its opponents argue that the promotion of "women's work" in all-female settings is a regressive policy, perpetuating segregation rather than promoting equality between the sexes. Others argue more generally that women should not receive special attention for jobs at all so long as men are under- or unemployed.

Creating employment specifically for women makes sense in at least three situations: (1) when the tasks to be organized are traditionally performed by females; (2) when cultural values require that girls and women be sheltered from contact with men who are not family members; and (3) when men are otherwise likely to gain control over the income earned from women's labor, for example, by selling the goods that women produce.

First, opposition to women's gainful employment should be significantly reduced if the task is one traditionally performed by women or defined as women's work. I am not suggesting that jobs for women be restricted to these tasks, but the prevailing sex-typing of activities within each community can create a natural occupational base for women that do not threaten to take jobs away from men, but rather generates new employment. Women in South Asia care for milch animals and raise poultry and vegetables in subsistence activities that could be upgraded in many areas to commercial production; they process foods into salable items such as ghee, ground spices, husked and puffed rice, or pickles and chutneys, and then make household items such as mats, baskets, cloth, and sometimes pottery. In Bangladesh, some village women make fishnets; in Kerala, women manufacture palm *gur* and process vegetable fibers. All-women's industrial and artisanal enterprises would be logical outgrowths of these activities.

Employment can be successfully generated in fields not defined as female, however. Women's cooperatives in Poona operate a match factory and an industry for manufacturing radio transformers. In Kerala, an industrial scheme is being developed at Ernakulam to employ women only for galvanizing, anodizing, and manufacturing pins, hooks and gem-clips and for operating a foundry. The Social Welfare Board of India has diversified its vocational training programs for women to include new occupations such as radio and television assembly, photography, and electroplating in addition to garment making, printing, hand looming and handicrafts, and dairy production.

Ahmed argues strongly that the employment opportunities most likely to attract rural women are those that are "least rural and least womanish"-that is, small industries that would teach women to operate and repair machines and to supervise, manage, keep accounts, and sell their products. Since these tasks will also attract men, a quota may be required to ensure that women participate. One way of doing this is to design some workshops for women only. The second condition under which an all-female work setting is desirable is where villagers fear that the chastity of the female and the honor of her family will be compromised if she mingles freely with men or is merely subject to their gaze or conversation. These fears are most elaborately symbolized by the institution of *purdah*, which regulates contact between the sexes by offering "separate worlds and symbolic shelter" to Muslim and Hindu women of certain social standing.

Women observing *purdah* must be assured of a protected working environment, at least initially, if they are to take advantage of employment opportunities outside the home. Among some tribes and lower castes of India, where women move about more freely, and among Muslims forced by economic necessity to forgo the luxury of female seclusion, women may still prefer to work primarily with other women, even if the culture does not demand it. Creating employment for women only is also effective in those instances where females are largely excluded from existing economic arrangements, especially where they perform much of the labor but acquire no control over the earned income.

The National Cooperative Union of India (n.d.) provides one such example. Laws which, in the past, prevented Hindu women from inheriting property effectively blocked them from membership in agricultural cooperatives, most of which are based on land ownership, regardless of their participation in agricultural labor or their interest in the economic decisions of the household. Credit societies made up of male members similarly block women from direct access to loans for their own enterprises. Even in cooperatives such as the *khadi* or dairy industry, in which women play a major role in production, shareholders are usually male household heads who represent the family's economic interest. Virtually all of the societies' elected officials and permanent staff members are men.

Restricting employment totally or primarily to women not only ensures that economic rewards will accrue directly to female producers, but also promotes economic and social self-reliance by inducing women to take on a variety of tasks that men would ordinarily perform, such as buying raw materials, keeping accounts, supervising other workers, and marketing products. In a mixed group the women's initial shyness and inexperience are likely to cause them to defer to men in most decisions, thus negating much of the potential for individual development inherent in the new employment.

The proposition that jobs in these modern, small industries be reserved for women in their early reproductive years derives from the simple argument that little demographic impact will result from employing women who already have large numbers of children or who are beyond menopause or widowed. Yet, frequently it is the destitute widows and women abandoned by their husbands who are the first to come forth. These women would be good candidates for income-generating activities based in or around the home; such as growing vegetables or raising poultry or fish for the market, spinning and weaving, and other traditional tasks. But the new employment in central workplaces could more effectively be secured for girls of marriageable age and married women in the early stages of their childbearing years.

The employment of unmarried girls is perhaps the most important step in bringing about social and demographic change. The opportunity to learn skills and earn money before marriage should awaken a girl to the possibility of becoming economically self-reliant and, at the same time, allay her fear of destitution or her dependence on reluctant relatives if she should remain unmarried or become widowed or divorced in the future. More directly, income-generating employment outside the home should offer an economically attractive and (with careful planning) a culturally acceptable alternative to early marriage and childbearing, particularly if the girl contributes part of her income to her family.

The lower age limit for recruiting unmarried girls should not be set so young that parents are encouraged to take their daughters out of school (if, indeed, they are attending school at all) in order to put them to work, but it should be set low enough to offer gainful employment to girls at precisely the age at which their parents are most concerned to have them married. In many areas this will be as soon as the daughter reaches puberty. Almost half of the fifty-six mothers interviewed in a small village in the Pakistan Punjab said that girls should get married between the ages of twelve and fourteen.

In rural India, in 1971, at least 14 per cent of girls between the ages of ten and fifteen were already married although the legal minimum age is fifteen; 18 per cent of girls of this age (rural and urban) in Bangladesh in 1965; 16 per cent in Nepal in 1971; and 1 per cent in Pakistan in 1965. Once the girls are working together, educational programs can deliberately promote postponement of marriage, at least until the age of eighteen or twenty. Direct financial incentives could also be incorporated into the work setting; some possibilities are suggested later in this chapter.

A similar argument holds for married women: those most amenable to social and demographic change are still in their early childbearing years. Women could be recruited from among those with fewer than, say, three children, with special efforts being devoted to delaying additional pregnancies and preventing births past the second or third child. Forty-five per cent of live births in rural India, in 1969, were fourth order or higher. An additional compelling reason for limiting employment to women in their early reproductive years is that younger women are likely to be more motivated to learn new skills and more open to acquiring new approaches to life.

The National Board of Bangladesh Women's Rehabilitation Programme restricts recruitment for its vocational training programs to women less than thirty years of age for exactly this reason. Older women, on the other hand, frequently admit their own lack of interest. For example, when women in a small village in the Pakistan Punjab were asked whether they would like to learn new skills such as sewing, they replied, "We have passed our time. It is time for our daughters to learn things".

THE PRODUCERS' COOPERATIVE

The concept of cooperative subsumes a number of organizational forms with a variety of function's-promoting group savings, obtaining credit and loans, buying raw materials or consumer goods, sharing agricultural services such as irrigation or fertilizers, manufacturing artisanal or industrial products, marketing, and organizing social services such as health care or housing, among others. In essence, a cooperative is a group of people who voluntarily form together, because of their common economic needs and interests, into an association in which decisions are made by members as a group or by elected representatives, and in which members share the costs and benefits of the enterprise. Cooperatives promote self help through group action.

Although the suggestion is controversial, I would argue that organizing women's economic activities into small, industrial producers' cooperatives offers a number of economic and social advantages over the promotion of individual entrepreneurs or the provision of jobs by public agencies. First, workers acquire an economic stake in the success of the enterprise by contributing their own capital (however small) toward membership shares and by participating in the distribution of profits.

Profit sharing disperses money over a large number of households rather than concentrating it in the hands of a few, thus raising the general level of living and encouraging expenditure in the local community. Second, members are generally required to save a portion of their earnings; the savings are credited to the individual member but pooled to provide loans to members or for group expenditures. Whereas private employers are unlikely to invest in public amenities, cooperatives generally allocate a portion of their profits to community projects such as schools or tube wells before distributing the balance as dividends. Third, registered cooperatives usually receive favorable economic concessions from governments in the form of easily obtained loans, lower interest rates, and lower prices for raw materials, special marketing outlets, and technical assistance.

In addition, by involving workers in decisions about the conditions of their employment and their role in the community, and by teaching management skills, cooperatives can act as agents of social change by breaking down the psychology of female dependency, mobilizing women to act on their own behalf, and creating a sense of group consciousness that may be essential to the achievement of such community goals as environmental protection or the reduction of birthrates. Whether other forms of organization of the workplace can deal with these issues as effectively is open to question.

Take the question of birth planning, for example. The immediate interests of the agrarian extended family are essentially pronatalist, while those of the wider community are likely to be antinatalist, especially where rapid population growth creates intense pressures upon available land or scarce educational facilities or jobs. Transcendence of immediate family interests requires that persons become aware of the socioeconomic costs to the community of their individual actions. Organizing women into cohesive associations could create competing loyalties between the family and the larger group, permitting new flexibility in reproductive ideals and behavior. Without an alternative base of information and support beyond the family, girls and women may be reluctant to resist pronatalist pressures from their kin.

In view of its many failures, critics are bound to question the promotion of a cooperative model. Its limitations are recognized, even by enthusiasts such as Ahmed, who argues that for Pakistan the combination of collective efforts and individual freedom inherent in cooperatives offers an attractive and plausible alternative to pure capitalist or socialist models for rural development. No one could deny that the cooperative movement has confronted a multitude of social, economic, and political obstacles in its long history in South Asia as well as elsewhere. Stories abound of bureaucratic mismanagement, membership apathy, political interference, and financial collapse.

A United Nations Research Institute for Social Development investigation of forty rural cooperatives of different types in Asia, Africa, and Latin America concluded that they rarely acted as agents of genuine social change for the rural masses because they were usually dominated by better-off inhabitants who were in a position to take advantage of their services and facilities. Staley and Morse, too, dismiss the cooperative model for small-scale industry because of its history of failure and stagnation. They choose free enterprise instead:

> The best strategy yet found by which a development-minded government can bring into being a vigorous, progressive, modern small industry is not to try to set up government-operated units, nor to sponsor manufacturing cooperatives. It is, instead, to devote equivalent energies and funds to modifying the economic, social, and political

environment in such a manner as to stimulate dozens, hundreds, or even thousands of private entrepreneurs to try their hands at organizing, modernizing, or expanding independently owned and managed small manufacturing enterprises.

Finally, others argue that the idea of cooperation is alien to many villagers and is doomed to failure for this reason. Because of their mutual suspicion and mistrust, one group of Muslim women near Jalchatra in northern Bangladesh strongly resisted pooling income from their jute handicrafts, insisting instead on individual savings accounts, even after a year of working together. In other instances, imposing a too-rigid model of cooperation may overlook or even destroy indigenous informal networks that have grown naturally out of such activities as savings and loan associations, mutual assistance in farming, or exchanging information and personal services.

Other forms of economic organization may be more appropriate. For example, several thousand self-employed cart pullers, sewers, street vendors, and rag pickers in Ahmedabad have been organized into a Self-Employed Women's Association (SEWA) which provides a number of credit and marketing services but is not technically a cooperative. The critics' arguments are compelling. Nevertheless, I would argue that, on the whole, cooperatives offer the most promising model for organizing small-scale industries among village women; that many pitfalls can be avoided with proper planning and supervision; and that the potential for socioeconomic transformation inherent in the cooperative approach surpasses that which is possible in other modes of organization.

Of course, the approach must be flexible, and under some conditions alternatives, such as private enterprise, will be preferable. But past failures should not necessarily lead us to abandon the principles of cooperation; rather, the principles could be adapted to current conditions in order to maximize their effectiveness. The idea of women's producer cooperatives is certainly not new in South Asia, but no one knows how many there are. Official registries are unreliable because many societies are not registered and because some that are registered are now dormant or defunct. Many of those registered are savings or thrift societies or consumers' groups rather than producers' cooperatives.

The Indian Cooperative Societies Act of 1904, stressing the development of agricultural credit societies, began what is now the oldest cooperative movement among developing countries. Women's cooperatives have been gaining in popularity since the early 1960s; by 1970-71 there were approximately 3,300 registered women's societies in India, with a total membership of 138,000. Of these, 1,100 were industrial societies with a membership of 24,000 producing goods worth Rs. 5.7 million (well over $500,000), and the balance were consumers of thrift and savings. Women's industrial societies have undertaken such activities as preparing pickles, jams, chutneys, and other foodstuffs, grinding and packaging spices, weaving and embroidery, rug making, knitting and doll making, and small-scale manufacturing and assembly of industrial components as ancillaries to larger firms.

Fifteen thousand women are members of registered all-women's cooperatives of various kinds in Bangladesh, but many of the societies are defunct. The Integrated Rural Development Program (IRDP) is specifically encouraging the formation of rural women's producer cooperatives in a program that is eventually to cover 1,900 villages of nineteen *thanas*, counties. These will be organized primarily around poultry raising and vegetable and fruit gardening. The program is to train 20,000 women in cooperative organization, agricultural skills, literacy, and family planning. About 3,000 Bengali women make jute handicrafts in all-women's cooperatives, which market their goods locally and export them through the Jute Works, but most of these are not registered.

Of the 30,000 registered cooperatives in Pakistan, with a total membership of almost 2 million, about 1,000 are women's societies, with a membership of 38,000. It is not clear what type these are. A former registrar reports that no women's cooperatives exist in the Northwest Frontier Provinces, even though women there do beautiful embroidery, which is usually sold through middlemen or shop agents. In Nepal, there are no cooperatives composed exclusively of women.

The government is consolidating the many single-purpose societies into larger multipurpose units, one to a village, in order to provide a wide range of services to farmers in conjunction with the village *panchayats*. It will probably be difficult for women to expand their membership or decision-making powers under these conditions despite the major role they play in agricultural and handicraft production. The Nepal Women's Organization (NWO) has not attempted to form cooperative societies in its training programs for rural women.

ADDITIONAL SERVICES AND INCENTIVES

If employment is to involve the worker in a genuinely developmental process, then additional services and incentives should be organized around the work situation. Among the most central of these are education in functional literacy, family planning, child care, and the establishment of living quarters for some workers. Financial incentives could also directly encourage delayed marriage and birth control.

The statistics on literacy in South Asia (with the exception of Sri Lanka) paint a dismal picture. According to the 1971 census, more than 89 per cent of women workers in India were illiterate. In Pakistan (including Bangladesh), in 1961, 93 per cent of adult women could neither read nor write; in Nepal, in 1971, 97 per cent were illiterate. Although women's illiteracy may not be a major obstacle to their work performance except at managerial levels, it does symbolize a state of social and psychological dependency on men (frequently their own husbands or brothers or sons) and on the small elite of women in the community who can read and write.

The workplace presents an ideal setting for education in functional literacy by facilitating group instruction and by anchoring the learning firmly in the work experience. Restricting employment to unmarried girls and young married women also creates an especially adaptable group who are more teachable than older or younger persons. One Indian study found that many students between the ages of fourteen and eighteen were able, after only two or three years' instruction, to pass the Primary School Leaving Certificate Examination, which is based on eight years of study for children beginning school at age six or seven. Young working women will learn especially quickly if the program's content is shaped by their immediate needs and experiences in their families, the community, and the workplace. One hour could be set aside each day for instruction.

If women can perform simple work tasks without knowing how to read and write, why should instruction be offered at all? There are at least two reasons for doing so: functional education improves basic decision-making skills and raises the learner's consciousness of community issues. At a minimum, all workers should know how to read and write simple instructions and to calculate wage rates by the hour or piece, simple interest rates on savings or loans, and prices for raw materials and marketed goods. These literacy skills are essential if workers are to protect themselves from exploitation by their own managers or outsiders and if they are to participate actively in cooperative activities.

Some membership decisions require rather advanced mathematical concepts. A small, very poor fishermen's cooperative in Bangladesh, for example, had to agree on the terms for accepting men who wanted to join after the original members had been paying monthly dues of 2 *takas* each (14 cents) for over a year. Would new members be asked to pay the full amount of accumulated dues, in which case no one could afford to join, or would they receive proportionately fewer of the benefits (for example, leased fishing rights)? If the latter, how these benefits to be distributed?

The second purpose is what Freire calls "conscientization," a process by which learners-not as passive recipients but as knowing subjects-achieve a deepening awareness of the sociocultural reality that shapes their lives and of their capacity to transform that reality. Education becomes a dialogue between teacher and learner, building on the concrete situation of the learner's life. It enables one to understand the origins of one's poverty, to cope with natural disasters such as floods and drought, to deal with community conflict, to expose the role of moneylenders, to develop improved agricultural techniques, and so on.

Discussions exposing the oppressive aspects of early marriage, the dowry system, the sexual double standard, and constant childbearing would also be included. Women become genuinely involved in their own education as they learn to read and write what Freire calls "generative words," while engaging in a critical analysis of the social framework in which they exist. Their education breaks through the "culture of silence" which results from the structural relations between dominant and dependent classes and from women's psychological and economic dependence on men.

Freire's philosophy gave impetus to the Bangladesh Rural Advancement Committee's (BRAC's) functional education classes in the villages of Sulla. With materials developed by World Education, BRAC organized classes for village women in the afternoons and for men at night, using local people with only five or six years' schooling as teachers. Each student receives a certificate of graduation at the end of the seventy lessons. To keep villagers from quickly lapsing into illiteracy, BRAC started a newsletter, Gonokendra (Community Center), which is distributed through all of the villages in the area.

FAMILY PLANNING

Women's isolation presents a major obstacle to community-level delivery of health and family-planning services. In contrast, the central workplace not only offers a convenient site for distributing family-planning information and supplies but also permits women to obtain birth control information and devices without the necessary knowledge or consent of other family members-a distinct advantage when husbands or mothers-in-law are most resistant.

Women also can derive social support from their coworkers for delaying marriage, postponing pregnancies, or forgoing additional births. The woman's identity as a worker begins to compete with her identity as a wife and mother; spacing and limiting pregnancies becomes a means of fulfilling her responsibilities as an employee and cooperative member. Birth planning takes on new meaning when it is offered in the context of raising the standard of living for the poorest sectors of the population through producers' cooperatives and alternative roles for women.

CHILD CARE

Child care on the job is controversial from a demographic viewpoint because the theory of role incompatibility specifies that women's work must clearly compete with childbearing and childrearing if fertility is to be reduced. Providing child care for working women would thus negate the potential antinatalist effects of their employment by enabling women to choose both employment and children. First, if women are to be directly exposed to an antinatalist environment at all, they must be encouraged to come out of their homes into a productive work setting in which they can learn new attitudes and behavior. Female employment must be facilitated, not impeded, if it is to have any effect on reproduction.

Second, rural women will bear at least two or three children in any case. The opportunity for gainful employment could influence (directly and indirectly) the timing of these births and the probability of having additional births. Direct exposure to family-planning information and services on the job will facilitate effective birth control.

Third, children already born need care if the mother is to work outside the home. If child care is not provided on the job, young children will be cared for by mothers-in-law, other relatives, older siblings, or simply neglected. Infant care on the job enables mothers to keep their babies close for prolonged breast-feeding, which not only has nutritional advantages for the child but also demographic advantages as a child-spacing mechanism. Older, preschool children will also benefit from group care.

Fourth, a working mother may otherwise take her eldest daughter out of school in order to care for younger children, sacrificing the daughter's future to the mother's immediate needs. Finally, the object of creating income-generating employment for rural women is not solely to reduce birthrates. Women have an equal right with men to paid employment, regardless of its demographic consequences.

LIVING QUARTERS

The lack of hostels where women can live or stay overnight discourages many from participating in rural development programs as teachers, health and family-planning workers, cooperative inspectors, or in other capacities requiring temporary or permanent lodging in the village. But local unmarried girls could also benefit from living in a hostel at the worksite: they would be marginally removed from intense family pressures toward early marriage, which derive in part from the drain on limited financial and space resources when the girl lives at home; they would not be exposed to men's stares when walking through the streets to work; and they could create an environment of solidarity and self-reliance which would be bound to carry forward into other aspects of their lives. Costs would be reduced if the young women shared in growing vegetables and raising poultry for their own consumption and contributed part of their earnings for room and board.

The community might well find the idea initially shocking, however, since even the most respectable arrangements for single girls often meet with disapproval. Cultural fears of public dishonor, deriving from the parents' loss of control over their daughters, could probably be overcome if living arrangements were chaperoned by a resident, older widow with a good name. And removing marriageable young women from the home could eliminate the prevalent fear of incestuous and privately dishonoring sexual relationships within the family itself. Keeping young girls confined to the home can also present a sexually volatile situation which propels parents toward arranging an early marriage for their daughters.

FINANCIAL INCENTIVES FOR DELAYED MARRIAGE AND BIRTH CONTROL

The producers' cooperative offers a number of opportunities for incorporating specific financial incentives for delaying marriage and for spacing and limiting births. Delayed marriage could be encouraged by offering a substantial bonus to girls who remain single to the age of twenty, perhaps splitting it between the girl herself and her parents.

Married women could receive bonuses for each year that a child was not born, with higher bonuses going to younger women of low parity. Incentives could be offered for the adoption of family-planning practices, such as the sterilization of the woman or her husband. The woman's right to determine the size of her family should also be emphasized. These incentives would have to be tied to an educational program in which the benefits to the woman and to the community of altered reproductive behavior would be clearly specified, however.

The central, albeit largely a priori, argument has now been set forth. The goals of promoting rural development, raising the status of women, and encouraging delayed marriage and birth control in rural communities could be met by creating income-generating employment in small-scale industries, specifically for women in their early reproductive years, in cooperatively organized central workplaces that offer additional services such as functional literacy programs, family planning, child care, living quarters, and financial incentives.

Probably no rural development programs in India, Pakistan, Bangladesh, or Nepal meet all of these criteria. An Indian program encourages village women to grow vegetables for their own consumption, an activity which may be worthwhile for its nutritional value, but one that contributes little to rural development and probably nothing to advancing the status of women or altering their reproductive behavior. Programs in Nepal encourage women in making home-based handicrafts, which are sold for small amounts through middlemen or directly to urban shops.

This activity might improve women's status slightly, if they controlled the income they earned, but would not generally motivate them to delay marriage or practice birth control. Some Pakistani projects do bring women out of their homes into workshops for weaving, sewing or embroidery, but they usually offer little opportunity for development of skills, nor do they encourage women to participate fully in decisions about their work. The women's cooperatives organized in Bangladesh and India do not always adhere strictly to cooperative principles, such as democratic participation and regular membership meetings. Some offer programs such as functional literacy or family planning but only on a sporadic basis.

Hostels are available in those training programs that require women to move to town temporarily, for example, in Dacca and Kathmandu, but are not utilized in conjunction with permanent local industries. Nevertheless, a number of programs are promising, even though they do not meet all of the criteria specified above. Each has a lesson to teach about the problems of recruiting women, of creating a viable economic enterprise, and other issues. They include a series of small women's agricultural cooperatives for growing vegetables and raising fish and poultry in Bangladesh; village milk cooperatives in India; the jute handicrafts industry in Bangladesh; dispersed workshops for food processing in India; and carpet-weaving factories in Nepal.

3

Cultural and Structural Obstacles in the Recruitment of Women Workers

Who among rural women will be willing-or able-to take advantage of new employment opportunities in the villages of India or Nepal, Pakistan or Bangladesh? Is it possible to overcome the major cultural and structural obstacles to women's work outside the home in those communities that advocate female seclusion, among other practices? Can cooperative work groups successfully transcend religious, caste, or class boundaries, or must the organizational structure inevitably reflect (or perhaps even intensify) the socioeconomic hierarchy of the community, and its pervasive factionalism?

An a priori assumption that women will eagerly come forward may well prove false: at an Egyptian garment-making factory, which was designed to test the impact of female employment on fertility, organizers discovered that they had to shift their initial choice of site because they could not recruit women workers at the first location. At the second site, however, more women volunteered than could be trained, most of them unmarried girls and not the married women whose employment had been anticipated. The assumption that unmarried girls and young married women will not be willing or permitted to work may prove unwarranted, even in a conservative Muslim community. The central question is, under what conditions will women and their families seek to participate in the new economic activities?

INCENTIVES FOR OUTSIDE EMPLOYMENT

Many rural women in the predominantly Hindu and Muslim countries of South Asia are already working outside the home, whether for wages in agriculture, as unpaid workers on their family's land, or in petty trade or service occupations. Among these women the incentive to work is apparently already strong enough to override cultural or structural constraints because official labor-force statistics generally exclude a range of economic activities among rural women (especially seasonal work), the following figures should be taken as minimal estimates of the labor pool.

The Bangladesh (then East Pakistan) census of 1961 showed that 17.4 per cent of females aged ten and over were in the labor force; of these, 92 per cent were in agriculture. The (then West) Pakistan census reported that 9.3 per cent of females aged ten and over were in the labor force; of these, 70 per cent were in agriculture. According to the 1971-72 national Labor Force Survey of Pakistan, females are more likely to be employed in rural areas (9.5 per cent) than in urban centers (3.9 per cent).

Although female labor-force participation rates for Bangladesh and Pakistan are considerably lower than those for Muslim Indonesia and Malaysia, and far lower than those for non-Muslim Southeast Asian countries such as Thailand, where women work freely in the fields and the marketplace, they are considerably higher than those for most Muslim countries of North Africa and the Middle East, where fewer than 5 per cent of women are generally reported as being economically active. With a rather liberal definition of economic activity, India's 1961 census reported that 31.4 per cent of rural females were economically active (about half of them unpaid) compared with 13.1 per cent under the more restrictive definitions of 1971.

Rates of economic activity in the Indian states ranged from just over 1 per cent of rural females in the Punjab to over 50 per cent in Nagaland and Tripura. In 1961, in the neighboring Hindu kingdom of Nepal, over one-third of females of all ages were reported as being economically active, almost all of them rural workers. Although labor-force participation rates among rural women vary considerably across the four countries and among regions and districts within each country, it is probably fair to say that in all areas the girls and women defined as being economically active are drawn disproportionately from the non-Hindu and non-Muslim minorities (especially tribals, Christians, Buddhists), from low-caste and scheduled-caste groups in the Hindu community, and from the lowest socioeconomic ranks among the Muslims. Wives of marginal farmers and of landless agricultural workers are particularly likely to be employed.

These introductory remarks suggest that in most villages and small towns of the countries under discussion here, there will be women who are already motivated to exchange an insecure, oppressive, and poorly paid job for one of higher status, better working conditions, and regular pay. Young tribal girls in the Vedchhi Intensive Area Scheme in Gujarat left their agricultural labor at below-minimum wages for papad production in the community center at Rs. 3 a day, and destitute wives and widows volunteering for heavy labor, carrying earth and bricks on Food for Work road-building projects in Bangladesh and India, would undoubtedly be happy to take a higher-skilled job in a small industry for a direct cash income. New rural production centers might attract women who are currently employed in less desirable circumstances.

Among classes of women not currently working outside the home, one would undoubtedly discover a significant number with a strong economic incentive to work if the opportunity were offered. These women are most likely to be widows or abandoned wives now solely responsible for their own support and that of their young children, if any, or wives and daughters living in households in which the male wage earners have low or sporadic incomes-usually landless laborers, marginal farmers, or unskilled rural workers. It is generally these women who first come forward when opportunities for work appear.

The YWCA handicraft-training program and workshop in Dacca, for example, has a waiting list of women without husbands, or women with brothers or other relatives to support, who are driven to work by economic need. Because those who are taken on for training contribute so heavily to the family income, husbands soon find their initial objections appeased by the extra money. The financial motive, strongest among low-income groups, becomes more pressing in times of personal, community, or national crisis. Several informants remarked that Pakistani women turn increasingly to employment in order to cope with inflationary pressures in that country. The impoverishment of some segments of the population is intensified following major national crises such as wars, droughts, or floods.

The violence and disruption accompanying the 1947 partition of India and the 1971-72 war between Bangladesh and Pakistan left a large population of widowed and abandoned women, many of them homeless, who were reduced to begging in the streets. A number of welfare programs were designed to assist these destitute women and to provide relief and rehabilitation through vocational training and employment. Poor harvests from droughts or floods also compound the problem of rural landlessness. As marginal farmers are forced to sell out or landless workers are unable to find employment, the whole family is left destitute and searching for work.

Even better-off village women may also have some financial incentive to work. Brahmin and Chetri women in one village located several miles from Kathmandu, for example, have said they would like to learn to knit or sew in order to earn their own money. They could buy a new sari or some jewelry, or new school shoes for the children, without having to ask the permission of their husband or father-in-law. The concept of an independent income for personal use in the extended family is an alien one however. For in its ideal form, the family combines the income of all members and distributes it according to need, with the allocation decisions being made be the household head. It is not known whether the Brahmin and Chetri women would be willing to work full time outside their homes year round. Such employment could be seen as threatening to the ritual status of the family.

NON-ECONOMIC INCENTIVES

Non-economic motives can also play an important role in inducing women to work. In one small study in Delhi, 70 per cent of one hundred middle-income women and 82 per cent of fifty low-income women declared they would continue to work even if their husbands' incomes were increased by the amount of their earnings. The latter group consisted entirely of scheduled-caste women working as servants, vegetable vendors, sellers of *lassi* or cow dung, quilt makers, and so forth.

One major Non-economic incentive to outside employment is prestige. Obviously, most jobs available to largely unskilled and illiterate rural women-and men-carry little prestige. The few prestigious jobs, such as teachers, government agents, and other community officials, are generally closed to women, who lack the education, training, geographical mobility, and cultural acceptability that such jobs require. As a consequence, rural women who work outside the home are mostly engaged in farm labor, petty trading (for example, selling glass bangles door-to-door), or in menial service (as sweepers and household servants). It is thus not surprising that most work is viewed as "prestige-reducing" rather than "prestige-enhancing" both by the community at large and by the women themselves.

Indeed, the mark of a family's prestige is to keep their womenfolk at home, not to have them exposed to strangers or low-status people in a public place. Because in rural areas it is predominantly the low-caste, low-income women who work outside the home (the same can be said for towns and cities except for a small minority of educated women in admired professional positions), female employment becomes identified as a low-status activity. Even selling articles made at home may be considered demeaning by some. In one Punjabi village in Pakistan almost all the women were engaged in spinning, pickle making, straw weaving, embroidery, crocheting, and weaving elaborate belts, while a minority sewed, knitted, and made pottery or other handicraft objects for the family's use.

But, according to Anwar and Bilquees, "The women generally disapprove of selling something made with their own hands. When asked about this, the women replied, 'We do not sell our skills,' 'People who sell their skills are Kammies low-caste'." Nevertheless, when there is good money to be made, women frequently become very proud of their ability to earn money from their skills. The Muslim women in the Sri Joni cooperative in Dacca who make jute handbags-although initially criticized for their behavior-came to be envied in the community when the value of their efforts became apparent. The young Muslim girls and women who have taken up embroidery in the village of Shah Jewana in the Punjab have gained considerable prestige, especially those who work full time and bring in a steady income.

Their prestige is enhanced with every new addition to the household's appliances or to their clothing, jewelry, or dowries. Young Muslim girls working as paramedics in the People's Health Center at Savar, Bangladesh, overcame the initial disapproval of their actions, acquiring prestige when villagers realized that the paramedics can provide them with notes granting immediate hospital attention for severe illnesses. The female paramedics, many of them local unmarried girls about fifteen or sixteen years of age, earn a small monthly salary, live at the health center, and receive six months of training in health care and family planning. The jobs are considered so desirable that there is a waiting list of applicants who wish to join the program.

On the whole, employment in small industry may not initially be viewed as prestigious by the local community since, at first, it attracts primarily those driven by economic need. The community's initial reservations will most likely be transformed into admiration and pride as the skills and productivity of the workers increase. As women become literate and learn managerial skills, taking positions on boards and training in distant towns, they will be regarded in a new light as they, their families, and the community begins to benefit visibly from individual incomes and cooperative investments. A small, tentative venture will begin to attract additional applicants as the benefits become clearer.

In the village of Shah Jewana only four women turned up when the announcement was first made in the mosque that Syeda Abida Hussein would buy their embroidery. But when the word spread that she was paying good money, thirty or forty others quickly joined. Ten years later, over two hundred girls and women were registered as regular embroidery workers, and the villagers were clearly proud of their accomplishments. A further motive which could be capitalized upon in recruitment is the women's desire to meet together outside the home. We noted that many rural women in South Asia already work outside the home either regularly or sporadically and seasonally, but others remain isolated in their homes or family compounds with their daily social contacts limited to immediate kin.

The usual meeting places for men-mosques or temples, tea shops, the "men's house" of the village, and the marketplace-are frequently closed to women. Rural women may pay occasional visits to their natal homes in another village, or gather together as passive observers of religious events, but, for many, opportunities for exchanges of information are few. Within the limited range of contacts, even an opportunity to meet other women for a few minutes at the river or well may be eagerly awaited. When women in one village of Nepal were asked which of their household tasks they found most onerous, for example, few mentioned having to go to the well several times a day to fill heavy clay or brass vessels with water.

Apparently, this was one of the few occasions on which women could socialize with one another. Brahmin and Chetri women in another village near Kathmandu work seasonally in their fields as a team, singing together and joking with the men as they plant the rice. But, except for the poorest households, this is the only time of year that women are out of their homes on a regular basis or interacting as a group. In parts of Bangladesh the women's lives are even more limited. In the Comilla District, for example, "the contacts the Bengali village mother has with the outside are extraordinarily limited. She may visit her kins people once or twice a year if they do not live too far away.

Though the mosque is a weekly meeting place for the men and boys, as is also the local market, the village women do not go to either." When the BARD in Comilla instituted literacy and vocational training courses for the rural women, the response was immediate. As Raper notes, "The benefits of the women's learning are clear in the villages, the courtyards, gardens, and households. But even more important is the fact that the women now leave their homes regularly and for a new purpose that they meet with other women regularly in the villages that they rarely, if ever, miss class, even during inclement weather."

How could the incentives be maximized for young women to work? The financial inducements are most straightforward: a steady income, at least equivalent to prevailing wage rates for male agricultural laborers. The woman herself should be able to set aside a part of her earnings for her own use rather than turning the entire amount over to the household as a whole. One way of accomplishing this without causing dissension in the family is to require that, say, one-tenth of her earnings are deposited in a savings account managed by the cooperative. Several of the cooperatives consider that compulsory savings plans are an essential ingredient of their programs.

Usually the elected management board decides whether a member may withdraw her savings for particular purposes or whether she should instead ask for a loan from cooperative funds. An appropriate withdrawal of savings might be the purchase of land that would ultimately provide a better income for the worker and her family in their old age; an inappropriate withdrawal would be one used to meet daily expenses for food and clothing. Direct cash payments to the family might also be considered as an initial incentive. A gift, equivalent to one month's wages, given at the outset with the stipulation that the women would begin training and stay on the job for at least six months, could sensitize the family elders to the value of the woman's work.

If the elders or the woman herself decided to withdraw her labor within the six-month period, the incentive payment would have to be returned, much like bride wealth at the time of divorce. The prestige incentive could be maximized by providing a culturally acceptable environment, as well as opportunities on the job for women to gain competence in literacy and other valued skills.

And the incentive to socialize with other women will be maximized by providing employment in a central workplace rather than in the home, by restricting employment to women, and by offering abundant opportunities for interaction on the job through functional literacy classes emphasizing discussion, or frequent meetings of cooperative members. Those who receive more advanced training in vocational skills and management will have the added opportunity to meet with women from other villages and to travel to distant towns or cities.

IMPEDIMENTS TO FEMALE EMPLOYMENT

On the basis of this brief review of positive incentives for rural women, at least those with low income, to seek paid employment outside the home, I would argue that the primary need is to overcome the major cultural and structural obstacles that prevent women who want to work from taking advantage of these opportunities.

The first of these is the natural suspicion that villagers are likely to feel when confronted with organizers promoting a plan for their benefit; other obstacles relate to the cultural requirements for observing *purdah* among both Hindus and Muslims; and others, to the simple fact that many rural women-as motivated as they might be-simply do not have the time to take on a regular outside job. They are, if anything, not an "underutilized human resource," as the planners are fond of referring to them, but "overutilized" in a very basic way. They work hard, all day, with few visible benefits from their labors.

REACTION TO THE PROJECT ORGANIZERS

Khushi Kabir, a young organizer of women's programs for the Bangladesh Rural Advancement Committee (BRAC), told of a village she had visited the day before in the Sulla area near Sylhet, where for several years BRAC has been working with the people to initiate health-care, adult literacy, housing, and agricultural programs. A health worker had previously arranged for the Hindu and Muslim women to meet with her individually in order to decide whether they wanted to start a women's group and, if so, what they would like it to accomplish. When Kabir arrived in the village on the appointed day, in the company of a Dutch male anthropologist, none of the Muslim women came out to meet with her.

A team of government family welfare workers who had visited the village a few days before had apparently broadcast their family-planning goals in a rather zealous fashion. When the city-bred Bengali woman and the bearded foreigner arrived a few days later, the Muslim women hid in their homes, fearing that the visitors were doctors who had come from Dacca to sterilize them. A number of Hindu women did show up, however, mostly wives past childbearing age and widows. They decided to start a rice-savings club and to plant potatoes for marketing during the next season.

The story highlights one of the major obstacles to organizing new programs: the villagers' suspicion of the organizers' motives. Their suspicion is, usually, a highly rational response to their concrete experiences of past victimization. Among the impoverished Muslim families scattered through the national forest near Mymensing in northern Bangladesh, for example, fear of outsiders was pervasive. A stranger could be a government agent, levying new taxes or looking for bribes; a forest service agent, sent to evict them from their illegal dwellings; or a spy for a band of thieves, who would steal everything they had right down to the last sack of rice.

The Roman Catholic mission at Jalchatra had taken decades to build a sense of trust among the local population of predominantly Garo tribes people through a comprehensive program of schooling, medical care, and agricultural assistance. One sister reconstructed the fears of the Muslim women this way: "What do these people want from me? What are they after? What is in it for them?" Mamdani tells of the reactions, in the mid-1950s, among the villagers of Manupur in northern India to family-planning workers who were trying to persuade them to use contraceptive foams: "The villagers searched for 'the clue' to what the Khanna Study was 'really doing.' Every detail of what the study members did was watched suspiciously.

One report states: 'Serious difficulties sometimes have attended seemingly minor matters. Despite careful preparation of the village authorities, mapping of the village gave rise to uncontrollable rumors of a rise in taxes, another war, or that the village was to be moved.'" Other villagers speculated that the visitors were missionaries, or contractors come to straighten the streets. The family-planning workers in this case were Punjabis, not foreigners, but their educated urban background proved to be just as alien to the villagers (and vice versa) as that of someone from another land.

And when missionaries/anthropologists William and Charlotte Wiser arrived in the Indian village of Karimpur, east of Agra to do a brief statistical survey, "even the dogs yapped and the donkeys escaped as fast as their hobbles would allow." The culture of suspicion and the structural conditions underlying it are aptly summed up in Banfield behavioral principle, derived from his observations of a village in southern Italy, "No one will take the initiative in outlining a course of action and persuading others to embark upon it (except as it may be to his private advantage to do so), and, if one did offer leadership, the group would refuse it out of distrust."

Although he centers his analysis on the phenomenon of

amoral familism -acting to benefit one's own nuclear family over the short term in an economy of scarcity, while assuming that others will do likewise-the principle may also apply to a number of communities in which the extended family predominates. Any outsider may be suspect, as well as members of the community who belong to different kin groups, one's neighbors, or other household members who are assumed to be acting out of a motive for personal gain. If new industries are to be successfully introduced into rural communities, and if women and their families are to cooperate actively in their planning and execution, the villagers' natural mistrust of the organizers must clearly be allayed.

Assuming that the organizers' motives are indeed honorable, the next step is to convince others that this is so. To this end, the central concern of the project should be with the whole development of the workers and not with the personal aggrandizement or enrichment of the organizers. It should also be designed so that workers will share in decision making, receive fair wages for their efforts, have a share of the profits, experience reasonable working conditions, and not be coerced into acting against their principles.

Ultimately, the demonstration effect will do. But initially it will be necessary to identify and utilize as sponsors or intermediaries those local institutions (for example, successful male agricultural cooperatives or *panchayats*), groups, or individuals who have the trust and admiration of a substantial portion of the people from whom workers are most likely to be drawn.

In addition, fears will be minimized if villagers are incorporated into the decision-making process from the beginning by the means of open meetings in which suggestions are elicited and proposals debated. In some villages meetings may have to be segregated by sex, but in others the men and women can meet together. In any case, it is essential that whole families participate and come to understand the nature of the projected scheme and its potential advantages or disadvantages if their womenfolk are to take on the new employment.

THE PRACTICE OF FEMALE SECLUSION

In regions of Hindu and Muslim influence in South Asia, the ideal of female seclusion remains one of the major inhibitors of women's participation in public life. Institutionalized in the practice of *purdah*, the ideal is expressed in avoidance rules designed to regulate contact between the sexes and to segregate most male and female activities both socially and spatially.

The manifestations of *purdah* most visible to the outsider are the virtual absence of women from the streets of towns and cities in some parts of Bangladesh and Pakistan; the segregation of those women who do appear in public into separate compartments in buses, trains, or waiting rooms, or their concealment by a curtain on the cycle rickshaws or scooter taxis to prevent strangers from seeing them (and vice versa); the form of dress which requires, at the very least, the covering of the head and shoulders with a sari or shawl, and, at the most, the covering of the entire body from head to toe with a burqa, out of which the woman peers through a small netting or thin cloth over the eyes; and, in many regions, the physical structure of dwellings, with high mud walls or bamboo or cane mats sheltering the region of household activities from view.

The practice of *purdah* is linked closely with other beliefs and practices relating to sexuality, honor, shame, and pollution; with the ideal arrangement of marriages for girls before, or as soon after, puberty as possible; and with structural conditions relating to kinship, the division of labor, and systems of social stratification in the society at large. In its most extreme form among Muslims, women remain totally secluded, leaving the home into which they were born or married only on rare occasions and then under the utmost protection. If a woman must go out, she will make herself invisible in her *burqa* and will be accompanied by other women or children or by a close kinsman, but she will never go out alone.

She will not gather with other women in public, or walk close to where men are gathered; and if she is accompanied by her husband or other kinsmen, she will walk a few steps behind. Within the home, if financial circumstances permit, she will share special territory with other women and children into which only the closest males are permitted. If someone who is not a close kinsman enters the house, women will be warned to hide, and not even their voices will be overheard. The women and children will eat apart from the men, and then only after the men have eaten their fill.

The degree to which *purdah* is practiced and the particular form of its observance varies considerably, depending on religion, caste, class, and region, among other factors. Although it is highly risky to try to sort out their independent effects, it is possible to make tentative generalizations. *Purdah* is practiced among Muslims more than among Hindus, and among Hindus more than among Buddhist, Christian, or other religious minorities. *Purdah* appears to have originated as a Muslim institution that was adopted by Hindus, in somewhat different form, in a process of cultural diffusion that has permeated South Asia.

Limiting the interaction between men and women outside certain well-defined categories, Muslim *purdah* restrictions "do not apply within the immediate kin unit, but only outside it," a rule that stresses "the unity of the kindred vis-à-vis the outside," whereas Hindu *purdah* regulates the interaction between a woman and the male members of the household into which she marries, but not of the household into which she was born. For these reasons, one would expect that Hindus would be more liberal than Muslims in permitting women to work outside the home.

Purdah is practiced among high-caste more than low-caste families at similar levels of income and education. *Purdah* in this sense becomes one aspect of the maintenance of the ritual purity of caste and subcaste, which, in Hindu tradition, is also bound up with rules for avoiding lower caste persons and "polluting" objects touched by them.

The practice of *purdah* among high-caste Hindus is linked with other conservative practices and values regarding the family, such as earlier arranged marriages, bans on divorce and the remarriage of widows, and a strong patriarchal structure of decision making. Indeed, among high-caste Hindus, women owe unquestioning obedience to their husbands-which in its extreme takes the form of religious worship-while husbands, in turn, owe unquestioning obedience to their fathers. Among lower-caste and scheduled caste Hindus, fewer restrictions are likely to prevail.

As von Furer- Haimendorf remarks of the Hindus in Nepal, "In this respect personal freedom and with it the right to moral choices increase as we descend the social ladder, and the women of lowly tenant farmers and agricultural labourers enjoy greater freedom in the choice of sexual partners than do the women of their high-caste landlords and masters." These so-called moral choices presumably also include the right (as well as the necessity) to move about more freely outside the home. Female seclusion is also stronger among higher-caste than among lower-caste Muslims. Although caste is technically a Hindu custom, Muslims in some areas have adopted such Hindu practices as prohibitions on divorce and the remarriage of widows, the giving of dowry rather than bride price at the time of marriage, and the caste system.

The seclusion of women becomes firmly tied to the maintenance of caste status among Muslims adhering to traditional values. *Purdah* is practiced more among well-to-do families than among poor families, within particular castes and levels of education. It is important to distinguish here between ritual status and economic status, the former being associated with caste purity, the latter with the material conditions in which the family or sub caste currently finds itself. Some villages of Nepal, for example, are heavily settled by Brahmins of high ritual status (by definition) but low economic status, most of whom engage in manual labor tilling the soil.

The tension between low economic status, which requires that women must engage at least seasonally in some economically productive activity outside the home, and high ritual status, which calls for their seclusion, leads to a number of compromises in the ideal. In times of severe economic need women will enter the labor force as agricultural laborers or in other capacities, but when conditions improve, they withdraw to their homes.

One explanation of the relationship between income and *purdah* within castes may be that the wealthy can well afford to keep their women in *purdah* while the poor cannot. Not only does an upper-class woman not have to work, but she can remain in separate quarters in the household and send servants or children on errands to the bazaar. Few among the village poor can afford to observe such restrictions regardless of their caste status. But several studies from India, Pakistan, and Bangladesh have suggested that in some situations *purdah* is more prevalent among lower-income than higher-income families.

No doubt education is a strong factor here: women in well-to-do families are likely not only to have a higher education, but, if they are employed, to be working in white-collar occupations, such as teaching in girls' schools or colleges, which protect them from contact with men. Lower-income women must wear the burqa for protection and status maintenance and, being little schooled or illiterate may hold to more conservative values. In looking at the relationship between class and *purdah*, then, one must distinguish between upper-class families that are highly traditional in their adherence to religious norms and family customs and those liberal upper-class families that increasingly reject restrictive attitudes and practices.

The bases of class stratification in rural South Asia are closely related to inequalities in the distribution of land, which in turn are related to inequalities in the distribution of income. Although the variations are complex, one can distinguish roughly among large landowners who employ hired labor or lease land to tenants in order to release themselves and their families from manual labor; small landowners who rely primarily on family labor (including that of women), with perhaps occasional hired labor, but who may abstain from manual labor if their status maintenance requires it;

sharecroppers and other tenant farmers, among whom women engage in manual labor at least occasionally; and landless laborers, among whom the women may frequently find employment as hired laborers alongside their men.

The relation of people to the land may be more useful than income in distinguishing life-styles of agrarian social groups, although the two are certainly related. *Purdah* is practiced more by upwardly mobile families and sub castes than among non-mobile families or sub-castes, especially among lower income groups. The adoption of elite norms of ritual behavior, encouraging the seclusion of wives and daughters in the home and their withdrawal from the labor force, is a common manifestation of upward mobility among both Hindu and Muslim low-income and low-caste families. Among Hindus, this is one aspect of the process of Sanskritization.

Its effects are clearly visible among peasants in some of the more prosperous regions of northern India. As reported by Mazumdar, "Recent studies on the changing pattern of village life indicate that improvement in prosperity, the spread of education, or acquisition of white-collar jobs by the lower castes invariably leads to a withdrawal of women from active employment outside their homes. This has been particularly noticed in the green revolution districts, where agricultural prosperity has led to a sharp drop in women's participation in agriculture."

The status of the entire kin group becomes tied to its ability to keep its womenfolk secluded in the home, much in the nature of the "conspicuous consumption" of nonproductive women among the upper classes that was identified by Veblen in the West. The more tentative the newly acquired social position, the more important the correct observances become. As Papanek remarks, "Observance of *purdah* in the lower middle class may function as a signal of status, especially for persons who have just achieved this class level." Even slight improvements in agricultural prosperity may permit peasant families to hire (sometimes female) paid labor when it is needed in their fields as a replacement for the work done previously by female family members.

Among Muslims, too, upward mobility is commonly associated with a strengthening of the practice of female seclusion in emulation of the traditional practices of higher castes. In Uttar Pradesh, for example, "There is a marked tendency among those non-Ashraf families lower-caste Muslims who have done relatively well to put their women in *purdah* and to withdraw them from the family work force. It is now said in praise of a husband that he is able to give his wife leisure to 'stay on bed,' instead of forcing her to work in the field".

Bhatty also tells of a newly prosperous family of the oil-presser caste in Uttar Pradesh in which the women of the household had previously helped to work the oil press and sell the mustard oil in the village streets. Now that the family has built a partly *pucca* (brick) house, the young daughter-in-law has taken to *purdah*, while the mother-in-law continues to work. Pastner, observing the same process in Baluchistan, calls the increased traditionalization of women in the face of the upward mobility of males an example of "negative modernization."

Observers have noted that the adoption of modern amenities, such as tube wells and latrines, by newly prosperous rural households also intensifies the seclusion of women by undermining two major excuses for leaving the home: to use the fields for elimination, and to gather water from the wells or the river. As a consequence, even these opportunities for visiting with other women are closed.

The withdrawal of women from the labor force, while heightening the family's ritual status, has an additional financial disadvantage beyond the direct loss of income. As girls and women become economic liabilities, the pattern of exchange at the time of marriage frequently shifts from bride wealth-a system generally practiced by tribal and low-caste groups, whose women are more frequently economically productive, and by Muslims-to the dowry. The family must now worry about how to raise money to find their daughter a husband of suitable status.

Purdah is practiced in towns (but not in cities) more than in villages. The difference between town and village is, of course, confounded by caste and class differences, for town dwellers on the whole are likely to be of somewhat higher economic and caste status than those living in villages or scattered in rural districts. Villagers, being poorer, are more likely to require that their women work in the fields, at least seasonally if not full time. Women who plant and weed and harvest cannot keep themselves covered from head to toe. They must forego the veil (although they will usually keep their heads covered) and may even tuck their clothing up around their legs to permit greater freedom of movement.

The observance of *purdah* in small towns is associated not only with the higher economic and ritual status of many town dwellers, but also with the greater likelihood of encountering strangers, or at least unrelated males, in the streets. For Muslims, this necessitates either the strict seclusion of women or the wearing of the *burqa* in public. Wherever there is an influx of outsiders into the area, one would expect an intensified concern with protecting the honor of females, not only in towns but in border regions or other newly prosperous areas as well.

Cultural variations across regions affect the practice of *purdah*. Within India, for example, norms regarding women's work outside the home appear to differ strongly by region, with far greater restrictions generally placed on women's freedom in the north (a region of strong Muslim influence) than in the south. Mazumdar goes so far as to call *purdah* a strictly northern phenomenon, reporting that participation rates of women in agriculture are generally high in the south, low in the north, and particularly low in West Bengal, where "the taboo on women in field work has penetrated even among the scheduled castes."

The caste system in general and the restrictions on high-caste activities are said to be less rigid in the Hindu kingdom of Nepal than in India. Within Nepal, Hindus in the Muslim-influenced southern Terai are more conservative than are Hindus in the north, where there is a strong Tibetan and Buddhist current. Among the latter, von Furer-Haimendorf argues that the relationship between husband and wife conveys "a relaxed and cheerful atmosphere" of closeness and warmth. The Nepalese Buddhists have simultaneously been influenced by Hindu tradition, however; the Newar people of the Kathmandu valley, about half of whom are Buddhist, have apparently adopted the caste system of their Hindu neighbors.

Although the impressions are difficult to verify, observers have also suggested that Muslim observances of *purdah* are stricter in Pakistan than in Bangladesh; within Bangladesh, they are stricter in the south (near Chittagong) than in the north; and within Pakistan, they are stricter in the north (near Peshawar) than in the south. There is little systematic research to substantiate these observations, however.

Purdah is practiced among women in their prime reproductive years more so than among younger girls or older women. Whereas the seclusion of Muslim girls begins at puberty, Hindu seclusion, strictly speaking, begins with marriage. Because the practice is so closely linked with the maintenance of family honor through protecting the sexual purity of its womenfolk, restrictions on interaction between the sexes should be greatest during those years when women are viewed as sexually most attractive, and, thus, vulnerable to possible illegitimate sexual intercourse and pregnancy.

The notion of the woman's sexual-reproductive value is quite explicit in the rules relating to unmarried girls, among whom a dishonoring sexual union could not only cause great shame to the family but could greatly reduce the girl's economic value in the marriage market (or, among groups practicing the dowry, greatly increase her cost). Even worse, the girl could become potentially unmarriageable and thus a permanent economic drain on the family's resources. Once the sexual value of the woman declines, either through aging (and the loss of reproductive capacity) or through widowhood, greater freedom of movement is generally tolerated. She no longer poses a major risk.

A widow's behavior may remain somewhat circumscribed, however, for widows are frequently expected to dress in a distinctive and unattractive manner (among traditional Hindus, by shaving their heads, wearing plain white saris, and walking barefoot) and to avoid certain ceremonies on auspicious occasions where their presence could bring bad luck. On the whole, though, widows and older wives are relatively free to move about outside the home. This brief summary of *purdah* observances, which may well be contradicted in specific instances, obscures many important variations and complexities, including the consequences of cross-cutting influences.

A high-caste married Hindu woman may experience more restrictions than a low-caste married Muslim woman, for example, and a low-caste Hindu woman of northern India leads a more restricted life than does a higher caste Hindu woman in the south. In some areas, certain religious minorities (although not Buddhists or Christians) may practice *purdah* to the same extent or to a greater degree than do Hindus and Muslims. The discussion perhaps also obscures the distinction between *purdah* practiced within the home in the presence of family elders, and *purdah* practiced outside the home.

The latter is more important with respect to recruiting women for rural industry, for we need to know the circumstances under which women are actually permitted to move about outside the home. *Purdah* observance within the home does have some bearing on these issues, however. To the extent that conversation between a young wife and her father-in-law or husband's older brother is considered a breach of proper conduct, it will be difficult for a woman to try to persuade reluctant elders directly to agree to a new form of social behavior. She may well work through other sympathetic family members, however-her husband, perhaps, or her mother-in-law-to affect a change of heart.

It is probably a major misconception to view the joint family as a solidary or impermeable institution which resists adoption of social change. Even if the family values the idea of female seclusion, the potential monetary advantages of permitting an unmarried daughter or young daughter-in-law to work outside the home may well outweigh the cultural resistance to the idea in the minds of the family's decision makers. And there may well be disagreement among these same decision makers which can be used to advantage. The points of fission in the extended family-the time when brothers decide to break up the joint household and establish independent residences with their wives and children, for example-can provide an opportunity for the adoption of new practices as well as a major financial incentive for female labor.

We must not gloss over the fact that in many instances it will be not just her husband, the elders in the household, or the community at large, but the woman herself who resists the idea of working outside the home. Bennett reports of the Brahmin and Chetri women in a village near Kathmandu that those who were forced by economic necessity to work in the fields looked forward eagerly to the time when they could stay home. This is not at all surprising in view of the onerous and unrewarding labor in which most employed rural women find themselves. In addition, because their work in the fields is generally considered a normal part of their domestic role, it does not translate into economic independence or greater power within the household.

If we take the view of the woman herself, then, it is clear that unless she must work for economic reasons she is likely to weigh the potential gains and losses of her employment quite carefully, in some cases deciding that the security of the home and what she perceives at her more privileged position there are not worth risking for some unknown quantity in the workplace. The obstacle of female seclusion could undoubtedly be more easily overcome if certain protections were offered to women and their families.

The most basic is an all-female work environment, including female supervisors, where this is considered a necessary precondition for women to work outside the home. Sentiment may initially require that the workplace be secluded from view by walls or bamboo shades, although experience is likely to show that these barriers become less necessary once the enterprise has gained legitimacy. In locales where it is still considered wrong for women to walk in the streets, even in *burqas*, or where they must travel some distance to work, some form of transport will be required, such as curtained cycles or scooter rickshaws.

Hostels may be required for some employees, such as unmarried girls whose parents are anxious to marry them early, workers from neighboring villages, or visiting trainers and supervisors. And the type of work itself must be considered respectable. In deciding on a product it is important to take into account local beliefs and practices; for example, caste restrictions among higher-caste groups on performing certain "lowly" tasks such as leatherworking or pottery making. This latter consideration is unlikely to pose real problems, since it is lower-caste Hindus, low-income Muslims, and religious minorities who are most likely to seek employment.

FARMING AND DOMESTIC RESPONSIBILITIES

A typical village of the rice-growing regions of Bangladesh is built on high ground in the midst of watery fields that stretch flat toward the horizon. Villages are joined by high roads or by paths through fields that are flooded during the monsoons. The houses, clustered together in compounds (*bari*) containing several households of a joint family and separated from other *bari*, are typically built of mud with a thatched roof, although sometimes the walls are of woven cane matting tied to bamboo frames and the roofs are tin. The houses must be repaired frequently. Surrounding the houses are smaller structures for sheltering animals and storing straw, a few fruit trees, and sometimes a small vegetable garden.

The *bari* usually centers on a large pond or "tank" in which people bathe themselves and their buffaloes, women wash dishes and clothes, and ducks dabble for food. The houses contain two or three small, dark rooms with, perhaps, one tiny window in each and a mud floor which is periodically coated with a mixture of mud and cow dung to give it a hard, clean surface. The house contains several charpoys (wooden frames strung with cord) for sleeping, some rolled-up bedding, and perhaps a chair or small table. The walls are decorated with pictures from old calendars, photographs of family members, and framed samples of embroidery. There is a separate cooking area with a mud *chulai* for cooking built into the floor, a few brass bowls and containers stacked on the floor or on shelves, and large earthenware jars to store water.

Rice and other staples are suspended from the ceiling in baskets or jars hung in woven jute *sikas*. The *chulai* burns leaves, sticks, or dried cakes of cow dung mixed with straw; smoke fills the dark room.

When the weather is good, the women do most of their cooking and washing out-of-doors in the courtyard, where a few skinny chickens peck in the dust and the children play. The goats and buffaloes have been taken to pasture, but at night they are tethered in shelters near the house. During the day the men of working age are all off in the fields; only young children and old men remain at home with the women.

When a stranger approaches, the women hurry indoors to hide or quickly cover their heads and faces. When the rice fields are bright green and the sun glints off the patterned water, the village looks beautiful and prosperous, but during the monsoons everything is flooded-perhaps even the house itself-and the cattle stand knee-deep in water. Access to other villages is cut off except by boat. It is within this setting that the women carry on their domestic activities. Our knowledge of how rural women actually spend their time is extremely limited.

Pilot studies by Sattar in the Comilla District of Bangladesh and by Anwar and Bilquees in the Lyallpur District of Pakistan contain helpful descriptions of the daily and seasonal round of activities among women in those villages, but systematic time-budget data which could throw light on regional, class, and caste variations in women's work have yet to be gathered. What is clear from the few available studies is that the time spent on different activities varies dramatically among different groups within the same village and among villages within the same region.

The daily round of domestic chores, combined with seasonal fluctuations in the demand for labor in the fields or for crop processing, appears to leave little time in the lives of most women for taking on additional activities.

In spite of the low percentage (under 10 per cent) of women counted as part of the rural labor force in Pakistan, for example, interviews with village women reveal extremely high rates of mostly unpaid labor in the fields or nearer home in crop processing. In four villages of the Lyallpur District in the wheat-growing Punjab at least 20 per cent of women in the five major castes cut wheat during harvest, at least 40 per cent thresh wheat, at least 27 per cent pick cotton, at least 60 per cent cut fodder for animals, and so on.

The general pattern is for higher-caste women (Rajput and Jat) to participate less in farm activities than do lower-caste women (Gujar and Baluch), although the relationship does not hold for all activities. Given the subsistence agricultural conditions that prevail in most regions, the question thus arises as to whether it is foolish to propose full-time, year-round Non-agricultural employment for rural women in South Asia. Even if cultural values did not restrict so many women to the home, would they have time to take on new activities? This section addresses briefly some of the major domestic responsibilities of rural women and suggests a few possibilities for circumventing these obstacles.

The major domestic tasks in which women engage, aside from their regular or seasonal participation in agricultural labor, include the processing of food and other crops for household consumption or for sale (rice, wheat, other grains and pulses, cotton, fruits and vegetables, nuts, oil, and so forth); collecting water, animal fodder, and cooking fuel; cooking, cleaning, and washing; and caring for children. In addition, women often fill their so-called leisure time with spinning, weaving, embroidery, mat or quilt making, or other production primarily for home use. In almost all these activities, both scarcity of raw materials and primitive technology require that women spend many hours every day on tasks of very low productivity. If women are to be free to engage in more productive labor, or if work outside the home is not simply to add to their already heavy burdens in the home, then clearly one of the first priorities is to reduce their domestic chores. Let us take the major activities in turn. Even if women do not toil directly in the fields, almost everywhere they are primarily responsible for handling the harvest. Women's work begins where their husbands' ends. Extracting oil from seeds; cleaning cotton; drying mango pulp; washing and cleaning jute; drying and husking corn; grinding corn, wheat, pulses, or rice into flour; peeling the tops of sugarcane for animal fodder-all take time.

Wives and daughters of small farmers are generally more involved in crop processing than are the wives and daughters of landless peasants who instead hire themselves out as agricultural laborers or as daily wage-labor in processing. Processing time has increased significantly in areas where irrigation now permits multiple-cropping and where new high-yield varieties offer more abundant crops. Far more attention should be paid to innovative means for reducing the work load associated with increased agricultural productivity through the introduction of more efficient intermediate technology in household-centered processing and storage activities.

Collecting water from a distant river or well for cooking, drinking, bathing, washing clothes and dishes, and watering poultry and animals frequently requires that women walk miles each day carrying heavy jars. Bennett calculates that an average household of ten members in a village in Nepal, with its own convenient well, uses about forty gallons of water a day, whereas households farther away from a water supply may use about twenty.

Households owning livestock need considerably more water because a buffalo consumes eight gallons a day, a cow three or four, and a goat about a half-gallon. The water is carried by women and children in narrow-necked, copper, brass, or clay vessels holding from three to eight gallons each.

The brass vessels are cleaned daily by rubbing them with ashes; the clay vessels are cleaned less frequently with sand. The Nepalese women wrap long cloths around their hips to support the vessels or else carry them, supported by a headband, in baskets on their backs.

Improved water supplies are a high-priority item in most rural development programs. Gravity-flow, piped water systems in the hills and tube wells in the plains will reduce women's work load significantly. It should be noted, though, that the insistence of public health workers on using boiled water adds to women's work, not only in time but also in the search for additional fuel. Other methods for sterilizing water should thus be encouraged.

Village women who also care for poultry and animals can spend hours everyday collecting fodder, washing and watering the animals, taking them to pasture, cleaning their stalls, and milking. In the arid, rocky regions of the Khyber Pass one can see tribal women leaving their villages at dawn to search for grass for their animals. Returning from the distant mountain valleys at noon, they carry tremendous loads on their heads. In one village located in a wheat-growing area of the Punjab women spend, on the average, over six hours every day finding fodder for their buffaloes and goats, caring for and milking the animals, and churning the milk.

Gathering time could be reduced by encouraging the planting of fast-growing fodder, such as protein-rich lucerne, on banks and idle fields close to the villages; by introducing more efficient techniques of chopping the fodder; and by using prepared animal feeds. The AMUL Dairy in Gujarat makes a highly nutritious feed by mixing oilseed byproducts, such as groundnut cake or cottonseed cake, with damaged cereals and cereal by-products, such as rice or wheat bran, and adding mineral supplements. AMUL's prepared feeds are cheaper and more nutritionally balanced and produce richer milk than the sometimes expensive cottonseed that farmers formerly fed their cattle. Prepared feeds could be manufactured locally by women's cooperatives.

The search for cooking fuel is another time-consuming task. Women of Nepal walk for miles in search of wood from the once-forested hillsides; now many hills are denuded, and they must go farther afield to find fuel. Even small saplings are pulled up for kindling. Elsewhere, women gather twigs and leaves for fuel, or collect dung, which is mixed with straw, formed into patties, dried on the mud walls of the house, and stored for later use.

The dung cakes give off a low and smoky heat. More efficient sources of fuel would include electricity, kerosene, butane, compacted sawdust, or crop by-products, solar heat, or methane gas produced in *Gobar* tanks from animal and human wastes and other biodegradable products. Methane gas produces a hotter, cleaner heat than does cow dung, while the remaining sludge is a richer fertilizer. Cooking time varies considerably by region, caste, and class. Women in south India, for example, are more likely to engage in lengthy meal preparations two or three times a day, cooking afresh for each meal, than are women in the north, who frequently prepare their staple foods (wheat *chapatis* and vegetables) only once a day, warming them up for other meals.

A typical midday meal in Bangladesh of rice, *dahl*, and vegetable requires that the husked rice be cleaned and cooked, the *dahl* cleaned, the vegetables peeled and cut, onions sliced, and all *masalas* (spices) cleaned, dried, and ground on a special stone grinder or between two stones, with water added to make a paste. The food is cooked over a wood fire on one or two *chulai*s. The *chulai* itself is rebuilt about twice a month. After the meal, the dishes and saucepans are taken to the pond to wash; the whole process may easily take several hours. More efficient stoves, cooking utensils, and facilities for food preparation (for example, spice grinders and oil presses) and storage would reduce considerably the time spent on cooking.

Child care as a specific activity tends to take up little of a woman's time because either she keeps her young children with her while she works, or she delegates their care to their older siblings (usually girls) or to other relatives in the household, perhaps a mother-in-law. But lack of alternative child care will interfere with some women's work outside the home. If women are not to neglect their children or to try to work with toddlers beside them, facilities for child care will have to be provided at the place of employment.

FACTORS INFLUENCING WOMEN'S DOMESTIC RESPONSIBILITIES

The extent to which women are tied to domestic and agricultural chores will depend, not only on the family's economic status and on the regional differences discussed above (themselves related to differences in agricultural productivity and in the division of labor by sex), but also on the structure of the household in which the woman lives and on her position in it. The Committee on the Status of Women in India argues that the joint family imposes greater constraints on women's freedom of movement than does the nuclear family, although to the degree that the joint family is correlated with higher caste or economic status, the relation may be spurious.

One could argue that the joint family is not only more culturally conservative, on the whole, but also that the economic vulnerability that pushes a woman into the labor force is mitigated by the joint responsibility of several male workers for the family's support. It is assumed, on the other hand, that the nuclear family permits a more egalitarian relationship between the husband and wife which would facilitate her employment outside the home; it is also more vulnerable to financial stress requiring an additional income. The 1968-69 National Impact Survey in Pakistan of 2,910 currently married women of reproductive age living with their husbands found that 25.1 per cent of rural women in nuclear households (about half of all rural households) were currently employed as compared with 19.2 per cent in joint households.

Corresponding percentages for urban women were 11.4 per cent and 7.8 per cent, respectively). The nuclear structure was apparently more conducive to female employment (in this case almost entirely agricultural) despite the fact that women in the sample nuclear households had an average of 3.5 living children as compared with 2.4 for those in joint households. The common assumption that the joint or extended family is not only the ideal but the typical family form in South Asia is challenged by Kolenda, who notes that in India, although the majority of people live in joint or "supplemented nuclear" families, the majority of households are nuclear or "subnuclear," that is, incomplete.

Nuclear households are more common in the south than in the north. The incidence of joint families in a community can be largely explained by the timing of their dissolution. Joint families are least frequent in communities in which brothers commonly set up a separate household at, or soon after, their marriage; more frequent where brothers commonly wait until the father's death to divide the property; and most frequent where brothers continue living together with their wives and children, even after the father's death. In trying to explain regional variations in the Indian family structure, Kolenda argues that these different patterns of fission in the joint household are shaped in large part by the bargaining power of women who, being "outsiders" and thus less committed to the maintenance of the extended unit, are assumed to have a stronger incentive to break up the household.

A woman's bargaining power, in turn, is derived from the relative amount of resources that the couple (particularly the husband) obtains from her or his own kin. In brief, couples are most likely to set up a separate household after marriage in communities that permit initiation of divorce by the wife, that emphasizes bride wealth rather than dowry, and that provide close linkages between the husband and his wife's natal family or linkage through her family's economic or social support to the couple. Couples are most likely to remain in a joint family, even after the father's death, in communities in which the wife's family provides relatively few resources compared with those provided by the husband's.

This analysis suggests that the bargaining power of women in the household may be more cause than consequence of nuclear family living, and that a woman who has successfully negotiated the transition from living in her father-in-law's home to living in her own home could, in turn, more successfully negotiate the right to work outside the home. It is a mistake to consider the joint household an insurmountable obstacle to female employment, however. For one reason, the differences in employment rates in the Pakistan survey are not great. For another, the joint household may provide considerable advantages for female employment in that it permits adjustments in the division of labor.

A mother-in-law or sister-in-law may well be willing to take on additional domestic responsibilities in order to permit an unmarried daughter or a young bride of the household to earn money, especially if the whole family will benefit from the earnings. In this sense the availability of other family members provides a supportive environment, freeing women who would otherwise be tied to the home. This brings us to the question of the woman's position in the family. Most village studies suggest that it is the older mother-in-law who, having achieved her life goal of retiring from domestic chores while her daughters-in-law take over, is most free both culturally and structurally to take on employment outside the home.

The primary goal in this scheme for creating employment outside the home, however, is to recruit unmarried girls and young married women in their early childbearing years so that their new status can have a maximum potential impact on delaying marriage, delaying the first birth, and spacing and limiting additional births.

Unmarried girls are likely to be relatively free of domestic responsibilities as compared with older married women if others in the household are willing to take over some of their tasks, and if they do not have younger siblings to look after. If they do have to care for younger children, then child-care facilities may also be necessary in order for unmarried girls to work. So, too, new brides who have not yet borne children may have more free time than after childbearing begins. The most difficult group to recruit would be married women with rapidly growing families, but as we have argued, the demographic impact of their employment will probably be limited in any case.

Recruitment of unmarried girls will have to be timed so that parents will have maximum incentive to delay their daughter's marriage. Among traditional Muslims, female employment may have to begin when the girl reaches twelve or fourteen in order for it to serve as an alternative to marriage; among Hindus, the most extreme pressures appear somewhat later; and among religious minorities, such as Christians, Buddhists, and some tribals, even later. Hardly any rural teenage girls will be enrolled in school. In Pakistan, in 1961, only 2.5 per cent of all females (rural and urban) aged fifteen through nineteen were enrolled, and the proportions were probably only slightly higher in India and much lower in Nepal. Having never attended school, having attended only sporadically, or having been withdrawn from school by the age of ten or twelve because schooling was not seen as a good investment for daughters, the girls are at a critical juncture with respect to their futures.

In Bangladesh, in 1965, only 13 per cent of girls between the ages of fifteen and nineteen were still unmarried, and virtually none remained single past twenty. Pakistan presents a far more favorable picture, with over two thirds still unmarried in their late teens, while India and Nepal range between these extremes. Although all four countries show a notable tendency for the marriages of females to be increasingly delayed, only in Pakistan is the marital timing even approaching the point where it could begin to have a significant impact on lowering fertility.

Offering supervised hostels as living quarters for unmarried female workers could, relieve space pressures in rural households as well as minimizing the threat of dishonoring sexual unions within the family. It could also permit unmarried girls from neighboring villages to take advantage of employment that would otherwise be denied them because of the difficulties in traveling over long distances.

In this chapter it has been argued that at least three incentives could motivate rural women to seek employment outside the home-money, prestige, and social contact.

These inducements could be strengthened by ensuring that the rural industries pay wages at least equal to prevailing rates for male agricultural workers; provide an opportunity for the acquisition of vocational and literacy skills; and encourage the formation of strong bonds of social solidarity in a central workplace. Against these incentives must be weighed several major impediments to the employment of girls and women outside the home: suspicion of the motives of the employer, cultural values favoring the practice of female seclusion, and a generally arduous round of domestic responsibilities that leaves women little free time to take on additional work.

In response to the question, under what conditions could women and their families be induced to take advantage of new employment opportunities, we could suggest the following criteria:

1. The potential workers and their families must perceive the concrete and immediate material benefits to be gained. In this sense, recruiting for paid employment differs from projects with deferred or less tangible rewards, such as literacy classes or nutrition or health-care training, in that it has a clear and immediate payoff. It has been suggested that family heads might even be offered some initial financial incentive to encourage them to permit an unmarried daughter or young daughter-in-law to work, if she is willing, and that care should be taken to ensure that both the family as a whole and the individual worker benefit from the new income. Saving a fixed portion of earnings should be mandatory.
2. Certain protections can be offered to workers within the framework of prevailing cultural restrictions on contact between the sexes. This would include providing for secure travel between home and the place of work, a protected work environment under all-female supervision,

and in some cases hostels or other acceptable living arrangements (for example, sharing the house of a respectable family) for workers, visiting female inspectors, training agents, and so forth.

3. The type of work must be acceptable to the woman herself and to her family. It is assumed that most of the proposals for small rural industries would be culturally approved, but certain caste-specific tasks such as leatherworking or fish canning may be unacceptable in some areas for some groups.
4. The motives of the employer must be considered trustworthy. New employment schemes for rural women would best be introduced under the auspices of an already known and trusted community group or institution, such as an integrated rural development scheme. The cooperative nature of the venture must be fully understood. To this end, villagers should be incorporated into the planning process from the beginning.
5. Major time-consuming domestic chores can be reduced. It could be argued that when women have no opportunity to earn income their household tasks expand to fill the time available. This is not intended to belittle the arduous nature of their work, but only to suggest that women might well shift their priorities if new opportunities for earning direct cash income were introduced. Most families can absorb some cutbacks and make adjustments in the division of labor by age and sex to accommodate women's work outside the home. In addition, the introduction of recommended labor-saving technology, such as oil presses, prepared foods, or centralized grain processing, can free women to use their time in more productive ways. Women are more likely to adopt the new technology if more productive and status-maintaining alternatives are available. Without new alternatives, women may resist rather than seek displacement from their former tasks.
6. Children can receive proper care. Child-care facilities at the place of work will permit young married women to

keep their children nearby and to breast-feed infants, an important nutritional advantage. Child care may also be required so that unmarried girls, who otherwise look after their younger siblings, can be employed.

7. Hours and days of work can be somewhat flexible, where necessary, to accommodate demands for seasonal agricultural labor. It is an open question as to the extent to which the new employment should compete, rather than integrate, with current patterns of agricultural labor among women.

Some forms of industrial production will require year-round operation, whereas others are more adaptable. Decisions on flexibility of employment should be geared to the conditions of each village. If a severe labor shortage during planting or harvesting seasons threatens to interfere with agricultural productivity, then it may be necessary to close the industry for several weeks. But if seasonal demands for female agricultural labor are not compelling, then the industry should probably remain in operation year-round. Indeed, removing some young women from the agricultural labor force will often improve the bargaining power over wages of those remaining.

The tension between the incentives and obstacles to working outside the home shapes the characteristics of women drawn into the rural labor force. In India, Bangladesh, Pakistan, and Nepal these workers include women who are experiencing the most intense economic need (women in families of landless laborers; the unskilled and illiterate; groups discriminated against by the dominant society, such as tribals, scheduled castes, and the Muslim minority in Hindu arcas); women who are most free of the restrictions of *purdah* (religious minorities, scheduled-caste Hindus, and low-caste Muslims); and those with fewest domestic responsibilities (frequently also the poorest segments of the population, such as women in families of landless laborers without their own crops to process).

Within each of these groups one generally finds an overrepresentation of destitute widows without families to support them who are simultaneously freer from the restrictions of *purdah* and relatively free of domestic responsibilities. Two canning factories near Peshawar in Pakistan, each with several hundred women workers in the busiest seasons, employ mostly widows or older married women.

Unmarried girls are also overrepresented in some employment schemes. Most of the tribal girls working in the *papad* center at Vedchhi are unmarried, as are the young Muslim women at the People's Health Center in Savar, Bangladesh; predominantly scheduled-caste Hindu volunteers for the rural women's training program of the Nepal Women's Organization at Jawalakhel, Kathmandu; and recruits for the garment-making factory in the village of Salah-el-Din, Egypt (despite the organizer's interest in recruiting young married women).

A combination of natural forces and deliberate policy would suggest that unmarried girls and, to a lesser extent, young married women with one or two children could be induced (if they are not already compelled) to take up employment in small rural industries, which would simultaneously expose them to new ways of looking at themselves, their role in the family, and their role in the community. These young women are most likely to be drawn from the poorest segments of the population, from groups of low ritual status in the caste hierarchy (both Hindu and Muslim), and from religious minorities.

The naturally pre-selected economic homogeneity of the group is particularly helpful in avoiding the tendency for privileged members of the community to accrue most of the benefits of the new enterprise for themselves, a phenomenon characteristic of programs, such as agricultural cooperatives, that include members with landholdings of widely divergent size. As Béteille remarks of agrarian societies placing a high value on hereditary privilege, "... Reforms directed towards greater equalization confront a number of challenging problems. Those who seek to implement such reforms find it particularly difficult to bypass the groups at the top and to reach down to those for whose benefit the reforms are primarily designed. In the absence of countervailing forces the privileged themselves become the principal beneficiaries of every type of innovation."

If women from the landless classes are most likely to be attracted to employment opportunities, a factor that would frequently discourage higher-status women from participating, then the chances are reduced of creating cooperatives that structurally reflect or exacerbate, rather than challenge, prevailing class distinctions within the community. Economic homogeneity builds on common experiences and aspirations to form a more cohesive group, while simultaneously encouraging the full development of the talents of all participants through on-the-job training.

Working Mothers and their Households

4

Working Mothers and their Households

We looked at the choices open to single women. We also saw how women approach partner selection: they hoped to find a husband whose earning capacity would allow them to escape the drudgery of their paid work. Given that the women in this chapter and the next have in the main, married men with steady incomes, the next question was whether they now had what they desired and why some were still in paid work. I wanted to know the meaning marriage had for those who had already embarked on this path.

They were the majority of the women I interviewed and I asked what happened to them after marriage. Some women have remained in the work-force while others have left. I wanted to know the reasons behind these choices. For those who remain employed, I was interested to know whether earning a wage in a monetised economy transforms women's relationships to the men in their lives and consequently shifts the gender contract between women and men. Pfau-Effinger uses the concept of a gender contract as opposed to gender relations which she sees as being more deterministic:

... the concept of gender contract emphasizes more explicitly the contribution of all actors, including women themselves, in the reproduction and changing of structures. The gender contract concept thus implies greater reference to the action dimension than the gender relations concept, which implies greater stress on structural factors. (Pfau-Effinger 1993:389)

Not all the issues of paid work and marriage would be addressed in this chapter. Markers of marital equity such as the domestic division of labour and the management of household finances would be discussed where comparisons were made between working wives and housewives. Here I look at the reasons behind working mothers' employment trajectories, their views on marriage and the question of autonomy.

PAID WORK AND LIFE-COURSE SQUEEZES

It was not so much marriage but children which were the deciding factor in the lives of the women in this chapter. It was very common for a child to follow quickly after marriage. The average number of surviving children each of these women had was three (range: 1-6). Although I did not ask them questions concerning fertility and family planning, one reason that I deduced from my questions on the preferred sex of children, was that children were viewed as important physical and financial supports for old-age. Since there were (and still is to this day) no adequate, affordable child-care services in the city, women often had no choice but to withdraw from the labour force during the years of child-bearing and child-rearing.

In the village, there was no disruption to mothers' productive work in the fields, as women could combine agricultural work with child-rearing. Women worked flexible hours on the farm and also carried their young ones with them to the fields. In other words, they could control the time and pace of their work and incorporate child-rearing into their routine. In the village, there was also a support network of kin to draw upon for assistance. In the city, without the assistance of kin, the stance of the government as to who should be responsible for child-care was a crucial determinant to women's ability to participate in the labour market.

The state views child-care as an entirely private, individual affair and there is no provision to enable women to combine paid employment and child-care. Even in the economic boom years of the early 1990s, when there was an acute labour shortage in Malaysia, women were merely expected to juggle their multiple roles as mothers, wives and workers. When foreign domestic workers (particularly Indonesian and Filipina) were hired in order to release professional, middle-class Malaysian mothers into the workforce, the government imposed a levy on their employment.

There is no comprehensive tax incentive for employers to provide child-care facilities, although the Ministry of Industrial Development has a special Industrial Building Allowance (IBA) for the purpose of encouraging manufacturers to provide accommodation and child-care facilities for their workers. Thus, the provision of child-care in Malaysia is minimal, haphazard and ad hoc. As affordable child-care is almost nonexistent for low paid women in Sarawak, they either have to stay at home to look after the children themselves or enlist the help of kin and friends for child-care in order that they may enter wage work. When they do get paid work, it is often near their home or else involves hours that conflict least with their domestic arrangements. With their lack of qualifications and in the employment context of Sarawak, wage work options for these women are limited to low skill, poorly paid work.

Fifteen (63 per cent) of the working mothers interviewed, entered paid work when they were single and left the workforce when they married and had young children: their participation in the labour market took second place to their duties at home. Three of the working mothers had had uninterrupted employment since they started wage work as single women because they relied on extended family members, neighbours and informal networks to provide childcare. Six working mothers had never been employed prior to their marriage and they entered the labour market only after the arrival of their children. They had married straight after school. There are no labour market statistics in Sarawak to indicate the percentage of married women who are employed and the sectors of employment where they work. I therefore do not know if women's employment in the formal sector of Sarawak generally has one life-course peak or two, with women working after they leave school and again when their children are school-age.

In Salaff's study of Chinese women in Taiwan, Hong Kong and Singapore, she found that women's labour force participation pattern is single peaked. Chinese newly weds often live with the husband's parents and new daughters-in-law would be asked to quit their job for housework so that other young unmarried daughters could continue their employment. This is particularly so for women who do not earn enough to justify paying someone else for child-care. This is contrary to the findings in Java where Wolf reported that motherhood did not necessarily push women out of the labour market. In rural Central Java, factory women were not migrants. Married women lived with their parents and continued factory employment, as factories were located nearby their villages thus allowing families to take care of children.

The majority of working mothers in my study migrated as single women for paid work in the city, then married and stayed on in the city. Only a minority lived with their parents in villages on the outskirts of Kuching. They therefore did not have a network of kin at hand for child-care. Those who were unable to hold down full-time jobs because of domestic responsibilities entered the informal sector of lowly-paid, part-time house-cleaning and laundry work. The story of Sue is an example of this.

Sue lived with her family in a squatter settlement about six kilometers from the centre of the city. Wooden planks were thrown on the soggy ground to make a path for pedestrians and motorcycles. Her house was on stilts. Old wooden seats were left on the outer verandah, which also acted as a laundry drying area. The zinc roof over the verandah was rusty and leaky and patched over with bits and pieces of thin plywood, collected from discarded boxes and crates. Although the roof of the house was low, it was cool because it was surrounded by coconut, banana and papaya trees. A bouquet of brightly painted flowers made from tin-can cutouts greeted visitors above the main entrance.

The living area was spacious and two settees were arranged at right angles against the wall. Two bedrooms opened onto this area. A stand-fan provided a cooling breeze on hot days. Separated by a low wooden wall, the cooking and dining area ran the width of the house. When I arrived for the interview, Sue was at the market and her youngest son was cooking some noodles with the radio blaring. I decided to sit on the verandah as it was cooler and this attracted the notice of her neighbours who gave me sidelong glances.

At 45, Sue had five surviving children, three of whom are married. She worked as a cleaner in an office for RM300 a month. Her husband drove an ESSO petrol tanker and earned RM700 a month. He also worked as a gardener, cutting grass and pruning hedges during the weekends, which added an extra RM400-500 to his monthly income. Sue also received another RM100-200 a month from the three older children. Sue's most educated daughter completed sixth form (although she did not pass the examinations). She was married to a Malay immigration officer and to Sue's chagrin was now a housewife at a border-post. Sue explained:

> It is a waste that she has schooling and does not work (Sayang dia bersekolah tapi tidak kerja). I gave her schooling. She should work but her husband does not allow her to. (Saya kasi bersekolah, dia mesti kerja tapi laki tidak suruh).

However, this daughter was most constant in giving her money. I have given Sue's own description of her work history. I think she does a better job than I can, given her complex employment history in numerous part-time jobs with multiple households.

> My husband's mother is Bidayuh and his father is Chinese. When we married, we lived in the village until the first two children were born. Later my husband found a job with a company that sells timber, sand and cement. The towkay supplied everything. I came here Kuching with one pot, clothes in a bag and one gunny sack of rice (Saya turun sini, bawa satu periuk, baju dalam beg dan satu guni beras). He drove a five-ton lorry and worked for the same company for six years.

After that, he became a driver for Telecoms. He worked there for three years and as it was a temporary job, he switched over to Sime Darby where he worked for the next twelve years. He was retrenched and found this present job through a friend. I only started to work when he started at Sime Darby in 1986. My children at that time were fourteen, thirteen, twelve and seven. The youngest wasn't born yet. They were old enough to look after themselves and we needed the money.

I started as a cleaner in the house of my mother's younger brother who was married to a Chinese woman. I cleaned and ironed and worked from 7:30 a.m. to 5:00 p.m. on Sundays only. I started on RM80 a month and by the time I left eleven years later, I was paid RM130. My Chinese aunt recommended me to my next cleaning job. I worked one full day and two half days in the week Mondays, Wednesdays and Saturdays on top of my regular Sunday cleaning job with my aunt. I was paid RM250 a month and I got lunch as well. I worked for six to seven years but stopped three years ago. My youngest son was between three to four years old when I started with the second employer and I used to take him along when I went to work. He was too scared to even go to the toilet. He was a very good boy. He didn't disturb anything in the house. While I did the ironing, he would sleep on the mattress. I would bring my own milk for him. I had to set the burglar alarm before I left the house in the evenings. It took me two evenings to learn how to operate it.

When I started work with my second employer, I was also cleaning for his sister twice a month and earned RM50. I worked for her for ten years. On Tuesdays, I worked for someone else for RM30 a day. On Thursdays and Fridays, I worked for another woman and got RM50 for two full day's work in a week. She gave me her used clothes and they were very nice clothes for my children and grandchildren. It was a pity that I was too fat to wear her clothes.

When I worked full-days, I got lunch as well. But I only worked for over a year with my last two employers. All the work that I did was recommended by my Chinese aunt. My sister was at first working in the office where I am working now but she gave it up because she cannot stand the air-conditioning. It is a permanent job and I get EPF. (Ini kerja tetap dan ada EPF). I paid RM36 for two sets of uniform. I wouldn't change jobs now, I'm too old. (... tidak mahu pindah kerja lagi, sudah tua). When I retire, it is more lucrative for me to look after women who have just given birth (Bila saya pencen, lebih lumayan jaga orang beranak).

It is good to be employed as we do not have to ask money from our husbands, it is embarrassing (... tak payah minta duit dari laki, malu). Last time, I used to see other people eating ice cream; I had no money to buy some. Now it is different (Dulu tenggok orang makan ais krim, pun tidak ada duit beli. Sekarang tidak sama.).

As in the agrarian village economy in rural Sarawak, which depends on the availability of household labour for farming, urban households are dependent on the cash-earning capacity of their members. In urban households, the number of wage earners to dependents must therefore be carefully balanced to ensure the survival of all. When the number of dependent children is greater than the number of wage earners in the household, the financial squeeze often means that women need to find wage work to supplement their husband's income.

In such cases, husbands often found employment for their wives and the burden of secondary earnings fell on married women. As there is no concept of a family wage, men do not feel that they have failed if their earnings are insufficient to support their families. There is no stigma, therefore, in assisting the wife in getting a job. The wife's earning capacity is held in reserve to be drawn on in times of the household's financial need. This is in contrast to the village economy where women combined their productive labour in the fields with domestic responsibilities continuously throughout their lives. The narratives of Marjorie and Jacky illustrate this.

MARJORIE (GARDENER, AGED 35)

Marjorie lived at the other end of the same squatter settlement as Sue. Her small wooden house was on stilts as it floods when it rains heavily. The entrance led to a small living area with a television set in pride of place. One of the bedrooms opened onto this area. A narrow dark corridor led to a kitchen at the back. Her husband built the house from leftover construction material from his work sites. Her eldest daughter, aged thirteen, served us Milo when I arrived one evening for the interview.

Marjorie is the eldest in her family. She left home at seventeen after spending a month in the village after finishing her Form 3 examination. Her first job was that of a domestic worker with her aunt (her mother's younger sister) in Serian. She was paid RM150 a month. She was not interested in child minding and said that her cousin was 'naughty.' When she scolded the child, the father would scold her in return. She left after a month. She found a job in the canteen of the Kuching Port Authority (KPA). Her father worked in a sawmill nearby and she went in to ask for a job. She was paid the same monthly wage of RM150. She enjoyed her work as many people ate there and she was kept busy. She met her husband who was a frequent customer in the canteen.

She left after six months when she married at eighteen. She left the work force for fourteen years and in that time had five children. Her husband earned RM800 a month as a construction worker and wages were calculated daily and paid twice monthly. There was no annual or sick leave and a day without work was a day without pay. He used to be in a work group of twenty but it had dwindled to six at the time of the interview. When his employment became precarious, he found Marjorie a job as a gardener with the Kuching City North council. At the time of the interview, she had been working for over two years. Her take home pay was RM400 a month. She said:

When I stopped work at the Kuching Port Authority and married him and had children, I was dependent on him to earn money (... harap dia saja untuk cari duit). Now that my job is going to be permanent, I will continue working until I retire (... sekarang kerja tetap, lanjut saja sampai pencen). I have to help him. One alone is not enough (Dia satu orang tak cukup). Things are expensive - school and books are expensive (Barang mahal - sekolah, buku pun mahal). I save nothing at the end of every month.

I was trained for three weeks and then they gave me gloves, boots and a uniform and I started work. Three of us work in a group and we are given an area to look after. We start at 7:30 a.m. and break off for lunch at 11:30 a.m. I take my own lunch. We start again at 1:30 p.m. and finish at 4:30 p.m. My husband gives me a lift to and from work. I like my job because it is not tiring and I will be made permanent after three years. When we go out to work, we also gain new experiences. If others can work, why not us?

JACKY (SENIOR SHOP ASSISTANT, AGED 32)

I went to meet Jacky and her husband on her day off and she took me to her house. I parked the car a short distance from the main road and we walked up a gravel path. She lived next door to her sister and another cousin was on the other side of her. Their love of plants was evident as the garden was luxuriant and overflowing. It was a spacious double-storey house, built of brick and cement on the ground floor and wooden planks on the first floor. As her baby was just beginning to walk, all the furniture was pushed against the wall, leaving a large empty space in the centre of the living room. The best part of the house was the balcony upstairs. It was cool and balmy and afforded a beautiful view of the hills opposite the house. This was also the place where Jim, Jacky's husband, nurtured his rare finds in the jungle. Jim worked for the same landscaping firm as Jacky. He acted as a seed and seedling collector in the jungle and also as the local interpreter for his boss who was an Englishman. When he was not out on his trips to the jungle, he cut the grass in the nursery. He earned RM850 a month. He was, however, an industrious man and earned an additional RM300-400 in commission on the sales of white goods and other products.

Jacky, on the other hand, worked as a senior sales assistant in the retail gardening outlet of the landscaping company. She was the eldest in a family of six children and was one of the most educated of the working mothers I interviewed. She married young, at eighteen. She became pregnant with her baby in sixth form and left school without taking the examinations. She started wage work when her baby was one year old. Her mother was able to provide child-care and she wanted to earn some money. A supervisor at this landscaping company introduced her and she was paid a daily wage of RM9 for working in the nursery. She could take home over RM300 a month (with overtime pay) and enjoyed her work as she made many new friends.

Her first child, a son, had Downs Syndrome and was frequently ill. She worked irregularly for two years in the nursery taking months off when she became pregnant with the second child. When she returned to work for the same company after the birth of her second child, she was placed in the wood cutting section. She had to work the plywood-cutting machine and was paid a lower daily wage of RM6. At this time, her monthly wage took a dip to about RM200 a month. She no longer enjoyed her job as she had lost all her friends in the nursery section. Furthermore, her eldest son was often sick and consequently, she left after a month. Her second son also had Downs Syndrome and she left the labour market for five years. Tragedy struck in 1992. Her two sons died within two months of each other. The eldest was six and the second was three.

After the birth of her third son, she returned to work in the same company. This time she was placed in their retail gardening outlet. She was paid a monthly wage of RM380. At the time of the interview, she had worked for two years there and was promoted to the position of senior sales assistant with a monthly wage of RM550. She often had to work overtime and, with commission on the sale of plants, she could take home as much as RM750 a month. This is what she said of her work:

My boss asked me to learn to use the computer but I'm not interested in working in the office. It's boring. I'm more interested in dealing with plants and customers. I am interested in plants even in my own home. But sometimes this job has its problems. Often the staffs are slack in their work.

They are only waiting to go home and they make big issues out of small things. The till is also often short.

Between the two of them, Jim and Jacky had a household income of RM2, 400. Jim paid RM130 a month for his motorcycle. He also bought the food. Jacky paid her mother RM200 a month for child-care and her sister RM100 for breast-feeding her child. She also paid for the electricity, her bus fare to work and the premium on her life insurance policy. She regularly saved money in the bank and was also involved in a revolving scheme with relatives in the village. She believed in continuing wage work:

If I work, I can help him and there is more to spend. One person earning is not enough. I'm also used to working.

The narrative of being in paid work to help husbands was recurrent. It was not only mentioned by Marjorie and Jacky but also by several others that I interviewed. It deserves some explanation. In semi-subsistence farming in rural Bidayuh areas, cash earning through seasonal wage labour in nearby bazaars is left to the men. Women take care of their families' landholding while men leave the village to earn cash during the lull stages of the agricultural cycle. Cash earning is seen to be in the province of men so 'helping men' through paid work is not a reflection of an emerging modern value associated with the western bourgeois family of male bread-winner and female home-maker, but is a continuation of an old cultural concept derived from the agrarian economy.

WORKING WIVES AND THEIR HUSBANDS

So far, I have discussed women's domestic responsibilities and life-course squeezes as the two major factors affecting women's participation in the labour market and turning to the third factor - the disparity between male and female earnings. Although this is relevant to all women regardless of their marital status, I have decided to discuss it in this chapter because comparisons of the earnings of married women to those of their husbands make the consequences of such income disparity more poignant.

The married working mothers in my study earned an average monthly wage of RM504 in comparison to their husbands' average monthly salary of RM1286. The women's monthly salary was 39 per cent of their husbands' monthly wages and yet, half of the eighteen married working mothers had the same years of schooling, if not more, as their husbands. Most of the women were overqualified for the type of work they did. There is also no correlation between their educational levels, years of working experience, the type of work that they did and the wages that they earned. On the other hand, the majority of the husbands of working mothers had additional credentials such as a driving licence for trucks and other technical and mechanical skills. Gender labour segmentation was not the only reason for the wage disparity between working mothers and their husbands.

Fifteen of the working mothers had a history of interrupted employment. They were employed when they were single and had been out of the labour market for an average of eight years each. In contrast, none of their husbands had had their employment interrupted by child-rearing and other domestic responsibilities. Kylie, who had three years more schooling than her husband but earned half his monthly wages, regretted being out of the labour market for thirteen years. She said that she would be earning much more if she had been able to continue in paid work without any interruption.

Given that the women's earning capacity was half that of their husbands, and in the absence of any meaningful welfare assistance, divorce or desertion by their spouses would trigger a survival crisis. Single mothers knew this only too well. Self-reliance and the difficulties of depending on men were therefore recurrent themes in the women's narratives when I asked them about the meaning of wage work for them and whether married women should remain in the labour market. I asked these questions of all the women I interviewed regardless of their marital or employment status. Below is a sample of what some of the women interviewed said:

We should continue working after marriage. We, women must earn for ourselves. Save our own money. We cannot depend on our husbands. (... Kita perempuan mesti cari duit sendiri. Simpan duit sendiri. Kita tidak boleh harap suami.) (Rosalind, single woman)

In this modern age, we should continue working after marriage. We can share expenses and help our own family. Also, should a woman divorce, she still has her own resources. (... Jika dia bercerai, dia masih ada pegangan.) (Cynthia, single woman)

It is not to say that when we marry, we can't work. If we can get someone to look after our children, we can work. I want to continue working after marriage and children. My mother told me, 'Don't stop working even if your husband asks you to stop because he might bully you or have another woman. What if he doesn't give you any money and your child has no milk?' I agree with my mother. It is better to have your own income, however small, as it is from the sweat of our brow. If we want anything, we can go ahead and buy it. We don't have to depend on others or ask for money from anyone. If we divorce, we don't have to depend on maintenance. With or without a man, we can live! (Marcia, single woman)

We should continue to work in order to support our family and for our own personal use. If we don't go out to work, we have to ask for money from our husbands and we can't depend on them. If they are good, they will give us some. If they are not good, they wouldn't. One day, they may get fed up. It is better to have our own income. (Agnita, working mother)

Mandy, a working mother who was ten years older than her husband had this to say:

I am still young, so I must work hard to save for my future and for my old age. What if my husband changes and leaves me? Who will help me? I save money for bad times and for when I need it.

Dorothy, who worked as a beer promoter, was divorced and with a son to bring up on her own knew only too well the unpredictability of life. She commented:

It is much better to work because the household of married people is not always steady. If we don't have a job, there is no savings. If we marry someone from a different place, how do we manage if he leaves us? Every day, I hear from my colleagues about men who are drunks, womanizers, who give enough money for children and the kitchen only. Some wives don't even have their own money to buy panties. We have to get the umbrella ready before it rains. Even if we are divorced, we still have a job. If we don't have a job, when there is a problem at home it gets worse. At least when you are working outside, you can release tension from the house. (Lebih bagus kita kerja kerana rumah tangga orang yang kahwin bukan selalu steady. Jika kita tiada kerja, tiada simpanan. Jika kita kahwin orang lain tempat, macam mana nak lari jika dia tinggal kita. Tiap-tiap hari saya dengar - laki kaki botol, kaki perempuan, kasi duit cukup untuk anak dan dapur saja. Bini tiada simpanan sendiri, sampai beli seluar dalaman pun tidak boleh. Kita mesti sedia payung sebelum hujan. Jika kita divorcekah, kita masih ada kerja. Jika tiada kerja, jika ada problem dirumah, makin teruk. Jika kita ada kerja, kita boleh release tenson dari rumah.)

Sally who was also divorced and a mother said:

I don't want to marry again. It is better to continue working especially if it is a good job. Nowadays it is also difficult to rely on a man (Sekarang, harap laki pun susah.) If your husband leaves you, you still have a job. If you don't have a job, you will have to look for one. You might as well keep on working even after marriage.

Reviewing what these women said leads one to ask why there was such insecurity about marriage. Unlike some Chinese men, who would have mistresses rather than divorce or abandon their first wives, the husbands of the women in this study do not earn enough to sustain two households. Abandonment or divorce is inevitable when men find new partners. Although there are no statistics on divorce for marriages under native customary rights, the women's perception was that divorce was more prevalent in the city than in the village. This could be because village elders often mediate in marital conflicts in rural communities. A married man in the village caught for adultery would be fined. If a child should result, he would have to pay for the maintenance of the mother and child. Although divorce is not a stigma in the village, adultery is and in a close village community, villagers can exert powerful sanctions through scorn, gossip and ostracism. In addition, the high labour turnover and men's geographical mobility in the urban areas meant that it was almost impossible to extract monthly maintenance from an errant husband.

The fact that the wives' wages could not support a family and were a mere 39 per cent of their husbands' monthly wage contributed in no small measure to their fear and anxiety about marriage and their desire to earn an independent income, however small. The break-up of a marriage, for a woman unable to earn a wage sufficient to support her family, could spell disaster. Many women who were separated or divorced from their husbands, and had no kin to look after their children, had to leave them in the Salvation Army Children's Home when they needed to seek wage work.

Husbands, on the other hand, differed in their opinion as to whether marriages were better now compared to those of their grandparents in the village. Of the six husbands that I interviewed, only one thought that marriages nowadays were more problematic. Two felt that it was the same, in that there would always be good and bad marriages. However, three of the husbands said that marriages were better now. Their opinion was that marriages nowadays were legally registered and therefore, men could not simply run away from their responsibilities unlike the marriages of old. Kenny, whose father was a school teacher who taught in different villages, illustrated this point by saying that his father had two wives in two separate villages.

However, only nine of the fifty women interviewed (18 per cent) felt that marriages nowadays were superior to those of their grandmothers' in the village. In the village, women worked alongside their men in the fields. They would go to the paddy farm in the morning together and return together in the evening. The family unit was primary and there was little time left in the week to be devoted to peer group leisure activities. To be sure, the men went off on hunting and fishing expeditions with their mates and the women wove and cooked together, especially during major cultural festivals, but these activities were not on a regular basis. Marriages in the city were different. Husbands and wives were employed in different locales and often had no idea of each other's activities throughout the day. With a six-day working week and shift work, the time that they spent together was further diminished. The majority of the women interviewed was anxious about infidelity and abandonment and held a pessimistic view of marriage.

> Nowadays even with a marriage certificate, men have girlfriends outside. Before, there was no marriage certificate but marriages were lasting. This is especially so for men who work in town. They always go travelling and like to go to pubs and karaoke lounges. Sometimes I ask my customers why they go for other women and they say that it is like food, they need variety. I told them that if I were their wife, they go out in front and I will go out behind. (Sekarang ada surat kahwin pun ada girlfriend luar. Dulu tidak ada surat kahwin, pun kahwin kekal. Laki kerja pasar, selalu travelling dan kaki pub, kaki karaoke. ... You keluar depan, saya keluar belakang.) (Dorothy, working mother, divorced - beer promoter)

> In our grandmothers' time, marriages were happier. Everybody just stayed in the village and other women had their own husbands. In town, men could tell us lies and we wouldn't know. In the village, they were too tired to go anywhere. Now, when my husband comes home after midnight from the army mess, I will ask him many questions. (Lydia, working mother)

> Women nowadays go for money (Perempuan sekarang janji duit ...) and don't care if the man is married or not. It is better not to be rich. I see middle-aged men bringing in young

women for a night in the best suite in the hotel and it makes me sick. (Tina, working mother - hotel housekeeper)

With shift-work, husbands and wives spend much less time together unlike before when they worked together in the farm and went home together. They spent more time together which makes for a happier marriage. (Jacky, working mother)

Given the constraints of child-care, life-cycle squeezes and anxieties about straying husbands, one could begin to wonder if it is indeed meaningful to talk of married women exercising choice as to whether to leave or enter wage work. However, many women I interviewed were committed to paid work. Marjorie mentioned gaining new experiences through work, Jacky spoke of being used to working and Dorothy talked of releasing household tension through work. Others were in paid work partly out of boredom in the home. Thus, women participated in the labour market not merely for monetary rewards but also for peer support and a social network outside the confines of the household. In the next section, I will attend to the age-old feminist question as to whether women's employment increases their autonomy and independence.

AUTONOMY THROUGH WAGE WORK

In the West where women's employment has been viewed as emancipatory, women's participation in the labour market has been perceived to be advantageous on two counts. First, paid work confers financial independence on women wage earners. Second, entry into the labour market is seen as an escape from the oppressive confines of domestic life. Analysis of the impact of women's entry into the labour market on their autonomy and status has long concerned feminists. However, dichotomous approaches which pitched productive labour in the public economic sphere against reproductive labour in the private domestic sphere dominated the debates in the 1970s and early 1980s. As pointed out by Stivens, '... in many of the discussions about autonomy, women are being judged as to how closely their state approximates that of the allegedly free and autonomous male subject/agent. Moreover, this is clearly the White, middle-class male of the liberal, humanist imagination'.

Similarly, Sharma when discussing the problem of the link between women's employment and their autonomy, in the context of India, said:

> If neither men nor women are expected to operate as though they had distinct and individual interests separate from those of the household and if household survival generally presupposes a high degree of financial and practical co-operation among its members, then perhaps we must formulate the problem differently. Instead of asking whether wages permit personal emancipation we should perhaps ask how they alter the nature of the individual's commitment to the household. (Sharma)

I agree with both Stivens and Sharma that an individualistic view of 'personal autonomy' does not take into account cultural differences in specific societies. Research in the south-east Asian region has shown that women's relationship to their earnings is very much integrated with their households. Wolf found that in Java, working mothers channelled more of their earnings into their households when compared to unmarried women factory workers. Similarly, Salaff documented that married working women in Singapore did not perceive their employment as conferring independence as their earnings went into supporting their families. In a situation where there is no minimum wage let alone a family wage, as in the case of Malaysia, married women's wages are very significant to their households. This is particularly so for the stratum of women workers in this study.

As with Salaff's working mothers in Singapore and Bangladeshi garment factory women, many of the women in my study paid for tutors for their children in order to improve their school performance. The working mothers that I interviewed did not want their daughters to end up with the same low pay, dead-end jobs they had. Without any state pension, they also viewed their children's education as an insurance policy for old age support. Many families were therefore committed to paying for extra tuition in order that their children may succeed in school. Many of the women in this study therefore re-entered the labour market in order to invest in their children's education. The narratives of Jean and Tina are illustrative of this. Jean (club housekeeper, aged 39)

Jean is the third in a family of seven children and the first five siblings in the family had only primary school education. Jean herself spent only four years at school. She did not choose to work in the city, but at seventeen her mother pushed her out to work in order to help the family. She worked as a domestic worker for a friend of hers and earned RM200 a month. She left after two years when she married at nineteen. She returned to the labour market fifteen years later after six children. When she rejoined the labour market, her children were aged 12, 11, 10, 9, 7 and 6. The youngest had just entered primary school. Her husband spent twelve years in the police force and left to be a driver on RM560 a month. He took up an additional job working as a bouncer for a seafood restaurant from 6:00 to 10:00 p.m. every evening.

That job brought in an additional RM380 a month. As the children grew, expenditure mounted and Jean was compelled to return to wage work. She had been working for the past seven years as a housekeeper in a recreation club and earned RM360 a month. She spent more than half her monthly wage on her children's private tuition fees. Her eldest son had a congenital heart defect and stopped school after the third year in secondary school. At the time of the interview he had recovered after an operation and worked as a store-keeper for RM320 a month. He gave Jean RM100 for living at home. Her second daughter finished fifth form and was taking computer classes in order to improve her chances in the job market. The rest were still in school. Jean said:

I will continue to work as my children need the money. I want my children to go academically as high as they can - to be doctors, teachers, engineers. Moreover, I am still young and should work. The children are old enough to look after themselves and it will be boring for me to stay at home. My husband gives me money but it is not enough. The more children we have, the more we spend. The older they grow, the more they need and the less I have for myself. Tina (hotel housekeeper, aged 33)

Tina is one of six women who started wage work only after marriage and children. She married at sixteen, immediately after Form 3 and had five children aged 15, 14, 11, 8 and 3. Her neighbour helped to look after her youngest child (her only daughter) when both she and her husband were at work. However, shift work suited her because when she worked nights, she could do housework in the morning and be at home when the children returned from school. Her husband was a clerk in a government office and earned RM1, 500 a month. However, with the children growing and four at school, his earnings were badly stretched. In addition, their second child had recently won a place in a prestigious government residential school for academically promising students. Although it was a non-fee paying school, he had to buy books and special uniforms for the many compulsory extra curricular activities in school. They too, sent their other children for private tuition.

At the time of the interview, Tina had been working for close to two years in a hotel as a housekeeper for RM450 a month. It was her first job. She commented:

I started work when my second boy entered the Junior Science College. My family is big and expenses kept mounting (... pembelanjaan makin bertambah). His husband's salary was not enough (Gaji dia pun tak cukup). As they go to secondary school, we need more money for books, shoes, school-bags, uniforms. My son in the Junior Science College spent RM3, 000 when he first entered the school. His books and uniforms were so expensive. The more activities they have, the more money is needed.

Before I started on this job, I did some direct sales. My husband is an Amway member and I joined Avon. I used to sell to my friends and neighbours but I earned only RM50-100 every four to five months. It was not enough, so I asked a neighbour to help me find a job. My husband didn't ask me to look for work but I wanted to help him and also to gain some experience outside. I was very shy at first as I had never worked outside the home before but I'm better now.

Although my aunt father's older sister and her husband are both farmers in the village, their children are all highly educated. They are university graduates and one is a YB title for a local assemblyman. I want my children to study as high as they can. I want my daughter to have high status (... berpangkat tinggi), to become a doctor. She could speak by the age of one and can talk very well now. I have to save for their further education.

It was obvious that for Tina, education was an important investment in her children's future and that she participated in the labour market to enable them to further their education.

In the absence of state child-care provisions, a woman's independence through paid work was not simply a matter of contributing to household expenditure; it also increased her dependence on other women. Kinship ties between women were significant as 48 per cent of the women interviewed felt that only female kin were eligible to care of their children. These women felt that those with no blood-ties would not do a good job. In this study, nine of the working mothers (38 per cent) depended on female kin for child-care. However, mothers and mothers-in-law who frequently provided domestic labour, especially child-care to their daughters and daughters-in-law, were often resentful of the extra burden placed upon them. Linda, a single mother explained:

My mother keeps complaining that because of my son, she can't work in the farm. She complains a lot. When she washes a bit of clothes, she will complain that her hands can't stand the detergent. I can't depend on my younger sisters either. They only go home to sleep and do nothing.

Returning once again to the question of independence, the answer as to whether women gained autonomy through wage work is complex and contradictory. Although women's earnings gave them greater discretion to manage their household contribution and personal spending, they were also more dependent on their support networks. The women's interests were therefore very much tied to their households and it was difficult to speak of a separate, individual 'autonomy.' Although single women enjoyed a certain measure of freedom, when they chose marriage and established a new form of family which was different from their village mothers, a new dependence on men emerged. This was because of the gendered nature of the capitalist labour market which rewarded them inequitably.

Working mothers in this chapter continued to participate in the labour market because of their household financial needs, for their children's educational future and no less because of the insecurity that they felt in their marriages. However, these were not the only reasons as women also remained in paid work because of its intrinsic rewards and their commitment as workers in spite of the less appealing nature of their work. As they could not afford private, commercial child-care, they had been assisted by their mothers, mothers-in-law, sisters, neighbours, husbands and older children. Thus, working mothers harnessed the resources and support networks available to them in order to earn a wage for their household's survival and for their own sense of security.

5

South and Southeast Asian Entrepreneurs Compared

Indian industrialists tend to have interests in a number of activities simultaneously and to engage in a large variety of activities over time. This is partly explained in terms of their trading background and in terms of the economic structure and the social setting of Indian society, which encourages rather than prevents diverse investments and the spreading of risks. The findings of the three empirical studies of central Gujarat, northern Malaysia and Central Java indicate that a personalized management style and diversified investment pattern are indeed a characteristic feature of Indian industrialists, but are certainly not uniquely Indian phenomena; they are equally characteristic of the entrepreneurial behaviour of Chinese and Muslim business-men in Malaysia and Indonesia.

All three groups of businessmen employ relatives and members of their own ethnic community for specific managerial tasks. The actual overseeing of the workforce is the responsibility of this intermediate stratum of supervisors and managers, relieving these entrepreneurs of the burden of direct supervision. Moreover, these relatives and members of the same ethnic community often provide access to the relevant government agencies and business communities with a view to securing the supply of raw materials, credit and other resources, and promoting the sale of the finished products. Within this framework, kinship and ethnicity represent an important organizational basis for entrepreneurship of these enterprises in India, Indonesia and Malaysia.

Quite unambiguously, all three groups of entrepreneurs prefer to create a distance between themselves and their workforce. Most of them employ labour on the basis of piece-rate and subcontracting arrangements, which allow them to hire and fire as it suits them. These labour relations enable the entrepreneurs to shift the onus for supplying work and for the terms of employment onto an intermediate group of subcontractors, or, as far as piece-work are concerned, onto the workers themselves. Creation of an intermediate stratum and the use of contract type of labour also partly explains their preference for employing migrant labourers who, according to the entrepreneurs, are more 'willing' than local labourers to work under agreements of contract or piece-rate. By organizing the work and the recruitment of labour in this wise, all three groups of entrepreneurs have transferred the adverse effects of fluctuations in demand for their products to the labour force, while still exercising control over the production process.

Economic diversification is also an important business strategy, not only for the rural industrialists in India, but also for the businessmen selected in Malaysia and Indonesia. Although there are large variations among the enterprises, most of the entrepreneurs in the three localities are able to make substantial profits from their business. Besides re-investing part of their accumulated surplus in their enterprise, many families have invested part of it outside the industrial or agro-industrial sector. A substantial number of them have purchased agricultural land, set up trading companies, or have invested part of their profits in new small-scale workshops and factories. Taken as a whole, the findings show that it is not uncommon for rural entrepreneurs in India, Malaysia and Indonesia to have more than one economic activity at the same time, or to be involved in them sequentially, often operating in different sectors of the rural economy simultaneously: in agriculture, trade and/or industry.

Another common characteristic of the three groups of businessmen in India, Malaysia and Indonesia is that commercial activities have been an important factor in this tendency towards economic diversification. A sizeable number of them have a trading background or have undertaken some sort of commercial activities before they started their enterprise. This has increased the amount of surplus available to these families and it has given them knowledge, contacts and experience in operating outside their traditional sectors of agriculture and artisanal production.

This is especially true of the members of the Patidar caste in the Indian case, for which agricultural trade has provided them with both extra capital and has given them the opportunity to establish economic activities outside farming but closely related to their own agricultural enterprise. The same applies to the Malay and Chinese owners of combine-harvesters who have a history of farming and various kinds of commercial activities. And even in the case of the iron-founders in Central Java, it turns out that the larger entrepreneurs, many of whom practice a business strategy of economic diversification, do not have an artisanal background, but originate from outside the region and belong to families with experience in other lines of business.

Following the commercial background and diversified pattern of investments by all three groups of businessmen in India, Malaysia and Indonesia, it could be argued that commercialism is indeed an important characteristic of the business strategy of rural entrepreneurs in South and Southeast Asia. Having said this, it would not be correct to dub them 'commercial businessmen' and conclude that the weakness in their entrepreneurship lies in their lack of knowledge of and interest in the technological side of the production process, as a consequence of which they tend - successively and/or simultaneously - to engage in a variety of business ventures.

As is shown in the analysis of the three empirical case studies, simultaneous investment in various economic activities has not prevented many of these entrepreneurs from re-investing. Additional capital has been invested to augment their outlets, to increase the size of their enterprise, to expand production, or to introduce technological improvements. Admittedly these changes have not occurred on a very large scale, but they are nevertheless significant enough to question the prevailing notion about commercialism being the characteristic feature of entrepreneurship in South and Southeast Asia.

In terms of forms of business organization, co-operation is what turns out to be a crucial aspect of the entrepreneurial activities of all three groups of businessmen in India, Malaysia and Indonesia. The discussions of the family firm and business networks in South and Southeast Asia have led to many lively debates. In the case of overseas Chinese, for example, the social cohesion provided by the traditional family structure and kinship ties is thought to promote the accumulation of wealth because of savings on managerial costs, the pooling of capital and relations of trust within the group. In contrast to this, studies on Muslim businessmen in Southeast Asia indicate that their Islamic background is not propitious to successful entrepreneurship because it does not provide them with instruments to form and make use of efficient organizational forms and economic institutions more complex than the nuclear family firm.

The findings of the Chinese, Muslim and Hindu businessmen in Malaysia, Indonesia and India show that family enterprises, partnerships and subcontracting relations - not to mention several other forms of economic co-operation, such as associations and co-operative societies - are of vital importance to the business operations of all three groups of rural entrepreneurs. The Indian case shows that the pattern of family business is not unique to overseas Chinese enterprises. Strikingly, a substantial number of Muslim businessmen in Malaysia and Indonesia operate through extended family enterprises, and partnerships are a common form of economic organization among all three groups of entrepreneurs.

The three empirical cases also establish that businesses in South and Southeast Asia are not necessarily family based or those family enterprises and partnerships are fixed entities free of conflict and immutable. All three studies found patterns of both family and non-family enterprises and business partnerships that are characterized by both a kind of jointers and conflict, and by a large number of changes over time. Subcontracting relations and networks are another important cooperative pattern in business organization among the rural entrepreneurs in all three countries. All of them tend to develop various kinds of linkages, partly with larger firms, partly among themselves. The case of the iron founders in Java, for example, highlights 'putting-out' relations between larger entrepreneurs and smaller businessmen.

Among other advantages, this system allows the former to expand their scale of operations without increasing factory size. Networks are found to be crucial for the functioning of many of the businessmen in Malaysia, Indonesia and India, and while the basis for building up networks varies (kin, caste, clan, and ethnicity), their deployment turns out to be quite similar across regions. The Malaysian case shows how Chinese businessmen use kinship and ethnic relations to build up business networks. At the same time, this case also unambiguously demonstrates that networks are not really more important for Chinese entrepreneurs than for those of other ethnic groups, such as the Malay businessmen.

In the Indian and Indonesian cases it initially appears that caste and religion are central features of business organization, but on closer analysis these can be seen as just one of the ways in which the wealthy business class forms networks to strengthen its economic position. Cogently, the differences in lifestyle within the Chinese business community in the Malaysian case, and its consequences for the functioning of business networks, again shows that the use of ethnic categories to explain entrepreneurial behaviour often tends to ignore the existence of heterogeneity within a business community.

Given this, it is obvious that the reason for a particular form of business organization flourishing in one place and not in another must certainly be more complex than the merely 'cultural'. Pertinently, the findings on the rural entrepreneurs in India, Malaysia and Indonesia indicate that both collective and individual types of entrepreneurial behaviour are present within one group. It is not so much collectivism or individualism which explains successful or unsuccessful entrepreneurial behaviour; of far greater importance is the flexibility to adjust social and economic forms of organization to changing circumstances in terms of space and time. Undeniably, the three cases manifest a tacit contradiction between the actuality of co-operation among relatives and an ideology of individualism or collectivism.

The Muslim iron founders of Central Java, for example, claim to work alone and attribute their success to their own efforts, but deeper investigation shows that they do in fact engage in several forms of co-operation, both within the family and outside. Conversely, the study of their behaviour in Malaysia and India indicates that Chinese and Hindu entrepreneurs tend to overemphasize the use of kinship ties, guanxi relations and joint-family structures, when in fact the day-to-day running of the business sometimes shows very little resemblance to these traditional ways. This indicates that the researcher must be wary of taking such proclamations by entrepreneurs at face value.

The bulk of the literature on South and Southeast Asian entrepreneurship stresses the symbiosis between entrepreneurs and the state, in terms of policy making, or the close relations which obtain between business groups and those who control the state apparatus. Studies on overseas Chinese businessmen in Southeast Asia often emphasize the close interaction between state and business to account for their entrepreneurial success. These studies argue that the intermediate position between the (colonial) state and the indigenous population goes some ways towards explaining the inclination among Chinese entrepreneurs to depend on state support by making use of politically secured economic privileges to accumulate capital.

Studies on Indian entrepreneurs and on Muslim businessmen in Southeast Asia indicate, on the other hand, that their profits are not based on production but are in essence rent incomes which derive from distorted market mechanisms following a high level of state intervention and regulations in these countries. This is perhaps a little too simplistic. The findings of the three cases in India, Indonesia and Malaysia show that rural businessmen use various strategies to develop contacts with government bureaucracy and the politically powerful. One tactic employed by these business entrepreneurs to promote their interests vis-á-vis the state is the formation of business associations.

In all the three cases, the business groups have discovered their common interests and organized formal associations to press their demands on the state. Such associations work to promote a degree of economic co-operation among businessmen and serve to represent the business community to outsiders. The Indonesian case in particular shows that business associations are also an important arena for factionalism and a means by which larger entrepreneurs are able to enhance their position in the rest of the business community. In such an instance, the study of the politics of business organizations provides an entry point through which it is possible to reveal deeper lines of division in local society and changes in social alignments.

Although most of the rural entrepreneurs in central Gujarat, northern Malaysia and Central Java manage to evade taxes and avoid government regulations, and although indubitably some have even benefited directly from government subsidies, they usually have a very negative attitude towards the economic policy of their provincial and national government. On many occasions, they emphasize that not only are their interests not served by government policy, in fact they are being frustrated. As entrepreneurs they consider themselves to be the backbone of the rural economy, providing employment and income for its population. They are very happy to claim a larger share from the government budget in terms of subsidies, but they feel strongly that they should be left alone to run their economic enterprises without any government interference in the form of labour laws, price regulations, and taxes and so on.

The history of economic development in the three localities in central Gujarat, northern Malaysia and Central Java shows that government policies have been pivotal in promoting the growth of small industry, hence nurturing regional capitalist classes. While acknowledging the link, it would be a mistake to presume that these small entrepreneurs depend entirely on state support. The three cases suggest that, even though there is state support for small industry, many of the most successful entrepreneurs have invested in business enterprises independently. Therefore the three groups of entrepreneurs should be viewed as agents in capitalist development rather than simply as products of state policy.

Typical of the behaviour of the three groups of businessmen in central Gujarat, northern Malaysia and Central Java is the utilization of various social and cultural strategies to enhance their social status and to build up social networks that may further their business interests. As rural entrepreneurs they belong to the newly rich classes in Asia who often employ their wealth to acquire prestige and power through investment in various social and cultural activities. Participation in social activities such as gambling, womanizing and drinking parties helps to establish personal contacts with potential clients and partners, and with government and bank officials. Other strategies include membership of and office-holding in educational organizations, business associations and co-operatives.

The principal goal of these activities is to develop business contacts, but they are also a splendid way to raise social standing, which in turn also contributes to entrepreneurial success, as all three cases demonstrate. On the whole, the recent economic wealth of the three groups of rural entrepreneurs in India, Indonesia and Malaysia has brought them the chance for more luxurious consumption, leisure time, a change in the nature of the work performed by both male and female members, and a more supra-local orientation in terms of economic activities and social contacts. Notwithstanding this tendency towards a more urban lifestyle and regional orientation, most of these entrepreneurs remain strongly based in their own local and ethnic community. Among the entrepreneurs studied, community, family status and family property are still important social criteria in the selection of both a marriage partner and a business partner.

Not only do they choose business partners from the same social and ethnic background, but they also strongly and explicitly emphasize the kinship ties and family relations that exist between the different partners. Entrepreneurial development in rural areas may therefore have various social outcomes, but it usually leads to some kind of economic differentiation, which may be marked by symbols of social exclusivity, as the three cases show.

In all three settings the entrepreneurial groups use social and cultural symbols to mark themselves off as separate classes, such as educating their children beyond the usual standard, adopting a distinctive lifestyle (often characterized by increased and conspicuous consumption), and creating exclusive social networks among themselves and with outsiders. In doing so, they are increasingly differentiated from the rural communities from which they arose and have more in common with town-based regional capitalists than with the farmers and other rural residents in their locality.

THE EARLY EUROPEAN INDUSTRIALISTS

The characterizations of entrepreneurs in India, Indonesia and Malaysia as 'commercialists', 'capitalist bureaucrats', 'statist capitalists', and 'dependent capitalists' have in common latent disapproval of the behaviour of the South and Southeast businessmen. Underlying this common view of a deformed, pseudo- or non-genuine nature of the capitalist class in South and Southeast Asia is the assumption that - either at present or in the past, either in Asia or in another part of the world - there once existed a class of pure, genuine and true capitalists. Without actually referring to the European path of industrial transition, it is this path and its generation of a class of industrial capitalists that is frequently invoked as a model or paradigm for the behaviour of the capitalists operating in South and Southeast Asia today.

It is generally assumed that the early European industrialists, i.e. those entrepreneurs who operated in Europe at the time of the Industrial Revolution - the mid-eighteenth to the mid/late-nineteenth century - did meet the characteristics of true and genuine capitalists which the present-day South and Southeast Asian entrepreneurs are said to be lacking. By 'Asian' mean assumptions that underlie Asian Studies, more in particularly studies in which references are made to the class of Asian capitalists. 'Asian' therefore includes both the studies on Asia by Asian scholars and by non-Asian, mostly Western scholars.

The 'Asian' assumptions about the early European industrialists are not invented, but often have their origin in notions that can be traced back in part to debates among European historians about the nature of the Industrial Revolution in general and the emergence of the early European industrialists in particular. Central to the 'Asian' notion of the Industrial Revolution is the idea that this period in European history has to be characterized, first and foremost, as a radical and sudden transformation of society. In this view, the changes that took place in Europe between the mid-eighteenth and the mid/ late-nineteenth century were sweeping changes which signified a break with the past in many aspects of economic life. The economic structure of Europe after the mid-eighteenth century was completely different from that of the period before. Two of the essential features of this radical and sudden transformation are generally thought to have been the emergence of a new production system, the factory, and the rise of a new producer, the industrialist.

The emergence of the factory-based production system arose from the demise of the putting-out and domestic system which had been the dominant forms of production during the period preceding the Industrial Revolution. The characteristic feature of the putting-out and domestic system was that production took place in small household establishments and domestic workshops. These systems of production were basically a combination of domestic work and commercial capitalism. At the top were rich men who were given various names by contemporaries, but who are generally described by historians as 'merchant-manufacturers'. They either placed orders with master craftsmen in provincial towns, who then produced the desired goods in small-scale domestic workshops, or brought in the raw materials which they distributed to peasant-workers to process in their own cottages, often using simple machines.

The characteristic feature of the merchant-manufacturer was that he did not actively participate in the production process. Basically, the merchant-manufacturer was a merchant, a trader, not an industrialist; he was an organizer of production and its financing, not a producer. Many of these merchant-manufacturers did not confine themselves to one line of business. They were often polyvalent, with multifarious and widespread activities and investments. A number of them had interests in several industrial concerns at the same time. In addition to their chief interests, they were also involved in farming, cattle-fattening, mining, malting, property ownership, retail trade and pawn broking. This behaviour could be observed among merchant-manufacturers large and small, several of whom had their fingers in many pies.

The versatility of businessmen and the absence of specialization in investment is therefore usually considered a trait which was normal at a time when functional specialization was little developed, but which became obsolete with the advent of the Industrial Revolution. Commencing in the mid-eighteenth century, factory-based production is generally held to have become the dominant system of production in Britain. What was new about this factory-based system was the concentration of production in organizations under unified technical management and ownership, the employment of labourers, and the widespread introduction of technological inventions, especially of power-driven machinery.

A vital component in the factory-based system was the increase in fixed capital at an unprecedented scale. From being commercial capital, a preponderant amount of capital became industrial, and from being floating and circulating capital, it increasingly became fixed capital, mainly as a result of the development of machinery, especially steam-power. The introduction of this new way of organizing production was established by a new type of businessman, the industrialist, who at the end of the eighteenth century was beginning to emerge in his own right and in growing numbers. This new businessman is generally considered to have differed from the old type of merchant-manufacturer in many ways.

Compared to the interests of the latter production lay at the centre of the industrialist's work and not at its periphery. No doubt, merchanting skills, a sense of market opportunities and an ability to deal with commercial problems were as important to the industrialist as they had been to the merchant-manufacturer. In contrast to the merchant-manufacturer, however, the industrialist is thought to have intervened much more thoroughly and widely in organizing production. He was viewed as a 'practical man', often his own technical expert. Instead of dealing largely in liquid resources, as was typical for the merchant-manufacturers, the industrialists are thought to have created very great elements of fixed capital and re-embodied them in the product over future time.

They short-circuited and eventually eliminated the various intermediaries especially the domestic small master and the merchant-manufacturer - who, under the domestic and putting-out system, came between the labourer and the wholesale buyer of finished goods. They organized production, brought together the capital and the labour force, selected the most appropriate site for operations, chose the particular technologies of production to be employed, devised new combinations of factors of production, were sometimes even innovators who initiated decisive economic change by breaking away from the constant trend towards equilibrium, bargained for raw materials and found outlets for the finished product. In short, it is generally held that the industrialists who emerged during the Industrial Revolution were setting 'a new pattern of the complete businessman', who gathered and merged a large number of roles in a single person.

Who were these new and complete businessmen, these first industrialists? Where did they come from and where did they acquire their capital to start their industrial enterprises? Central to the 'Asian' notion of the early European industrialists is that these industrialists did not belong to the category of merchants or merchant-manufacturers. There are some indications that, in the early eighteenth century, large traders who had earned money from the international trade had invested some capital in industry. 'The impression gained from the literary sources is that, in the west of England at least, the leading textile entrepreneurs were often exceedingly wealthy merchants'.

Central to the 'Asian' notion is that such an extension of activity was not common among the European merchants, nor was it common among the merchant-manufacturers. On the whole, rich merchants and merchant-manufacturers in Europe are thought to have rarely invested the profits of their mercantile or putting-out ventures in industry; it was still rarer for them to be active partners in industrial firms. It is generally believed that those merchants and merchant-manufacturers who did own part of an industrial undertaking were merchants or merchant-manufacturers first and foremost, and their industrial activities were of only secondary importance to them.

This 'Asian' notion that the early industrialists in Europe did not originate from the ranks of the merchants or merchant-manufacturers follows Marx's description of the second road to capitalism according to which a section of the existing merchant class began to 'take possession directly of production', thereby 'serving historically as a mode of transition', but becoming eventually 'an obstacle to a real capitalist mode of production and declining with the development of the latter.'

This view has been extended by Maurice Dobb who emphasizes that even though in the early days of the Industrial Revolution certain sections of merchant capital did turn towards industry and began to control production, at most they might have prepared the way for capitalist industrialization, and may in a few cases have reached it, but they did not bring about any thorough transformation. Following this line of thought, the instigators of the Industrial Revolution in Europe are thought not to have originated from the traditional dominant classes of merchants and merchant-manufacturers but to have come from those social strata which had so far played a less prominent role in economic life: the class of independent, self-sustaining yeoman farmers and small and middle-scale craftsmen.

This notion owes a very great deal to Maurice Dobb's study in which he argued that it had been Marx's first road to capitalism which had been the dominant way in which the transition from feudalism to capitalism in Europe took place. According to this 'really revolutionary way', a section of the rural and urban producers themselves had accumulated capital and had taken to trade, and in course of time had begun to organize production on a capitalist basis, free from the handicraft restrictions of the guilds. It is from the social stratum of independent, self-sustaining peasant-kulaks and small and middle-scale craftsmen that the early European industrialists are usually held to have originated. Being 'new' men, who did not originate from the classes that dominated the old social structure, these new producer-capitalists had every interest in dismantling the various barriers and guild privileges that were part and parcel of the traditional domestic and putting-out system of production.

This idea of the 'common' origin of the early European industrialists, as defended most prominently by Maurice Dobb, is closely connected to a more general belief that the chief agents of productivity in the early stage of European industrial development were mostly self-made men. This belief was widely prevalent in the nineteenth century and is clearly shown in the writings of contemporaries such as Samuel Smiles, in his best-seller Self-Help, published in 1859, and P. Gaskell in his detailed account Artisans and Machinery.

It is this belief of the 'self-made man' who sprang from a 'humble origin' among peasant- kulaks and craftsmen which has strongly influenced the 'Asian' notion of the early

European industrialists. The logical consequence of such a view, the early European industrialists are held to have been independent businessmen. Whatever profits they accrued were the fruits of their own hard work. There was no government assistance; all of them had to survive in an open, free market economy characterized by fierce competition. Born in humble circumstances (this is a standard expression), i.e. from modest or even poor families, they had started life as wage-earners, often working with their own hands; but, thanks to hard work, thrift, mechanical ingenuity and character, they had been able to set up their own business, to develop it and eventually to become wealthy and powerful.

Bearing in mind the putative humble origin of the first industrialists and the fact that the introduction of the factory system is thought to have required large concentrations of fixed capital, it is therefore generally assumed that 'capital had been a serious problem during the industrial revolution, and that innovators and entrepreneurs had been hampered by its scarcity'. However, 'of serious shortage of capital we hear strangely little'. Presumably a business was launched with the savings of the industrialist himself and grew by the assiduous plough-back of profits. And indeed, 'it has often been said that the early industrialists ploughed back their profits into their business'.

This way of financing industry through ploughing back of profits was possible because of the stringent frugality and unremitting thrift these industrialists are said to have widely practiced as part of an overall sober lifestyle. Their origins were often humble, and they were as hard on themselves as they were on others; business was their consuming interest and they continued to lead the simple lives to which they had been early accustomed, practicing a stringent personal economy and a rigid austerity, which maximised their savings. They withdrew from their business each year only a small part of its profits for their personal needs, or else they paid themselves a small salary, hardly any higher than a skilled workman's wage.

This practice of taking but a small part of the profits for

their personal needs and leaving the remainder to accumulate in the business led to constant reinvestment and to a rapid growth of capital. Establishing and expanding an industrial enterprise by saving out of income has frequently been regarded as the only form that accumulation can take or at least the only form it took during the Industrial Revolution. This frugal living and saving behaviour of the first industrialists is considered to be the result of a pattern of deferred gratification, which may be defined as 'readiness to forgo present gratification in order to attain greater gratification of the same or another need at a later date'.

It is this postponement of immediate gratification in the expectation of increased future benefits which is generally held to have been a guiding principle among the early industrialists in Europe. This method of industrial expansion through saving and reinvestment, although in the first instance imposed by necessity, is said to have quickly acquired a virtue of its own in the minds of these early European industrial entrepreneurs. In this, they followed the prevalent ethic among the bourgeoisie who are held to have valued hard work and condemned idleness, and who frowned on spendthrift behaviour and praised savings.

Fine virtues though they may be, frugality and saving of themselves did not automatically lead to increased production. The regular reproduction of capital by the early European industrialists, involving the continual investment and reinvestment of capital for the end of economic efficiency, is therefore usually not associated with a specific saving and frugal behaviour but with an overall attitude among the members of this class. Characteristic of this overall outlook, this very specific kind of ethic is the continual accumulation of wealth for its own sake, rather than for the material rewards that it could serve to bring.

Weber claims that it is this combination of a work drive and a sober way of life that is the essence of the spirit of modern capitalism. Those entrepreneurs who are associated with the development of rational capitalism in Europe are said to have been characterized in their behaviour by an integration of the impulse to accumulate with a positively frugal lifestyle. 'When the limitation of consumption is combined with this release of acquisitive activity, the inevitable practical result is obvious: accumulation of capital through ascetic compulsion to save'.

It is this capitalist spirit, this combination of a work ethos and a sober way of life, which is usually associated with the category of early European industrialists. Even though it was part of an overall ethic among the bourgeoisie of that time, its exemplary protagonists are said to have been present among those who initiated the process of industrial growth in Europe. Within the class of early industrialists, the capitalist spirit is generally thought to have been the way of life, the form of consciousness that was best suited to the categories of yeomen and small and middle industrialists, and was not to be found in the 'hunger for money' and 'greed for gain' mentality, common among the monopolist merchants and usurers who dominated the period preceding the Industrial Revolution.

It was Weber who considered that the motivation underlying this spirit of capitalism was of a religious nature: the Protestant ethic, the desire to acquire property not for enjoyment but for augmentation in the service of God and as a sign of His blessing. Although he emphasized that 'we have no intention whatever of maintaining such a foolish and doctrinaire thesis as that the spirit of capitalism could only have arisen as the result of certain effects of the Reformation, or even that capitalism as an economic system is a creation of the Reformation', religion is often considered to have been of importance in stimulating the principle of deferred gratification among the early European industrialists during their initial phase of capital growth.

The fact that many, nay the majority of eighteenth-century industrialists belonged to non-cornformist sects definitely reinforced their tendency to abstinence, hard work and thrift, and helped to keep them faithful to their simple and frugal way of life, even when they had made a fortune, and to discourage them from conspicuous expenditure or aping the upper classes;

thus religion was a factor in the rapid accumulation of capital. In a nutshell, 'Asian' assumptions about the early European industrialists consist of the following characterizations. Industrial growth in Europe was set in motion by a specific type of industrialist who had a peasant- kulak/yeoman or craftsman/artisan background and a single-minded devotion to his business. For him, it was not the process of circulation that was the decisive factor but it was the production process that lay at the centre of his activity and concern.

Instead of following a policy of diversification like the merchant-manufacturers had done in earlier days, the early industrialist pursued a strategy of capitalization with resolute consistency by focusing all his energy on developing and expanding his business. He possessed a strong work ethos and practiced a stringent personal economy and a rigid austerity. He reinvested the results of his labour ethos and his sober way of life by expanding production and realizing continuous technological improvements. His behaviour was identical to the pursuit of profit, forever renewed profit, by means of continuous reinvestments of his surplus through expanding and improving production, all of this with no other purpose than to generate more surpluses on ever-expanding scale.

To what extent is this characterization of the early European industrialists, on which the 'Asian' assumptions are based, a valid characterization? At the risk of stating the obvious, it is important to emphasize that a type of characterization as the one described above basically ignores the possibility of diversity. Findings gleaned from economic historical studies show, for example, that the characterization of the early European industrialists as described above does not give a true representation of the category of first industrialists in France, nor does it give a true representation of all the categories of early industrialists in Britain. Several economic historical studies of France point out that the first French industrialists - i.e. those operating between ca. 1815 and 1870 - have to be characterized as conservative and consumption-oriented industrialists who were more intent in enjoying their wealth, power and prestige, than in pushing up the indexes production. With rare exceptions, French enterprise was organized on a family basis, mainly restricting its clientele to an intimate circle of friends and relatives. The French businessman was considered to have been insufficiently enterprising, preferring security behind tariff walls and seeking support from the state rather than investing in modern techniques and pushing into new markets.

In an almost similar line, economic historical studies of Britain point at the entrepreneurial failings of the second- and third-generation industrialists in Britain who operated at the end of the nineteenth century. They emphasize the waning of the entrepreneurial energies of the founders' descendants for whom the industrial enterprise ceased to be an end itself and increasingly became a means for earning money to support a luxurious lifestyle. With the members of the family more actively pursuing their own interests outside industry, many of the industrial firms were gradually allowed to run down.

This overall 'decline of the industrial spirit' in the later nineteenth century was caused, in part at least, by the fact that many of the industrial entrepreneurs were too busy becoming gentlemen, living and spending on a lavish scale. They were often held to have been more focused on spending their wealth than on earning money through productive activities. These views of the first industrialists in France and the second/third-generation industrialists in Britain do to a large extent give a stereotyped picture of their behaviour.

Economic history with regard to the industrial revolution in France and with regard to the late nineteenth-century industrialization in Britain has gone through a process of renewal and reappraisal. Here it is enough to emphasize that these views, despite their stereotyped nature, point to the possibility of diversity among the early European industrialists. They indicate that the 'Asian' assumptions about the early European industrialists have to be questioned for at least these two categories of early industrialists in Western Europe, one of them operating in Britain, the country that was the first in the world to industrialize. Following this, the test case of the 'Asian' assumptions about the early European industrialists seems to be the first industrialists in Britain, operating between the mid-eighteenth and mid-nineteenth centuries. These industrialists belonged to the very first industrialists in the world and are therefore considered to be the classical case of the emergence of a class of industrial capitalists.

Before I discuss the findings of various historical studies of these first industrialists operating in Britain at the time of the Industrial Revolution, it is important to emphasize that this field of study is still blighted by a lack of detailed research at the factory level and of reliable quantitative data on the origin and nature of the industrial entrepreneurs. On top of this problem of data scarcity and unreliability of the data used, many studies turn out to be based on biased samples.

This in itself should make us suspicious of the validity of the 'Asian' assumptions about the origins and behaviour of the early European industrialists, as presented in the previous section. This suspicion increases when we take a closer look at the findings of the economic historical studies of each of the various aspects of the origin and behaviour of the first British industrialists. In this overview, I do not pretend to give the subject an exhaustive treatment but focus only on those aspects of the emergence of the first industrialists in Britain that are important to understanding the discussion on the nature of the capitalist class in South and Southeast Asia today.

In contrast to the notion of the Industrial Revolution as a radical and sudden transformation of society, recent research and analysis support the view that industrialization in Britain was a gradual process during the classic industrial revolution period. This being so the inescapable conclusion has to be that business organizations and procedures prevalent in the pre-industrial persisted into the industrial economy where they co-existed with other forms.

Furthermore, recent insights into the history of technology of the eighteenth and nineteenth centuries challenge the view of rapid and universal technical change embodied in conventional notions of the Industrial Revolution. The substitution of machinery for labour, which is an essential feature of the Industrial Revolution concept, was an equally uneven and protracted process as was the introduction of the factory organization. It is equally unlikely that the early stages of industrialization required such a hefty leap in investment as has sometimes been supposed. Capital requirements by the factory entrepreneurs were similar to those of the existing merchant-manufacturers; a relatively small proportion of their capital needed to be laid out in fixed plant and machinery.

There is evidence too that many of the first industrialists used various capital economizing devices to escape large outlays of fixed capital. Payne argues that only a handful of the major pioneers of the Industrial Revolution would therefore apparently qualify to be called innovating and genuine entrepreneurs, while the vast majority of such businessmen appear to have been imitative. The nature of the growth pattern was often conservative, being frequently characterized by sheer multiplication of existing plants and processes producing a fairly limited range of related products.

Many small industrialists during the mid-nineteenth century did not even want to grow because they wanted to remain independent entrepreneurs who could run their enterprises all by themselves. They were able to make comfortable profits, which strengthened their resolve not to increase the scale of their operation beyond the size which would have involved partially entrusting their businesses to managers recruited from outside the family circle. All this made possible the continued existence of numerous small, often weakly-financed family concerns, many of which chose to specialize in the exploitation of only a limited portion of the full spectrum of demand for related products.

Instability in production was a common phenomenon among the first industrialists in Britain. The mortality rates for these firms were high; getting started was relatively easy, but staying in business turned out to be much harder. Many bitter individual failures occurred, particularly during the early decades of the nineteenth century, when many new firms were established. Instability was also common in the organization structure among these first industrialists. Many firms were partnerships, often small, family-linked partnerships. A characteristic feature of these partnerships was 'their rapid turnover, the frequent changes among their members; partnerships were unceasingly created, supplemented, terminated. Indeed, their death rate was high; many factories or works had a chequered history and changed hands at frequent intervals, while many industrialists moved from mill to mill - several times in some cases - during their career'.

All the evidence points to the fact that plurality of interests was common among the entrepreneurs of the Industrial Revolution and it has been pointed out that, especially in the eighteenth century, men of capital were frequently interested in several enterprises of different kinds. In his study, Industrial Capital and Landed Investment, E.L. Jones, for example, remarks that 'the economic interests of the truly affluent and most powerful in trade, industry, and land did overlap in England'. Industrial and commercial wealth was invested in land, while landowning and commercial wealth flowed into mining and industry. Many of the richer industrialists were as it were *brasseurs d'affairs* - rich people who had their fingers in several different pies, who were simultaneously involved in, say, trade, banking, landowning, mining and industry.

Following this brief description of the economic behaviour of these first industrialists in Britain, there is a common question which must be asked about these men: where did they come from and from where did they obtain their capital to start their industrial enterprise? Following Maurice Dobb's view, derived from Marx, the really revolutionary transformation of production and the breaking of the control of merchant capital over production was accomplished by men coming from the ranks of former craftsmen. Some of the first industrialists were indeed craftsmen who had assumed the role of manager and owner of the means of production by investing their capital in the employment of other smaller craftsmen.

Undeniably the class of artisans was the breeding-ground

for several famous machine-makers, including the greatest of them James Watt, who was an instrument-maker before becoming interested in steam-engines. On the whole, however, the rise among the craftsmen of a richer, capitalist element did not take place on a large scale. It now seems that the role of merchant-traders in the formation of the industrialist class is not as negligible as has often been maintained. Their initiative in industrial investment did not come from the foreign trading companies, but lay with the humbler provincial middle bourgeoisie, of which the members were less privileged and less wealthy but more broadly based.

Though important this category of traders was surpassed by businessmen who were already engaged in industry, i.e. by the group of manufacturers or merchant-manufacturers in domestic production, and owners and managers of already centralized establishments. Pertinently, many businessmen played the dual role of merchant-trader and merchant-manufacturer simultaneously.

By the end of the eighteenth century, for example, many merchant-manufacturers established spinning mills and calico printing works or one or the other, while continuing to put out work to domestic handloom weavers. During this same period, many merchants gained absolute control over production by becoming manufacturers themselves. As a result, merchants and manufacturers were often united in one person.

On the question of the sources of capital, i.e. the financing of industrial enterprises, both at the time of their foundation and during their expansion, a large amount of data has been collected by various scholars. The idea that many, if not most, industrialists were self-made men - which was a popular view during nineteenth century - was exposed as a myth by twentieth century economic and social historians. The number of industrialists, even in the Industrial Revolution, who began without capital or connections of any kind, was a minute fraction of the whole. In many enterprises, capital from diverse sources was used. Small partnerships were common, usually consisting of a group of relatives or friends, though sometimes a stranger was admitted as a sleeping partner.

Most firms were started with initial capital which had been accumulated through pre-factory system manufacturing or merchant-manufacturing activities, or through the trading of industrial raw materials or finished articles. Small artisan entrepreneurs for example often obtained outside help in order to found large factories. 'Of course we can find some which were founded solely on "artisan" or "commercial" capital, but generally speaking an entrepreneur had to rely on various sources to collect enough capital to found a sizeable new undertaking'.

There can no longer be any doubt that the founders of factory industries obtained capital from diverse sources, but that these sources were of unequal importance; industry itself supplied most of the capital for its own transformation, while commerce provided an important supplementary reservoir. The part played by bank capital seems to have been very small. Institutional sources hardly played a role in the supply of capital. Both private bankers and their joint stock descendants were commercial bankers, not investment houses. Overall, therefore, external supplies of capital were 'less important than the personal or family funds which the industrialists scraped together and ventured in the new productive equipment. The power of heredity and the vitality of the family as an economic group stand out whenever we examine the history of the pioneer manufacturers'.

In order to expand, the pioneer 'firms usually borrowed - on mortgage, bond or note of hand from family and friends, solicitors and attorneys (or through their agency), or from other manufacturers or merchants with whom they had connexions'. Payne shows that 'although the firms that were limited were by far the most important in their spheres of activity, judged by size of unit and amount of fixed capital, the vast majority of the manufacturing firms of the country continued to be family businesses in the mid-1880s'. He even suggests that 'the over-representation of non-conformists among the entrepreneurs who attained prominence may be explicable not in terms of their religious precepts, their superior education or their need for achievement, but because they belonged to extended kinship families that gave them access to credit which permitted their firms, and their records, to survive, while others, less well connected, went to the wall'.

Taken together, these economic historical studies reveal the variety of the sources of capital which had been used for establishment, the resorting by the first industrialists to the resources of their relatives and friends, on a personal basis, and the movement of capital between various branches of industry. In spite of all these financial sources, it is often emphasized that what permitted the Industrial Revolution to proceed at a relatively swift pace was the fact that enterprises increased their capital by ploughing back the greater part, or even the whole, of their profits immediately, regularly and almost automatically. Entrepreneurs who operated at the inception of the Industrial Revolution are said to have immediately reinvested most of their profits (and even the interest on capital) in order to finance expansion.

It is probably true that this state of affairs enabled a number of enterprises - possibly most of them - to finance expansion entirely from their own sources. However, although there is every reason to believe that most of the additional capital required for expansion was indeed provided from the savings of the industrialists, this does not necessarily imply abstemious frugality and unremitting thrift as part of an overall sober lifestyle on the part of the industrialist's family. In the first industrial period, many industrialists did indeed live relatively simply: they resided close to their works, often in an adjacent house; the daily tour of the various departments was part of their way of life; they spent long hours at work, twelve or more a day, and closely supervised everything which went on in their factories.

However, 'once they had built up their businesses and secured their fortunes, they nearly always relaxed somewhat, withdrawing more money and adopting a more comfortable way of life. Some of them bought landed estates and built themselves large mansions'. We must therefore not overemphasize the frugality of these early industrialists. They were conscious of the need to save money, for this was the source of investment funds, but they also quickly espoused new pleasures in the guise of consumers. They were eager to acquire a new standard of living and slowly began to separate themselves from the rest of the middle class.

More and more successful business families sent their sons to public schools and many of them bought large mansions in which they employed servants and pursued a lifestyle of luxury and conspicuous consumption. E.L. Jones, for example, remarks that much of the money which passed out of industry into land was squandered on prodigious bouts of port-drinking, on assemblies, race meetings, fox-hunts, and pheasant battues. Resources were dissipated on unproductive activities like the gyrations of armies of flunkeys, the sonorities of private chapel building, the ordered informality of landscape gardening, the contrived futility of mock ruins and follies. A share of industrially created wealth constantly disappeared in these bonfires of good living for a small, landed class or was immobilised in their ornaments.

During the first phase of European industrialization, the 'status of many families which produced industrialists was rather low, and even when they had made fortunes, industrialists were heartily despised by the traditional ruling class for their low birth and bad manners, and for decades they remained beyond the pale of "gentle" society'. In England, social standing depended to a greater extent than elsewhere on the ownership of landed property. The purchase of landed estates by the first industrialists was therefore part of a widespread emulation of aristocratic lifestyles by the wealthier sections of the entrepreneurial class.

New aspirants to the landed gentry came from many industries, sometimes acquiring land by marrying into this class or even from time to time into the aristocracy, more often by straightforward purchase. It is evident from the terms of the marriage settlements between aristocrats and bourgeois heiresses that considerable material gains were necessary to induce the great families to contract them. Those industrialists who entered county society through the purchase of land wanted to seal their new status by reaching new heights of splendour in their residences, extensive landscaping of their park, and projects for improvements on their farms.

These changes in the lifestyle of the members of the industrialists' families were not restricted to the males only, but affected the life of the women as well. In his study, Leisure in the Industrial Revolution, Hugh Cunningham, for example, describes the lifestyle of the middle-class women in mid-nineteenth century Britain in the following ideal form:

The perfect lady of the mid-Victorian years removed not only from worldly concerns, but also from household ones, was a symbol of her husband's wealth and status. Conspicuous leisure and conspicuous consumption were a mark of status, their utility for purposes of reputability lying in the element of waste common to both - waste of time and effort, or waste of goods. Dress for women, therefore had to be both expensive and impractical for productive labour; designedly uncomfortable, it testified in a general way to woman's economic dependence on man, and specifically to the status of a particular man. These concerns with status led, as is well known (and was much deplored at the time), to late marriages, so that the husband, well set in his career, could keep his wife in the manner which she had been led to expect as daughter.

Overall, consumption and leisure were quickly becoming part of the lifestyle of the new industrialists. In this, they followed a general pattern of changes in lifestyle by members of economically upwardly mobile classes in society, as described by Thorstein Veblen in The Theory of the Leisure Class. In this study on social climbing in late nineteenth-century America, first published in 1899, Veblen emphasizes that 'in order to gain and to hold the esteem of men it is not sufficient merely to possess wealth or power. The wealth or power must be put in evidence, for esteem is awarded only on evidence'. He shows that in many instances conspicuous abstention from labour therefore became the conventional mark of superior pecuniary achievement and the conventional index of reputability; and conversely, since application to productive labour is a mark of poverty and subjection, it became inconsistent with a reputable standing in the community. Habits of industry and thrift, therefore, were not uniformly furthered by a prevailing pecuniary emulation. Conspicuous consumption of valuable goods was also a means of reputability. This need of vicarious leisure, or conspicuous consumption of service, was for example a dominant incentive to the keeping of servants.

The ultimate industrial consequences of this draining of capital are hard to assess. The opportunity costs of land purchases were high and economic growth could surely have come faster without them. While part of the fortunes made in industry did leak into landownership and into a conspicuous lifestyle, from the common-sense point of view it appears that since manufacturing did expand, the counter-attractions of wealth and rural life may have retarded but could not block industrialization. Continuous investments and reinvestments in industry by these early industrialists therefore did coincide very well with an increase in wealth and conspicuous consumption.

There seems to be little doubt that social ambition provided an immensely powerful motor of business activity at the time of the Industrial Revolution. The pursuit of wealth was the pursuit of social status, not merely for oneself but for one's family and this often meant the acquisition of a landed estate or the purchase or building of a great house.

Coleman therefore argues that 'no more then than today was the maximization of profits an end; it neither was, nor is today, the only means employed. The ends are more intangible and varied: profits are a path to prestige, power, status, personal satisfaction, adventures made, purpose and achievements gained'. In a similar vein, P.L. Payne states that those who have argued that this pursuit of non-economic ends inevitably involved a haemorrhage of entrepreneurial talent as the nineteenth century progressed, should perhaps balance this against what might be called the demonstration effect of conspicuous consumption or social elevation on the new men crowding in to emulate those who had already succeeded. One cannot help believing that many new thrusting firms would not have come into existence, or small established companies grown, had not their founders or owners, or their socially ambitious wives, seen or been aware of the tangible results of commercial or industrial success. These manifestations of success served to encourage the others.

The foregoing social and economic profile of the early industrial entrepreneurs clearly indicates that many of them were drawn from exactly the same class as before. The new industrial changes in late eighteenth-century Britain were linked organically and personally to an older economic world at every stage. Only to some extent was the industrialist who emerged during the Industrial Revolution a new man. Continuity rather than discontinuity was the rule. Many of the first industrialists in Britain originated from the traditional dominant class of traders and merchant-manufacturers, who followed a strategy of diversification of their economic and social interests along with expanding their industrial affairs.

Guided by a short-time horizon, these industrialists often did not reinvest their profits in the same enterprise but were notoriously quick to spread their risk by investing in different types of economic activities, either simultaneously or successively. Mobilization of capital and organization of the work was often done along the traditional, pre-capitalist lines of family and kinship. Although many of the first industrialists in Britain followed a lifestyle of frugality and sobriety, for many others investments of capital in their economic undertakings coincided with a lifestyle of luxury and consumption.

It is generally assumed that the emergence of the capitalist class in South and Southeast Asia is a historically unique phenomenon and the factors leading to it are so specific that they cannot be compared with the rise of the early industrialists in Europe. Any comparison of current industrialization in South and Southeast Asia with the

European path to industrial transition is often regarded as historical determinism and therefore out rightly rejected. To a large extent, this is of course correct. History does not repeat itself mechanically. A nineteenth-century pattern of development could hardly be repeated in detail today.

All processes of change have their own prerequisites, which will differ from country to country and from one time to another. That the emergence of a capitalist class in South and Southeast Asia would be an exact duplicate of the rise of the class of industrial capitalists in eighteenth- and nineteenth-century Europe is of course ridiculous and should indeed be rejected out of hand. Having accepted this, there is some danger in arguing that every comparison of the emergence of the capitalist class in South and Southeast Asia with the rise of the class of industrial capitalists in Europe is always to be regarded as historical determinism and therefore to be rejected under all circumstances.

The rejection of general theoretical models for comparative study after the 1970s led to a concentration of research on Asia in its own right. The subsequent trend has been to emphasize the cultural uniqueness of business organization in different contexts, as seen for example in the literature on Indian business communities and Chinese business networks. Cogently, the terminology employed to characterize the class of present-day capitalists in South and Southeast Asia shows that this has not prevented comparisons with their European counterparts from taking place, but has 'forced' these comparisons to get below the surface and thereby to become unverifiable. As a result, most references to the pseudo- or non-genuine capitalist nature of the present-day South and Southeast Asian entrepreneurs are based on assumptions about the origins and nature of European industrialists of which the validity is seldom questioned. Viewing the persistency and value attached to these characterizations, it is important that these assumptions are made explicit and are tested on their tenability.

Economic historical studies on the early European

industrialists, as discussed in this chapter, show that most of the 'Asian' assumptions about the European industrialists are not tenable, not even for the 'classical case' of the first industrialists in Britain. They point out the fact that, because of lack of detailed research at the factory level and because of lack of reliable quantitative data, little can be said with certainty about their origin and nature. This in itself already casts doubt on the validity of the 'Asian' assumptions about the early European industrialists. From the findings of the economic historical studies on different sections of the first industrialists in Britain, as they were presented in the foregoing section, it appears that these 'Asian' assumptions are based on a stereotyped model and present us with a distorted view of the emergence of the class of industrial capitalists in Europe.

These 'Asian' assumptions/myths about the emergence of the class of industrial capitalists in Europe have already often been challenged and invalidated by European economic historians for quite some time. In his study, British Entrepreneurship in the Nineteenth Century, published in 1974, P.L. Payne, for example, argues that the pioneer industrialists do not fully deserve the notion of high quality of entrepreneurial performance that is usually attached to them. Based on an overview of the studies available at that time, he questions the assumption that drive and dynamism were characteristic features of the British entrepreneurs of the Industrial Revolution.

It is a curious fact that studies which have made so many contributions to a revision of old myths regarding the history of South and Southeast Asia have seldom made use of new insights among the European economic historians to question their own view of the origins and nature of the class of European industrialists on the image of which they have characterized the emergence of the present-day capitalist class in Asia as being of a deformed, pseudo- or non-genuine capitalist nature. The fact that scholars studying Asian society do not question their assumptions on Western society, but accept these notions as the true image, is not simply a matter of ignorance, but more of a choice for ideology over knowledge, as argued by Heather Sutherland (1993).

She emphasizes that the common view of Asian 'economic backwardness' as being rooted in the failure of Asian societies to maintain the 'proper' distinctions between political and economic spheres is based on ideologically inclined misreading of European history. Her conclusion that 'all too often, our ideas of the past are dominated by an idea of "progress", derived from simplified myths about European industrialization and growth' could equally well apply to our ideas of the present: 'While recent research has modified our views of those sturdy entrepreneurs who set us happily upon the right path, the comforting folk-tales still lurk in our memories and influence our assumptions'.

It is this simplified image and lack of historical perspective regarding the roots of European capitalist development that has enabled scholars studying Asian society to conclude that South and Southeast Asian industrialization seems to merit a terminology specific to the region. Based on an unchallenged, stereotyped impression of the behaviour of the early European industrialists, who are characterized as true and genuine capitalists, it is relatively easy, but highly questionable, and to argue that the present-day South and Southeast Asian industrialists should be characterized as a class of deformed, pseudo- or non-genuine capitalists.

Moreover, our evaluation of the specific characteristics of Asian entrepreneurs has undergone several changes over time. In the 1960s and 1970s entrepreneurial characteristics of personalized management, economic diversification, collectivism, familism, close state-business relations and an emphasis on social status, were soundly criticized by both Western and Asian scholars and policy makers who considered them to be one of the main causes of the backwardness of Asia. These critics argued that impersonal management practices, individualism, open competition and frugality were the only ways to compete successfully in the modern world economy. Following the rise of East and Southeast Asian economies, this notion was widely challenged in the 1980s and 1990s.

It was then argued that the personalized management practices in diversified enterprises, collective forms of business organization along traditional lines, close state-business relations and an emphasis on social status, have all been crucial factors in bringing about the Asian miracle. More recently, this view has been challenged again. The Asian crisis of 1997 seems to have set the stage for a return to the earlier notion that the specific characteristics of Asian businessmen are responsible for the lack of economic progress in Asia. In these analyses, the origin of the Asian crisis lies in the inability of Asian businessmen to practise impersonal management styles, to confine themselves to one line of business, to operate independently of others and within a free market economy with minimum government intervention, and to delay consumption expenditures by making sacrifices now for the sake of future benefits.

These changing views on the behaviour of Asian entrepreneurs again underline the need to develop a theoretical model for the comparative study of regional business classes that can help to explain the similarities and the differences in their practices and characteristics, but that is not arbitrarily based on a Western or Eastern model of economic behaviour. Now that a significant body of knowledge about economic development in Asia has been produced, the time has come to look again at European history and contemporary developments, employing insights gained from the Asian experience, and also for experts on Europe to look at the Asian examples.

Such a comparative analysis needs to take into account the wide diversity in forms of business organization and entrepreneurship within and between Asia and Europe, and should look for the conditions that promote or inhibit the growth of industrial entrepreneurship and investment without relying on Euro-centric stereotypes of entrepreneurial behaviour. If the processes such as those described in this book are understood within the overall framework of the expansion of world capitalism - which while exerting certain pressures towards uniformity also interacts with local structures and cultures, thereby producing many variations - we will be able to account for both similarities and differences in entrepreneurial behaviour at various times and places. Therefore, one aim of comparative analysis should be to describe and account for various forms of entrepreneurship without resorting to stereotypes of what constitutes 'correct' capitalist behaviour or capitalism proper.

As already discussed, both the structural and cultural modes of analyses by themselves have proved to be unsatisfactory for constructing such a comparative approach. Both types of explanation, even when employed in combination, tend to be deterministic, ignoring the role of human agency. The structural approach views the macro-economic or political environment as the main determinant of entrepreneurial development, while the conscious human actor is all but forgotten. In cultural analyses as well, actors seem to be entirely constrained, although now by their cultural 'baggage'. This neglect is curious because the study of entrepreneurship, which often concerns unusual individuals and singular success stories, should take the lead in exploring the interconnections between individual agency and wider social structures and cultural traditions.

The continuing hiatus between structural and cultural analyses and disregard of agency reflect the failure of entrepreneurship studies to catch up with recent advances in social theory. Two developments concern us here. First, with the collapse of the traditional boundaries dividing the social sciences there is an increasing interest in tracing connections between, for example, the social and the economic. There is a new awareness that the study of economic behaviour - whether that of markets, firms, or individual entrepreneurs - cannot be abstracted from the social institutions and systems of meaning in which it is situated. In fact, this is an excellent field in which to explore such interconnections because business relations are a prime example of economic activity embedded in social relations.

The case studies presented in this book reflect this understanding by presenting entrepreneurs as social actors not merely as economic agents. These case studies also demonstrate the impossibility of carrying on business without the support of webs of social connections and more or less institutionalized structures, as well as the central role that trust and familiarity play in maintaining such relations. This insight serves to shatter the hoary myth of the self-made man (itself part of early capitalism's official ideology). As the three empirical cases in this book demonstrate, entrepreneurs are critically dependent on others for their success; moreover, they usually become entrepreneurs as a group of some kind rather than as individuals. It is important to stress that these characteristics are not confined to Asian business classes.

A second theoretical development has taken place in the anthropological concept of culture. From a cultural perspective, an entrepreneur's perception of the economic situation is crucial to his actions, and this perception is filtered through a cultural lens. However, the prevailing static notion of culture as a given 'factor', that either promotes or inhibits entrepreneurial activity, needs to be replaced by an understanding that culture is constantly recreated, invented and negotiated by conscious actors.

A 'culture' may provide motivation or an ideological base for entrepreneurship, but an entrepreneurial culture can also develop as a result of involvement in the market. In fact, both happen simultaneously; just as culture is never static, the economic 'base' is in constant flux and human actors are constantly acting upon and reacting to it. Thus, a businessman develops economic interests within a particular socio-cultural setting and makes decisions based on his culturally conditioned understanding of his situation, but at the same time he may transform his cultural orientations, and those of his community or class, in the cause of his pursuit of his economic interests.

What is needed, then, is a theoretical framework which integrates the analysis of political and economic structures and marries an understanding of cultural context with a concept of human agency. Such a model should enable individual action (the innovating, risk-taking entrepreneur) to be related to the macro-economic processes that constitute development, and it should facilitate the analysis of specific cases without being too context-dependent. For the study of entrepreneurial behaviour at the micro-level, and especially as a means of incorporating agency into the analysis, Bourdieu's theoretical apparatus could be useful. Bourdieu has shown how in the pursuit of their goals people, though constrained by their cultural inheritance (habitus) and external structural factors, employ strategies which are based on the conversion of one kind of 'capital' (social, cultural, economic) to another.

This approach might be particularly apt for the study of entrepreneurs. As the case studies in this book illustrate, it is common practice for businessmen to allocate resources to the building up of social capital (networks) and symbolic capital (social status), and in the purchase of socio-political influence - investments which in turn help in their business activities and in the further accumulation of economic capital. Thus typical activities such as the wining and dining of business associates and bureaucrats, demonstrative expenditures on marriages, and buying the latest model BMW, can be seen as rational investments in the accumulation of capital, in Bourdieu's broad sense of the term.

While Bourdieu's theoretical apparatus can help in this kind of micro-level analysis of entrepreneurs' activities, it leaves out the linkages between the micro- and macro-levels. One scholar who has explored this problem is Baumol (1990). He argues that the common identification of economic stagnation and decline with a decrease in the number of entrepreneurs or a waning of entrepreneurial spirit is based on wrong assumptions about what entrepreneurs are doing. Their main objective is not the well-being of society but their own personal well-being, defined in terms of wealth, power and prestige. Entrepreneurs in society, according to Baumol, play a variety of roles, some of which may not be constructive and which may even be damaging to the economy. The role perceived to contribute the most to personal wellbeing depends on the context within which an entrepreneur operates, and wealth, power, and prestige are not always acquired in ways that contribute to economic development.

A third approach to comparative research is the Weberian institutional approach advocated by Biggart (1991). When social actions are repeated over time and are assigned similar meanings by self and others, they become institutionalized; institutionalized action is economically efficient because making decisions and carrying them out becomes simpler when the actor can predict and understand the actions of others. Biggart suggests that societies have varying deep-rooted 'institutional logics' which pattern business relations as well other social institutions.

Therefore the Muslim businessmen in Indonesia operate most frequently in individual enterprises along subcontracting relationships; the Chinese entrepreneurs in Malaysia organize their companies along extended family relations and within ethnic business networks, and the Hindu industrialists in India work within joint-family businesses and in partnerships with caste-members. Although there are important differences among these forms of organizations which lead to variations in labour relations, in the nature of subcontracting relations, in investment patterns and the like, they are all 'network logics'. It could therefore be argued with Biggart that this approach can bring together the micro- and the macro-levels as well as address the problem of structure and agency by focusing on the intermediate range - the institutions that shape economic activity and their reproduction through social action.

By looking at actors' strategies, which are goal-oriented (aimed at accumulating power, prestige, and wealth), within the context of certain constraints (the socio-cultural and macro-economic environment), the actions of individual entrepreneurs or business groups can be integrated into a more general history and sociology of capitalist development. Such an approach also addresses the important question of motivation, which so concerned Weber, for social goals and ideational orientations are seen to be inseparable from economic strategies of accumulation. The actions of entrepreneurs, like those of any other social group, cannot be understood in terms of their economic 'interests' alone.

Like everyone else they are also driven by the desire for prestige, social status, or political influence - all non-tangible goals which are nonetheless salient for them. A shift from the structural and cultural determinants of entrepreneurial development towards a focus on human agency leads to the view that small-scale entrepreneurs are not mere products of wider economic processes or cultural systems, but are actors who are themselves bringing about these capitalist transformations. Businessmen, small and large alike, act consciously, both collectively and individually, to further their political, social, or economic goals.

The strategies of the rural entrepreneurs in India, Indonesia and Malaysia, as discussed in this book, such as social climbing, accumulation of social capital and development of socio-political influence, are employed by these businessmen to boost not only their individual interests, broadly defined, but also those of their own class or social group. If this is so, research on rural capitalists can provide a means for studying processes of class formation, which also has economic and political implications for the societies concerned. A first step towards such an analysis is to acquire more in-depth knowledge about entrepreneurs in different parts of Asia and Europe, both now and in the past.

6

Women in the Indian Labour Force

Women's participation in market economic activities in India is low compared to most other parts of Asia. There is also wide regional variation within the country. Detailed field studies as well as large survey data reveal a high sensitivity of women's measured participation to definitional changes. Minor alterations in the definition result in the inclusion of, or exclusion from, the labour force of a few million. Debates on the nature of women's work, to a great extent, are constrained by these definitional problems; therefore considerable effort is wasted in classifying economic activities and women's participation in them. Consequently much of the macroeconomic research on women's work is descriptive and based on data sets which are not necessarily comparable with each other.

It is not difficult to trace the genesis of this ambiguity. Unlike most countries of East and South East Asia, India has not experienced rapid economic growth on a sustained basis in the contemporary period. The long term trend growth in the real GDP over 1951-1990 was 3.5 per cent per annum, and for per capita income, 1.5 per cent per annum over the same period. The GDP growth rate exceeded 5 per cent per annum for the first time in the 1980s. Moreover, the growth process has been uneven across regions and has not been labour intensive. Consequently evolution of labour markets has remained stunted. Large parts of the country have stayed within the peasant sectors in which it is difficult to differentiate between activities related to self-provision and the market.

In support of this argument a few statistics may usefully be quoted here. The latest available labour data show that about 70 per cent of the Indian work force resides in the rural areas and over two-thirds is engaged in a largely subsistence-oriented agriculture.

Over half the workers are engaged in activities termed as 'self-employment' or 'unpaid family work'. A substantial section of the population is engaged in unskilled jobs. In the absence of significant changes in the structure of the labour force, pre-industrial configurations continue to influence the work pattern.

Research on women's work has been extensive since the mid-1970s, and a number of studies have tried to highlight women's (in) visibility and importance in the economy. However, as stated above, there have been problems relating to the definitions of work, enumeration and coverage, which have marred construction of systematic profiles for temporal and regional comparison. The classification of female workers has been subject to question, since some scholars find their work to be non-standardized. Since the regional variation in the levels of development is high, cross-regional comparison of many features of the work force have not been found to be very meaningful.

The only broad contention that has been agreed upon is that there are very wide, often inexplicable, differences in the labour force characteristics across regions and over time. Also, most studies on women in the labour market have not covered the decade of the 1980s, the only time when the country experienced a relatively high growth rate. This paper is written with a view to constructing profiles of labour participation, activity and sectoral distribution of female workers, identifying the causes of the wide variation in women's work participation across states, and understanding their earnings behaviour. The main data used in the text are drawn from the National Sample Surveys (NSS) of India and the Ministry of Labour.

AGGREGATE PARTICIPATION RATES

No two decennial censuses in India have had comparable definitions of workers in the recent decades except those conducted in 1981 and 1991. Since the 1991 reports are not available as yet, census data are not used for comparing labour participation rates. The NSS, since its twenty-seventh round of data collection in 1972-1973, has conducted quinquennial surveys on employment/unemployment in which comparable definitions have been used.

These surveys, though conducted on a less than 1 per cent sample, are highly representative at the aggregate level. They are also more accurate than the census data, since their collection is staggered round the year to capture the effect of seasonality. The NSS uses three alternative criteria for enumerating workers: the usual status (US), the current weekly status (CWS) and the current daily status (CDS). More than one definition is deemed necessary in the Indian setting since the (pre-industrial) nature of work is difficult to capture by any single definition. Participation according to each of these is discussed in turn here.

A person is included in the labour force as a main worker by the usual status if he/she has spent a major part of the last 365 days in gainful economic activity or is actively seeking/available for work. If a person works for (inclusive of is available for) only a minor part of the year he/she is deemed a subsidiary worker. There is virtually no difference observed in the total (main plus subsidiary) as well as main workers' participation rates (US) over the said years, for both male and female workers, in rural as well as urban areas. A fluctuation of 1 to 1.5 per cent is observed from one round to another but this could be attributed to sampling errors.

The other two measures have a reference period of a week. Because of the short reference period, these measures exhibit a high degree of sensitivity to frequent withdrawal from and entry into the labour force. According to the CWS a person is deemed to be in the labour force if he/she has worked or is available for work for any time during the reference week preceding the date of interview; while according to the CDS the labour participation is calculated as a proportion of the number of person-days worked (plus available/seeking work) to total person days on an average day in the reference week. The participation rates by CWS/CDS are 20-25 per cent lower than by US (main plus subsidiary) among women. While this pattern is observed even among male workers, the magnitude of the drop is much smaller.

There are three main observations that call for attention here. The first is the low and invariant participation of women, owing to which the gap between the male and female participation is large. The second is the high and persistent presence of female subsidiary workers, in the range of 8-10 per cent of the population in rural areas and 3-4 per cent in urban areas. This forms about a fourth of the total female labour in each case. The third is the visible gap between the usual and current status participation rates. All three have their origin in the nature of constraints faced by women in a relatively slow-growing, poor agrarian economy.

Women's work participation is closely related to their overall work burden, which in turn is dependent upon the level of development of an economy. In India commercialization and division of labour have all along been low. To a great extent this can be attributed to slow economic growth and the associated low labour absorption. In large parts of rural and urban areas women are engaged in self-provision, due to which families are able to sustain themselves at amazingly low earnings levels of $2-3 per day. Aside from self provisioning, women also have reproductive responsibilities, due to which their temporary withdrawal from the labour force often renders them subsidiary workers. The birthrate in India is still in the range of 30-32 per thousand populations.

Again, because of the slow economic activity there is relatively low labour demand, due to which wages and incomes are low. Also, agriculture, the single largest employer, is a seasonal activity in which women's role is quite rigidly defined. They participate only in certain activities, mainly sowing, seed bed preparation, plant care, weeding and harvesting, and frequently withdraw from the labour market for short periods. The fact that over the fifteen-year period women's participation is virtually unaltered suggests that economic growth has barely kept up with demographic pressure.

LABOUR PARTICIPATION BY AGE

Data on age distribution in Indian demographic- and socio-economic surveys are very weak. This is because the respondents often have little idea of their exact age. This bias can somewhat be neutralized if the age brackets are kept relatively large. The NSS tabulates data by fifteen year age brackets for the population belonging to age 15 years old and above, and by five-year brackets for those below 15.

The age group (30-44) years has the largest participation rate both among men and women. The reasons appear obvious. Younger men and women are in education in the earlier age brackets. Some women join the labour force after completing their reproductive responsibilities (i.e., after the age of 30-35). Next, given the fact that the average life span of an Indian during the 1980s was 55 years, both men and women tend to drop out of the labour force after the age of 45 due to poor health. Figure 2.2, which shows the age specific participation for 1987-1988 by five-year age brackets (for earlier years this was not tabulated), confirms the usual inverted U shaped curve with a peak at the age of 35-40 in both rural and urban areas.

There is a striking similarity between the data from the different rounds which suggests that not much change has occurred during these fifteen years. A significant feature, though, is a drop in the labour participation rates of both men and women in rural as well as urban areas, in the age groups 5-9 and 10-14 years, between 1983 and 1987-1988. A fall is also observed in the 15-29 age brackets in all groups except urban women.

Over this period the NSS data on school attendance report that in the 5-9 age group, the ratio of rural male school attendees to total in that age group rose from 49.6 per cent to

52.5 per cent, whilst the ratio for rural females rose from 35.5 per cent to 40.4 per cent. The corresponding increases in urban areas were from 71.1 per cent to 73.0 per cent (males) and from 65.9 per cent to 67.9 per cent (females). For the age group of 10-14 the increases were from 61.5 per cent to 66.1 per cent (males) and 33.9 per cent to 41.9 per cent (females) in rural areas; and 78.5 per cent to 79.9 per cent (males) and 67.0 per cent to 71.9 (females) in urban areas. These statistics show that during this period female school attendance has increased much more than male, which may account for the decline in labour participation in young age groups.

An important exercise in understanding the age-specific labour participation rates is to compare age cohort participation rates. The NSS authorities tabulate data by fifteen-year age brackets and the time span between 1972-1973 and 1987-1988 is fifteen years, permitting only a two point comparison. This is unlikely to yield meaningful results. The decennial census permits a comparison of ten-year cohorts for labour force of age 20 and above. A cohort comparison was done using data from the 1961, 1971 and 1981 census reports, but it did not yield meaningful conclusions owing to incomparability in the definition of workers. The results are therefore not presented here.

LABOUR PARTICIPATION BY EDUCATION

These data show that in virtually every case there is a U-shaped pattern; the illiterate enter the labour market in largest proportions followed by the just literate and then the middle school graduates. Except for urban women, the participation of secondary school graduates is the lowest, and participation then rises for university and college graduates and above. (For urban women the increase in participation begins at the secondary school education level.)

Arguably the markets faced by the illiterate (thereby also the poor) are mainly the informal unskilled ones-both in urban and rural areas-in which entry is not very difficult. At the same time the compulsion to work for survival by the poor is acute.

University graduates also have a compulsion to work owing to the large number of years of education put in. The intermediate education groups neither have such high supply compulsions nor is the demand for their skills strong. Thus those in the middle education groups do not participate, or else do so only as subsidiary workers. This is particularly the case for women.

REGIONAL VARIATION IN LABOUR PARTICIPATION

There is wide variation in the inter-state labour participation levels of women workers. Their participation in the capacity of main workers ranges from less than 10 per cent in Punjab to over 40 per cent in Maharashtra. An age-specific standardization of the distribution (not presented here) reduces the variation by a bit but large differences still persist. The coefficient of variation across states is above 50 per cent. Several attempts have been made in the literature to explain the interstate variation in female work participation. In a recent exercise, under the (implicit) assumption that India is predominantly an agrarian economy, Sundram argues that women have household responsibilities which hamper their labour participation, and that women withdraw from the labour market when affluence increases.

He also argues that, given the fact that women tend to work in informal systems where it is possible for them to simultaneously undertake household responsibilities, access to physical resources within the household will enhance their participation. While Sundram's model is statistically significant, it is ahistorical and based on supply side logic only. More important, it is unlikely that the vast regional variation in women's work can be explained by such a simplistic formulation. In another group of exercises it has been suggested that women work more in paddy growing areas. It is argued that they mainly work in monotonous and low paying occupations such as transplanting and weeding for which male labour is hard to get.

This explanation does not, however, hold uniformly for the whole country since the eastern states, which are mainly paddy growing, exhibit very low labour participation rates compared to the millet zones in central and western India. Socio-cultural reasons are also argued to inhibit women's participation in the labour force. Among the major constraining factors are caste and religion. Since India has had slow economic growth and limited presence of market forces, non-economic factors continue to assume an important place. In this context one important constraint is *purdah* (or 'seclusion') which is widely (though not exclusively) practised in the east and north and on which a lot has been written. While this explanation carries a lot more weight than the other propositions, there are gaps in knowledge here too, such as why *purdah* affects women differentially across regions, given that it has been prevalent in most parts of the sub-continent.

A MACRO-LEVEL ESTIMATE OF PARTICIPATION PROBABILITY

This paper estimates a simple model to explain inter-state and micro-level variation in women's participation, based on some of the factors discussed above. There are clear regional patterns in women's participation. According to the main worker criterion, the eastern states, namely West Bengal, Assam and Bihar, along with the ones in the north, namely, Uttar Pradesh, Punjab and Haryana, show very low (less than 20 per cent) female labour participation rates. Orissa, an eastern state, also shows a fairly low participation, although higher than in the other eastern states.

These states also have a high proportion of women working as subsidiary workers. In contrast, the states in the west and south, namely Rajasthan, Gujarat, Maharashtra, Madhya Pradesh, Andhra Pradesh, Karnataka and Tamil Nadu, show a relatively high participation rate (greater than 30 per cent). (Kerala, another southern state, is the only exception.) These states also have a low proportion of women subsidiary workers. This pattern of dispersion broadly coincides with the geographic 'north and east' versus 'south and west' divide of the country. Each of these regions has historical/cultural as well as agro-climatic characteristics which distinguish them.

In the Indian context, to some extent, participation in the labour force has its genesis in the historical shaping of land systems. The eastern and northern regions, which receive high rainfall and/or lie in the fertile Indo-Gangetic plains, have historically been under land control systems which are characterized by a complex hierarchy of intermediaries involving castes and classes (the *Zamindari* system). Manual work on land is tedious (and low paying) and the social values attached to it have traditionally been such that it is to be performed by persons belonging to the lowest rungs of the society.

In this multi-layer structure, people have traditionally tended to emulate the behaviour of those higher up in the hierarchy. Both men and women thus tend to shun manual wage-work, and this may tend to support the institution of *purdah* as a means of avoiding it. Since agriculture was (and still is) the dominant occupation, its influence has spread over other occupations, including those in urban areas. In the south and west, regions which are characterized by relatively low rainfall, aridity and rocky terrains, historically the land systems (the *Ryotwari* system) assigned less rigid caste/class/sex roles to the populace.

In these regions, unlike the *Zamindari* areas, land has been relatively more equitably distributed and the castes that control it belong to the middle cadre in the hierarchy of castes. The tendency to emulate the life styles of the landed does not inhibit others from working on land, since people belonging to the middle and landed castes themselves are not averse to working outside the household. Women's work participation in these areas has also been aided by the fact that historically these areas have been sparsely populated and the sheer demand for labour has pulled women into the labour force. Again, agriculture, the principal employer, exercises influence on the other sectors, including those in urban areas; hence the overall participation rate is high.

Within this broad north/east-south/west divide, the inter-state variation can be explained by socio-economic factors which govern the supply and demand for labour. Several micro studies show that women's work burden in peasant societies is uniform at about 8-10 hours a day in diverse settings; the difference lies in what they do in which setting. One way to analyse work is to divide it between market-oriented jobs (Wm) and expenditure saving activities (Wd). Wm is that component of work which is usually enumerated in the calculations of labour participation rates. Wd is that component of work which is not directly income generating but is economically and socially useful to the household; and if not performed, the household may have to expend money to buy the corresponding goods/services. Typical examples of these activities are animal care, food processing, weaving, tailoring, stitching, etc.

The choice between Wm and Wd depends upon the relative economic and social advantage derived from each activity. In each region, labour force participation depends on the choices available to workers (how attractive the returns are to Wm, relative to Wd). Two considerations warrant attention. First, dispossessment is an important reason for women to join the labour force. Agricultural land is the major resource in most of India and those who do not possess it join the labour force for survival (the returns to Wd become very low). Landless women in almost all cases are able to do little else other than manual jobs; they thus join the labour force in the capacity of casual labourers.

Second, in a slow growing economy those women whose income (socio-economic status) is high do not join the labour force, since they do not find it meaningful to compete for work with low wages and difficult conditions. Instead, they engage themselves in 'status production' activities which Papanek describes as those which enhance the status of the household through human/ physical capital formation in the domestic sector (i.e., the returns to Wd are high relative to Wm).

The choice between Wd and Wm is also influenced by human capital endowment. It was noted earlier that some education tends to inhibit women's participation rate while more education may promote it. It is argued here, and empirical studies also show, that the demand for labour in the Indian markets for the less educated is not very high. In the face of slack demand conditions, those who can, withdraw from the labour force. By the same argument, the better educated tend to join it, because demand for highly educated labour is stronger. In an attempt to examine the empirical validity of the above explanation, grouped data on women's labour participation rates from fifteen major states of India (disaggregated by rural and urban areas), as obtained from the NSS surveys of 1977-1978, 1983 and 1987-1988, have been pooled together. A Chow test permits such a pooling. The dependent variable is the percentage of women participating in the labour force to total women (US main), standardized for age distribution across states.

The independent variables include two dummies, one for differentiating the erstwhile *Zamindari* and *Ryotwari* regions (NSD: 1=west/south) and the other for identifying the rural and urban areas (RUD: 1=rural). The reason for introducing the latter is to differentiate between labour markets in the two locales as the activities in them are different. Next, the percentage of women casual labourers (the dispossessed) to total women workers is included as a proxy for compulsion to work in the market (CL). Income is included (monthly per capita household expenditure, MPCE) to control for income effects on work decisions (ideally this should exclude the woman's own earnings, but this was not feasible with the data).

The model is estimated using a Generalized Least Squares (GLS) procedure since the off-diagonal elements in the variance-covariance matrix may not be zero in pooled panel data sets. The estimated equation is as follows (t values in brackets):

LFPRf=8.08+0.305 CL"0.039 MPCE+14.182 RUD+15.671 NSD

(3.921) (2.404) (6.934) (6.457)

R=0.764 n=90

All variables are significant at 5 per cent level with the correct signs.

In sum, it is suggested that at the very broad level, agro-climatic conditions and land systems shape women's work participation, while within each region; choices/compulsions operate according to the socio-economic status of households.

A MICRO-LEVEL MODEL OF PARTICIPATION

Microeconomic exercises in understanding labour participation are very scarce for India; there is therefore, little to draw upon from the literature. The model here has been tested using primary records of the NSS for the province of Maharashtra, using persons age 10 and over for 1987-1988. Separate estimates are made for rural and urban areas. The dependent variable is labour force participation; if the woman participates the variable assumes value equal to unity, and zero otherwise.

The model tested is essentially the same as before, with a few changes that are pertinent in micro-level estimation. An age variable (dummy) is included (1 in ages 30-45 and zero otherwise). This takes account of the childbearing activity prior to age 30, and the tendency to retire from the labour force after age 45 as health deteriorates. In an alternative specification, age and age squared are included in place of an age dummy. The number of children in the house is an equally important factor in keeping women from work. However, data on this variable are not available, and instead, the overall size of the household is included as a (poor) proxy.

Two sociological explanatory variables included are marriage and religion. A dummy variable has been introduced that assumes a value zero for the married and unity otherwise. Under the assumption that certain religions influence work participation, another dummy is introduced which assumes a value zero for Islamic women (since they practice seclusion the most) and unity otherwise.

The two variables used for representing withdrawal of women from the work force by the affluent and high castes are the monthly per capita expenditure and the caste status. The former is a continuous variable, and for the latter a dummy variable has been constructed which assumes a value unity for the 'scheduled' categories (socially and economically least advantaged) and zero for others. Next, female-headed households have been identified to be the poorest in India. The participation of women in these households is expected to be high. The variable is measured by a dummy assuming value zero for female-headed households and unity otherwise.

The impact of education on participation is measured by constructing two dummy variables; one for up to secondary grade education (junior education), and another for education beyond secondary level (senior education). Continuous years of education variable would have been ideal but that is not possible here since data are available only for completed years of schooling at discrete intervals. Next, under the assumption that technical education would encourage people to participate in outside work; an indexed variable has been introduced, which assumes a next higher value as the technical grade rises.

The model is fitted using the logistic regression method. The choice of this method over probit is made because much of the literature on this subject bases itself on the logit model. In specification one, all the variables in the equation on rural female participation are significant and bear the right signs. In the urban participation equation too, eight out of the ten coefficients are significant. Household expenditure and market status do not seem to be important in urban areas. It can be argued that the demand conditions here offer a wider choice of jobs, thereby permitting women the possibility of working for a wage/salary without compromising their social status. This is corroborated by a positive sign on the higher education coefficient, which is negative in the equation for rural women. Specification two also shows very similar results, with only minor differences. The estimates confirm the hypotheses discussed.

EMPLOYMENT STATUS

The ILO classifies workers according to whether they are employers, own-account workers, employees or unpaid family workers. In the Indian setting, it is less useful to separate the first two categories since 'employer' as a category is statistically insignificant as well as non-exclusive. This is because the peasant sector in agriculture has a multitude of owners who are mainly self-employed but also hire-in/out labour. Next, it is useful to disaggregate employees into regular and casual workers since the work availability and earnings of these two are quite different. The category of unpaid family workers was not tabulated separately for 1977-1978 and 1987-1988, but was merged with the self-employed.

In the rural areas a majority of both men and women are self-employed. The next most important group is casual labourers and then regular employees. A higher proportion of women are casual workers compared to men, and a lower proportion is regular employees. Since casual workers hold an inferior position compared to regular employees, women occupy an inferior position in this category of workers. In the urban areas the largest group of men is regular employees, while the largest group of women is self-employed. This is due to a higher rate of commercialization in urban than in rural areas, particularly in the male labour market.

A breakdown of the self-employed into unpaid family workers and own account workers is available for 1972-1973 and 1983. These data show that in rural areas a major proportion of self-employed women are actually unpaid family workers, who are engaged in work which generates money income, but who have no control over their earnings. By contrast, a major proportion of men in rural areas are own-account workers. Fewer urban women workers are unpaid family workers, possibly owing to a higher degree of commercialization of the labour markets in urban areas. This is inevitable in a stagnant economy facing demographic pressure.

There is distinctly a gender specific concentration of workers by status, and to judge whether this has changed over time, a Duncan index is computed. This index shows that over time there has been a reduction in segregation by employment status, larger in rural than in urban areas. However, this is computed based on only four observations.

Age specific data on worker employment status at two points of time, were examined to observe any change in the age-status roles. Workers in prime working ages in the Indian context (15-44) are more likely to be employees than workers in younger or older age groups. There is no discernible trend seen over time.

WOMEN'S EMPLOYMENT BY INDUSTRY

A priori it should be mentioned that workers in the primary sectors-mainly agriculture-have a lower status in the labour force, and earnings are low compared to the non-agricultural sectors. This shows that over three-quarters of the labour force in the rural areas is concentrated in the primary sectors; more so among the women workers. In the urban areas too, almost a third of the women and about a tenth of the men are engaged in agriculture. In each case there are a higher proportion of women (than men) in agriculture, which strengthens the earlier findings about their lower status in the labour force.

In the rural areas there has been a shift away from agriculture, of about 9 per cent among men and 5 per cent among women workers, and a corresponding rise in the other sectors. In proportional terms women's employment has increased most in manufacturing and men's in services in rural areas. In contrast, in the urban areas there has been little or no sectoral shift observed over this period. It is not encouraging to note that agriculture is a significant and only very slowly diminishing occupation in urban areas.

A more detailed (two digit) breakdown of agriculture and allied activities in rural areas shows that livestock is the only agricultural activity in which there has been a significant increase in the proportion of women workers. This is perhaps due to the stepping up of rural diversification programmes during this period, in which the principal activity promoted was animal husbandry. A corresponding two-digit breakdown of the manufacturing activities in urban areas shows a minor rise in the share of women workers in the industry groups of chemicals, electrical machinery, and others, but the absolute share of these in the overall employment structure is so small that the changes are insignificant.

More striking, unlike in most of South and East Asia, there is no visible growth of employment in the 'sunrise' or export industries, and no visible alteration in the composition of the labour force. A Duncan index of dissimilarity was computed to judge the differences in the gender distribution of workers and the shift over time. For the rural areas this index assumes values 0.07, 0.08, 0.10 and 0.11 in the four survey years, whilst the corresponding figures for urban areas are, 0.30, 0.33, 0.32 and 0.34. There is a small movement towards dissimilarity as industry diversification has occurred over time. However, the results should be interpreted with caution because the dominance of one sector reduces the sensitivity of this index (as is the case here with agriculture in the rural sector).

The industry distribution results support part of the findings of the employment status distribution that the relative position of women in the labour market is inferior to that of men, but it has not deteriorated (compared to men's) over the period.

EMPLOYMENT IN ORGANIZED AND UNORGANIZED SECTORS

Workers in India are engaged in economic enterprises as diverse as modern automated industries and household and cottage enterprises. For analytical purposes, it is useful to distinguish the organized sector - i.e., those protected by various labour laws-and the unorganized sector. Agriculture and allied activities are almost wholly outside the purview of the organized sector except some plantations, some livestock activities and specific agricultural services. Hence the nonagricultural sector alone is discussed here.

The size of the organized sector was low (less than 10 per cent) when compared to the size of the total labour force of about 260 million (including agriculture) in the early 1980s. In the early 1970s the percentage of male workers in the nonagricultural sectors who were not organized was 68 per cent. By the 1980s this proportion rose to about 72 per cent. For female workers these percentages rose from 83 per cent to 85 per cent over the same period. It is evident that the share of the unprotected labour in the total labour force is larger for women than for men, and raising over time for both sexes.

THE ORGANIZED MANUFACTURING SECTOR

Most modern medium and large industries in India fall under the organized sector. The most striking feature found is that up to 50 per cent of women in the organized sector are concentrated in three industries: textiles, cashew processing and tobacco processing. The much talked about employment of women in the garment and electronic industries is perhaps outside the organized sector. In most high growth sectors (i.e., those which have experienced employment growth of 50 per cent or more) the absolute number of women has been too small to change the pattern. On aggregate the growth in employment has been less than 15 per cent over the ten years.

Among the export industries that have shown promise of high earnings in recent years are textiles, garments, electrical machinery (including electronics), gems and jewels, engineering goods, processed food, and petroleum products. Women's employment is important in textiles and cashew processing, but not the others.

OCCUPATIONAL DISTRIBUTION

Studies on occupational distribution find that women seem to be concentrated in a small number of occupations. In rural areas there is a predominance of both sexes in agriculture, which, though decreasing over time has stayed large. The urban areas show a concentration of workers of both sexes in production and transport. The next highest concentration of women workers appears in agriculture, followed by services, and then professional occupations. Over the decade there is a significant rise of women among professionals, administrative and clerical staff, and a corresponding fall in agriculture. There is considerable gender segregation in the occupational distribution (the Duncan index is about 0.28 for both years).

DAYS OF WORK

The definition of work is such that any work up to four hours is counted as a half day, and more than four hours work is counted as a day. Thus, data on days worked has deficiencies. A coefficient of variation calculated on the Maharashtra data (mentioned earlier) shows an extremely small figure. In spite of this, effort was made to set up a model to explain variation in the days of work put in by female labour for Maharashtra. All the known explanatory variables combined were unable to explain more than 1 per cent of the variation in both rural and urban areas. Arguably, it is labour demand which largely determines hours worked in India (evidence for this is the fact that a quarter of women, according to the NSS survey, would opt to work more if more work was available).

EARNINGS BEHAVIOUR

As stated earlier, primary data for the whole country are not available; therefore the NSS data set, available for the state of Maharashtra, has been used for estimating the earnings functions. Separate equations are estimated for rural and urban areas. The model estimated is based on the classical human capital theory of the Mincer type which uses individual attributes of workers to explain variations in earnings. Earnings behaviour in India has been studied by Tilak (1979), Datta (1985), Rao and Datta (1989), and Acharya and Jose (1991), among others. Most studies, however, base their findings on small samples drawn on individuals belonging to a section of the society, or a specific geographical setting.

Analyses based on large and random samples are few, if any. In a recent global survey of literature done by Terrell (1992), not a single Indian study is quoted. It is with this backdrop that the present study is undertaken. The explanatory variables are age, age squared and five education dummies representing completion of different levels of education. In a statistical sense the equations are good fits with all the coefficients significant at 5 per cent confidence. The square of age bears a negative sign as expected. The education (dummy) coefficients increase in magnitude with increasing education as expected, implying that the mean earnings rise with education. The R value, particularly in the urban equation, is high, though it is not unacceptably low in the rural equation, given the fact that these equations are fitted using cross-section data.

A two step self-selection correction procedure, suggested by Heckman, has been followed and these results are in columns two and four. In both the equations the lambda (selection) terms are statistically only significant at the 10 per cent level, neither the R values nor the coefficient values of the explanatory variables change significantly, implying that the coefficients of the uncorrected equation are not biased.

The Mincer model is expanded to include variables such as occupation and marital status. The occupation variable is a dummy, with a value of unity for professional and technical-type occupations and zero for lower and unskilled jobs. Marital status is also represented by a dummy assuming a value of unity for the unmarried and zero otherwise. The estimates show that all the coefficients in all four equations, other than marital status in the rural women's earnings equation, are statistically significant. Lambda is no longer significant at 10 per cent level.

Columns one and three on the one hand and two and four on the other, which are the estimates for the uncorrected and corrected versions of the model, show a fall in the magnitude of most coefficients when compared with their counterparts. This shows that part of the education effect works via choice of occupation. The marital status coefficient indicates that married women are paid less than unmarried ones. The occupation variable is highly significant, with the expected sign. All the coefficients are statistically significant at the 5 per cent level and bear the right signs in both rural and urban equations.

The gender wage gap is next disaggregated using the Oaxaca (1973) decomposition formula. This offers a method by which the wage gap due to explained or measured factors (Xs) can be separated from the unexplained or unmeasured ones. The difference between the mean of male and female wages can be explained as,

$$W_m - W_f = \sum (B_{mi} - B_{if}) X_6 + \sum_i B_{mi} (X_{mi} - X_6)$$

where W is the mean wage, the Xs are the means of explanatory variables and the Bs are the coefficients of Xs. The subscripts m and f refer to male and female, and subscript *i* refers to individual *i*. The total wage gap explained in rural areas is 35 per cent, and in urban areas it is 26 per cent. Thus, a large portion stays unexplained. This is often thought of as the upper bound to gender discrimination, although demand side factors and unmeasured individual characteristics may also be important. This decomposition exercise is perhaps the first of its kind on Indian data.

SOCIAL AND INSTITUTIONAL ASPECTS

Traditionally, Indian women are viewed as housewives; their principal functions are restricted to reproduction and homemaking. Although this is not true for all Indian women, nevertheless, the status of women's work continues to be viewed as subsidiary. The whole analysis of this paper bears testimony to this. Indian society is segregated owing to its incomplete transformation into a market economy. As a result, there are few economic practices common to all segments and regions. As far as market work is concerned, marriage and childbirth affect participation, but in ways specific to class and region.

In rural areas most women continue to work, while in urban areas many withdraw from the labour force. The affluent can afford to drop out more than the less affluent. Women in the formal sector, particularly the government, are more likely to continue work since the law permits certain concessions such as maternity leave and paid leave. However, women with several children are likely to drop out of the labour force, whatever their employment. The laws that have been enacted that seek to regulate women's work include the Maternity Benefit Act and the Equal Remuneration Act.

The Maternity Benefit Act seeks to protect women during pregnancy by allotting those three months of paid leave and regulating their work conditions to prevent damage to their health. Both this act and the Equal Remuneration Act are characterized by poor enforcement. The enforcement mechanisms are virtually non-existent in the unorganized sectors. The Equal Remuneration Law was enacted to prevent discriminatory practices with regard to labour recruitment and pay. Its main features are as follows:

1. Both men and women should get equal remuneration for the same work or work of a similar nature.
2. In order to comply with the above provision, the employer should not reduce the rate of remuneration.
3. The higher of the two rates is final.
4. Discriminatory practices in recruitment, promotion, training, transfers, etc. are prohibited.

Often differential interpretations are attached to the above. The words 'same work or work of similar nature' is interpreted to suit the employers' advantage. Thus women's work is often graded as being qualitatively different as and of less value than men's. Moreover, many women are employed for seasonal work and often are not given regular wages (or salaries) as per the stated law. Closely related to this is the Minimum Wages Act (1948) which stipulates that men and women get an equal minimum wage. Again, in the absence of other regulating mechanisms, this is seldom enforced outside the organized sector. Eighty per cent of women work in the unorganized sectors and these women are not effectively covered by the Minimum Wages Act, Contract Labour Act or the Inter-state Migrant Work Act.

In the agricultural sector, minimum wage is prescribed for all manual work. There is also a provision of equal pay for equal work. There is, however, no administrative machinery to follow it up. In the organized sector (in non-agriculture) there are laws which provide for minimum wages for each job skill and these are equal for both the sexes. Work hour regulations, paid leave, medical insurance, job security and maternity leave, are all part of the package available to the organized sector workers. There is administrative machinery to support the legislations and powerful trade unions to follow them up. The organized sector, however, comprises only a small section of the work force and hence the impact of the laws is only partial.

There is no legal prohibition about gender-segregated advertisements. It is not uncommon to see advertisements that exclusively seek applications from one gender or the other. Women in India are largely semi-literate and are socially and politically ignorant.

Because of the lack of awareness and the resulting disempowerment, they are unable to fight for what is legally theirs. Coupled with an inefficient and half-hearted enforcing system, the situation is one of discrimination and exploitation. Certain workers are totally unprotected by the law. This is because they are inaccessible. They include home workers, domestic workers, vendors, hawkers and construction workers.

This chapter attempts to put together existing secondary data on women's labour participation, their work status and occupations, the industry groups they are employed in, and their earnings, in a temporal and regional framework. The period covered is from the early 1970s to the early 1980s.

The results indicate that there has been little change in women's participation rates over time but that wide regional variations exist. The major reasons for these variations lie in the historical shaping of land systems, the choices people exercise in working for a wage vis à vis work at home, and some socio-cultural influences. There has been a rise in the casualization of the labour force owing to economic stagnation and demographic pressure. Gender segregation exists in the work of men and women by industry and occupation.

Individual earnings functions of both men and women show that the classical human capital theory is applicable in the Indian conditions. An attempt was also made to correct for self-selection bias in the earnings functions; it was found that this bias was not prominent. Oaxaca decomposition exercises showed that up to 25-35 per cent of the male-female wage gap can be explained by measured variables.

Women's relatively weak economic position is also reflected in weaknesses of the institutions affecting women's position in the labour force. This weakness is related to the level of economic development and to demographic pressure in labour supply.

11

7

Male-Female Wage Differentials in Korea

This chapter examines the factors that restrict female employment and cause wide wage differentials between men and women workers, in order that specific policy proposals can be made to improve the economic status of female workers in Korea. The central hypotheses are that the Korean labour market is segmented into high-wage and low-wage firms (or sectors), and that employment problems of women such as low productivity and low wages are related to their being employed in low-wage firms (or sectors). Even though the female labour force has experienced many kinds of mobility (regional, industrial and occupational), and increases in skill level, it will be shown that women workers are mainly hired in low-wage firms (or sectors) requiring only a low level of skills. As a result, they usually cannot escape from disadvantages with respect to wage and employment opportunities.

In the section on pp. 186-193, we analyse the male-female wage differential in the segmented labour market. In order to formulate public policy that will reduce discrimination in the labour market and misallocation of resources, and also achieve more equitable income distribution, one has to find out how much of the gender wage disparity is due to inequality of treatment and how much is due to differences in characteristics. Our empirical results show that the elimination of wage discrimination in Korea could result in an increase of the ratio of average female to average male wage from 51 per cent in 1989 to approximately 80 per cent.

In the section on pp. 193-200, we argue that any policy to promote sexual equality should be based on the reality that the Korean labour market is segmented and hence should be sector-specific in nature. We examine existing institutions, and suggest three types of government policies and programmes to reduce gender disparities in wages and employment opportunities: those for high-wage firms, those for low-wage firms, and general ones.

CHANGES IN THE STRUCTURE OF FEMALE LABOUR SUPPLY

As Korea has developed into a semi-industrialized country, female participation in economic activity has increased. Over the period 1963 to 1990, the size of the female population aged 15 years or over has grown at an annual average rate of 2.6 per cent while the size of the female labour force (employed workers plus unemployed workers) has grown at an annual average rate of 3.5 per cent. By contrast, the two comparable growth rates for males were 2.5 per cent and 2.7 per cent, respectively, over the same sample period. Profound structural changes in the female labour supply have occurred, such as urban migration, increased participation of married women in the labour force, and higher levels of education. The discussion below examines each of these changes in detail.

The female labour force participation rate raised from 36.3 per cent in 1963 to 47.0 per cent in 1990. Over the same period, the labour force participation rate for males gradually declined from 76.4 per cent in 1963 to 73.9 per cent in 1990. Two additional factors are likely to promote a further increase of female participation in future economic activity. First, the demand for married women is expected to rise as the rural unskilled labour supply is almost exhausted. Second, the increasing numbers of highly educated women coupled with changes in females' individual and social perceptions about jobs and work should result in growing labour force participation by more-educated females.

Migration has been remarkable for both men and women. The majority of the male and female working population (59.4 per cent and 64.1 per cent, respectively) was located in rural areas in 1963, but these proportions had dropped to only 18.7 per cent and 22.8 per cent respectively in 1990. Out-migration in younger age groups was particularly striking. In 1990, the age groups 15-19, 20-24 and 25-29 comprised only 1.7 per cent, 4.9 per cent and 6.0 per cent, respectively, of the 3.5 million rural labour force populations. Meanwhile, the age groups 30-39, 40-49 and 50 or over comprised 14.6 per cent, 20.8 per cent and a striking 51.9 per cent, respectively. It is useful to note that there is little difference in the age distribution of the rural labour force population between men and women.

The massive urban migration led to a concentration of the labour force in urban areas as well as an aging rural labour force. According to estimates made by Tai Whan Kwon (1978, 1988) using data from the Population and Housing Census, the volume of rural-urban migration was 3.5 million between 1960 and 1970, 4.4 million between 1970 and 1980 and 1.9 million between 1980 and 1985, making a total of 9.8 million of the rural population who moved into urban areas during the period 1960-1985. Using the same data, Jin Do Park estimated the extent to which the increase in the urban labour force population can be attributed to the migration of the rural labour force population.

Unfortunately, Park utilized time series data spanning only from 1965-1980. Park found that 53.0 per cent of the increase in the urban labour force population between 1965 and 1970 could be attributed to rural-urban migration. His figure for the period between 1970 and 1980 was 44.0 per cent. We expect to see a further decline in the contribution to the urban labour market made by rural-urban migration in the decade of the 1980s, which is likely to continue in the 1990s. At the infant stage of industrialization between 1963 and 1970, Korea experienced a dramatic upsurge of labour force participation by young unmarried women aged 15-19. Participation rates of those 20-24 were also high until the marriage age of 25-29 years, after which women tend to reduce their labour force participation.

Once they are in the mid-30s, they once again return to the labour force and there is a second peak between ages 40-44, followed by a substantial decline thereafter. In 1990, the labour force participation rate of young unmarried women aged 15-19 declined due to increasing enrolment in middle or high schools. In contrast to the period between 1963 and 1970, however, in 1990 participation rates of women in all other age groups rose. Between 1960 and 1990 the education level of the labour force in Korea experienced a substantial improvement.

In 1960, 79.5 per cent of employed men were composed of elementary school graduates, while 9.1 per cent, 7.8 per cent and 3.1 per cent of employed men were middle school, high school and college graduates, respectively. The comparable shares in 1990 were 21.6 per cent for elementary school graduates, 19.2 per cent for middle school graduates, 41.9 per cent for high school graduates and 17.4 per cent for college graduates. A similar trend is detected in the case of employed women. In 1960, middle school, high school and college graduates formed 3 per cent, 2 per cent and 0.2 per cent, respectively, of all employed women, while elementary school graduates formed the majority, at 95 per cent.

Though the elementary school graduates still were the largest group of female workers (40.7 per cent) in 1990, the share of high school and college graduates increased significantly to 20.0 per cent for middle school graduates, 31.0 per cent for high school graduates and 8.3 per cent for college graduates.

CHANGES IN THE DISTRIBUTION OF EMPLOYMENT BY STATUS

The proportion of working women engaged as employees (i.e., persons who are engaged in paid employment) among employed women in the labour force has raised steadily from 21.8 per cent in 1963 to 56.6 per cent in 1990. This means that the proportion of working women engaged as own-account workers and unpaid family workers have shrunk correspondingly. Not only did the informal sector shrink drastically, but women workers' status has also been improving from temporary or casual job status to regular or permanent status.

But it should be noted that a large informal sector still continues to be a major characteristic of the Korean labour force. Furthermore, as indicated by the fact that 13.2 per cent of male employees and 22.6 per cent of female employees are casual or daily workers, female workers undoubtedly experience greater employment instability than male workers. We will investigate this issue further in the industrial and occupational compositions of the labour force and in the section on pp. 179-180, which discusses segmentation of the labour market into high- and low-wage paying firms.

CHANGES IN THE DISTRIBUTION OF EMPLOYED PERSONS BY INDUSTRY

In 1960, 69.3 per cent of female labour was employed in the agricultural and fishery sector, while the rest were distributed among the social and personal service sector (13.1 per cent), the retail and wholesale sector (9.3 per cent) and the manufacturing sector (6.3 per cent). By 1990, the majority of female employment was in the low-income sectors of retail and wholesale, and manufacturing (56.2 per cent), while the rest were in the agricultural and fishery sector (20.4 per cent) and in social and personal services (15.4 per cent).

Among the major industries where the female labour force is heavily concentrated, the manufacturing sector showed the highest growth rate of employment in the 1960s and 1970s, but was surpassed by social and personal services and the retail and wholesale sectors in the 1980s. A further categorization of the manufacturing sector by a two-digit industrial classification shows that 73.4 per cent of female employment in manufacturing was in textiles, clothing and leather, and 11.1 per cent in food and beverages in 1966, which changed to 42.5 per cent in textiles, clothing and leather, 22.8 per cent in fabricated metal and 10.4 per cent in food and beverages in 1989. It is to be noted that the textiles, clothing and leather industry is a labour-intensive, simple assembly and processing type of industry.

On a three-digit classification of the fabricated metal industry, 68.9 per cent of female workers employed in this industry are in the electrical machinery equipment manufacturing industry, in which the female workers constituted 48.6 per cent of total employees in 1989. The electrical machinery equipment manufacturing industry mainly produces home appliances and assembles intermediate products into final products; therefore unskilled women are often employed in this industry as the work required is standardized, simple and repetitive. The majority of female workers in manufacturing are employed in labour-intensive, assembly and processing type of industries including textiles, clothing and leather, food and beverages and electrical machinery equipment manufacturing industries.

The two sectors other than manufacturing and agriculture with large female employment in 1989 were the wholesale and retail industry, and social and personal services. 82.0 per cent of female workers in the retail and wholesale sector were employed in establishments with less than five employees, while 7.9 per cent were employed in establishments with 5-9 employees. The comparable shares of female workers in the social and personal services sector in firms of these sizes were 54.0 per cent and 7.9 per cent, respectively. Since a majority of female employees in the tertiary industry are hired in the establishments with petty capital and small size, it can be conjectured that these women are faced with instability of employment.

Before proceeding to the occupational composition and its change of female labour force, it must be emphasized that female employment is concentrated in low-wage industries. Those industries where the majority of female workers are employed, including textiles, clothing and leather, other manufacturing, electrical machinery equipment manufacturing and scientific measuring and controlling machinery sectors tend to pay wages lower than the average for manufacturing as a whole. On the other hand, a relatively high wage is paid in machinery, transportation equipment, and chemical and primary metal sectors where male employment takes a majority share.

The wage indices of the textiles, clothing and leather, electrical machinery equipment manufacturing, other manufacturing, and scientific measuring and controlling machinery sectors, where female workers are heavily concentrated, are 74.3, 97.0, 72.3 and 91.1, respectively, which are in sharp contrast with the wage indices in those sectors where the majority of male workers are employed (149.1 in the basic metal, 118.2 in the machinery manufacturing and 139.3 in the transportation equipment sector). The manufacturing sector is a low wage sector relative to the service industry. Among tertiary industry, however, the retail and wholesale sector, in which female workers are heavily concentrated, is a low-wage sector. On the other hand, females are a minority in the high-wage sectors of electricity and gas, construction and banking and insurance. This apparent industrial segregation of the sexes, with men concentrated in high-wage sectors and women concentrated in low-wage sectors, causes larger male-female wage differentials.

CHANGES IN THE DISTRIBUTION OF EMPLOYED PERSONS BY OCCUPATION

There have been considerable occupational changes for women between 1963 and 1990. The share of farm workers has been rapidly declining and there have been dramatic increases in the share of clerical workers, professionals and managers, and production workers. However, a more detailed study indicates that the female employment structure by occupation reflects industrial segregation. We first examine the distribution of female production workers by three-digit occupational classifications.

Female production workers are primarily employed in sewing, weaving, spinning, textile apprenticeships, electrical and electronic assembly, unclassified electronics, shoemaking and bakery. Among the total of 118 three-digit classifications of production and related occupations, twelve occupations account for 69.0 per cent of female production workers.

As has already been mentioned, female production workers are mainly concentrated in the low-wage manufacturing sector industries such as paper, textiles, clothing and footwear, electrical machinery assembly, and food and beverages. A raising demand for unskilled or semi-skilled labour in the assembly and processing of textiles, clothing and footwear and electronics where precision and exactness are required drove female workers into the occupations of sewing, weaving, spinning, shoemaking and electrical and electronic assembly. Thus, whereas Mi Hye Roh (1990) and Soo Bong Uh (1991) argue that occupational segregation generates the severity of wage differentials between male and female workers, we would argue that it is industrial sex segregation which gives rise to occupational segregation between different sexes. That is, female workers employed in the low-wage industry are driven into the low-wage occupations within the same industry, and the crowding of female workers to low-wage occupations in turn generates the severe male-female wage differentials.

The same phenomenon is evident in sales-related occupations. According to the Occupational Wage Survey, there are a total of six occupations by a three-digit classification in sales-related occupations. However, the single three-digit occupation of salespersons and shop assistants accounts for 98.5 per cent of total female workers in sales-related occupations. According to the Report on the Employment Structure Survey, which provides the statistics on the industrial distribution of women working in sales-related occupations, the retail and wholesale, and food and lodging industries accounted for 90.6 per cent of female employees in this category in 1989. This industrial concentration leads to the occupational concentration observed.

In service-related occupations, there are twelve three-digit occupations. The three categories cook, cleaner, and non-classified services, constitute 85.4 per cent of women in service-related occupations. As 95.8 per cent of women in services industries are distributed in the wholesale, retail and lodging and social and personal service industries, it can be conjectured that again the industrial characteristics determine women's occupations as well. Female workers in production, sales and service occupations comprise 75 per cent of total female workers, excluding those working in agricultural and fishery occupations. We conclude that the argument by Mi Hye Roh and Soo Bong Uh, urging government policy to reduce the degree of occupational segregation in order to reduce male-female wage differentials, is not convincing. Rather, more efforts must be put into reducing industrial segregation.

The one case where reducing occupational segregation seems important is in the context of the administrative, professional and management occupations. There are seventy-seven occupations by a three-digit classification in the cases of professional workers, of which nurses and non-classified nurses' account for 44.6 per cent of total female professional workers. Similarly, four occupations (typist, bookkeeper, transport conductor and telephone operator) account for 47.0 per cent of total female clerical workers whereas there are in total nineteen occupations by a three-digit classification. By contrast, only 1 per cent of managers are female, which reflects social custom in Korea that male workers are reluctant to be supervised by a female manager. Therefore, female professional workers are forced to take the role of assisting a medical doctor or the male managers or administrators in white collar occupations.

INDUSTRIAL DUALISM, SEGMENTED LABOUR MARKETS AND FEMALE CONCENTRATION

Even though female employment is concentrated in labour-intensive, assembly and processing industries and in low-wage occupations, it is important to examine whether the industrial segregation of the female labour force is improving or worsening, since this may have important effects on female employment opportunities. Research concerning the relationship between industrial dualism and labour market structure has been done in the past among others by Bluestone,

Wachtel and Betsey, Thurow, and Piore. Dualist theories argue that the primary labour market consists of workers for monopolistic core firms, whilst there is a secondary labour market supplying competitive periphery firms. Increased subcontracting is argued to have intensified dualism in the developing countries in the 1960s.

Cho analysed industrial dualism in Korea. He defined a low wage as two-thirds or less of the median wage received by male workers in the manufacturing sector in Korea. He then calculated the percentage of low-wage workers within a firm. Firms were then categorized into four classes: the top class of high-wage firms, the middle class of high-wage firms, the middle class of low-wage firms and the bottom class of low-wage firms if the share of low-wage paid workers in the firm fell in the ranges 0-24 per cent, 25-49 per cent, 50-74 per cent and 75-100 per cent, respectively.

The first characteristic is that the middle class of high-wage firms is very weak in Korea. The distribution of firms has a sandglass shape, clearly indicating a dual industrial structure. This type of industrial dualism may cause the labour market to be segmented into the primary labour market and the secondary labour market. Cho further demonstrated that there were indeed significant wage differentials among observationally equivalent workers between high-wage firms and low-wage firms.

The second characteristic is that the firms' distribution changed after 1973 and it is not until 1989 that the firms' distribution again becomes similar to that in 1973. The reduction in the share of the top and middle class of high-wage firms in 1978 and 1984 suggests the increase in importance of low-wage firms in the industrialization process since 1975. As the economy turned its attention to the heavy and chemical industries, the increasing number of subcontracts given to small and medium size firms was apparently accompanied by the quantitative expansion of low-wage firms.

Another factor may have been expanding employment of unskilled and semi-skilled workers within the top class of high-wage firms, associated with the increase in number of assembly factories specialized in mass production. As the number of low-wage workers employed in the top class of high-wage firms increased, the share of the top class of high-wage firms declined between 1978 and 1984. But as the economy enjoyed a boom over the period between 1986 and 1989, the profitability of those firms increased. Furthermore, the negotiating power of labour unions in large scale production sites became strengthened after the massive strike waves of 1987. Therefore we can conjecture that the industrial dualism in Korea is shrinking rather than expanding. The concentration of women in low-wage firms intensified during the heavy industry phase after 1975 but diminished again by 1989.

DISEQUILIBRIUM OF LABOUR SUPPLY AND DEMAND IN KOREA

In contrast to the 3.1 per cent average growth rate per annum of total employment across all industries in Korea between 1960 and 1990, female and male manufacturing workers' employment grew by 9.7 per cent and 7.1 per cent, respectively, over the same period. Recently, labour shortage has emerged as a serious problem in Korea. The labour shortage problem is especially marked in the manufacturing sector, where low-wage firms are in the most difficult situation. In particular, there is a severe shortage of production and related workers.

The number of vacancies and the vacancy rate by industry. As of March 1990, Korean industry was 192,100 workers short of full capacity, with a vacancy rate of 4.3 per cent. This rate compares to one of 1.8 per cent in 1985 and 3.2 per cent in 1989. The manufacturing sector faces the most difficult labour shortage problem: in 1990, 78 per cent of all vacancies were in manufacturing. Within the manufacturing sector, the textile, clothing and leather, and the metal assembly industries were heavily hurt by the labour shortage problem, with vacancy rates of 8.3 per cent and 4.6 per cent respectively. As was discussed earlier, these are the sectors where female workers are massively employed. The mining industry, one of the declining industries in Korea, also experienced a relatively high vacancy rate (7.11 per cent in 1990). By contrast, the retail, wholesale and lodging industries, the banking, insurance and real estate industries, and social and personal services each have a vacancy rate barely exceeding 1 per cent.

The data on vacancy rates by occupation confirm the pattern given in the industry data. As of March 1990, 86.3 per cent of the total number of vacancies was in production or related occupations. The labour shortage in production is relatively recent, as information on vacancies over time shows. One cause of the shortage may be the increase in the number of college graduates and a decline in those with high school education who might enter production work.

Korea's Ministry of Labour provides occupation-specific information which allows a more systematic study of the degree and the scope of male and female labour shortage. The job opening rate is measured by dividing the number of job offers by the number of job seekers. A job opening ratio exceeding 1.0 represents labour shortage, while labour surplus is represented by a rate below 1.0. The average job opening ratio is 1.18 across all occupations registered in the National Employment Stability Institute. Separate ratios are calculated for vacancies for females and for males (since 1990 it has become illegal to issue sex-specific job advertisements).

The job opening ratios for women are high in many female labour-intensive occupations: 1.58 for female nurses, 2.05 for female nurses' assistants, and as high as 8.51 for female weavers and 8.11 for female shoemakers. The on-going labour shortage suggests the necessity of revision in customary discrimination practices against women in order to solve the labour shortage problem, which will be discussed in the section beginning on p. 197. In spite of the current serious labour shortage in Korea, we observe a substantial number of discouraged female workers in the age group 25-39 and among highly educated married women. Statistics on both the unemployment rates and the hidden unemployment rates of men and women by age group and education level are compiled in the Report on the Employment Structure Survey, 1983, 1986 and 1989.

The hidden unemployed are those in the survey who were not actively searching for work because they believed no suitable work was available. The (open) unemployment rates of male and female workers in 1989 were 3.0 per cent and 2.2 per cent, respectively. But the hidden unemployment rates of male and female workers in 1989 were 3.3 per cent and 16.7 per cent, respectively. Even though women's open unemployment rate is lower than men's, the women's hidden unemployment rate is more than five times that of men. In 1989, the number of women who were out of the labour force but willing to work if reasonable work was available totalled 1,319,000, far exceeding the total number of workers in shortage in Korea, which was 192,100.

Analysed by age group, the hidden unemployed women are heavily concentrated in the age groups of 25-29 and 30-39. The hidden unemployed rate of females aged 15-19 was highest but the absolute number was only 4,000 persons, which was relatively small. Analysed by education level, the hidden unemployment rate is highest among women junior-college graduates. In 1989, the hidden unemployment rates for women of middle school, high school, and junior-college and university graduates were 13.7 per cent, 21.2 per cent, 30.8 per cent and 18.2 per cent respectively. Reducing employment and wage discrimination in Korea seems essential to utilizing women's human resources adequately.

MALE-FEMALE WAGE DIFFERENTIALS

According to the Occupational Wage Survey, women's wages were 45.4 per cent of men's in 1971 when the survey was conducted for the first time. This percentage fell to 41.2 in 1975, but then reversed its course and edged up to 42.9 in 1980 and to 52.8 in 1989. Historical figures from the Yearbook of Statistics, issued by the Japanese Government-General of Korea, reported that the ratio of Korean women's earnings to Korean men's was 53 per cent in 1930 and 54 per cent in 1935, and the Industrial Labour Force and Wage Survey for South Korea in 1946, conducted after the liberation from Japanese rule in 1945, reported that the ratio was 57 per cent. Thus the wage gap remained fairly constant until 1946, then got steadily wider up to 1975, then it started again to narrow very slowly. While women's labour force participation has risen dramatically, it nonetheless remains the case that the gender wage gap has remained wide.

Data published in the 1989-1990 ILO Yearbook of Labour Statistics suggest that Japan and Korea exhibit the largest wage differential by sex of any country. Several factors account for the large differential in Korea. Cho's (1991) work discussed above suggested that women were disproportionately employed in low-wage firms. We believe that intense competition for securing employment in high wage firms produces labour queues. Taking advantage of this situation, high-wage firms often show preference for male workers. One customary practice is that only male workers are hired through regular job opening advertisements, while female workers get their jobs through personal connections such as recommendations from friends and relatives. This type of discriminatory practice may be called 'discrimination at the port of entry', and tends to produce unequal job opportunities. Since a large fraction of human capital stock possessed by individuals is acquired from learning on the job or on-the-job training, discrimination at the port of entry will generate unequal on-the-job training (or learning) opportunities over individuals' working lives and subsequent wage inequalities between men and women.

Seniority is very important in the determination of wages in Korea. Under this wage system, female workers are at a disadvantage because they tend to quit their jobs because of marriage, child birth or child-care problems. Shorter job tenure limits the prospects for wage increases for female workers, even though there is few gender differentials in the wages of the newly hired workers aged 17-19 or 20-24. The small number of highly-paid middle-aged or older female workers, coupled with the tendency for married women who reenter the labour force after raising children to be paid wages similar to those of young unmarried female workers, leads to the large wage differentials between male and female workers.

Wage differentials between male and female production workers are small up to age 25, but for female production workers wages tend to decline after age 25. For those female production workers who reenter the market after age 30, low wages prevail and the gap relative to male wages increases continuously. A similar phenomenon affects female white collar workers. Female workers tend to receive infrequent and inadequate on-the-job training and receive few promotion opportunities. Female white collar workers are assigned to secondary jobs such as typing and bookkeeping and serve as assistants to male white collar workers. This implies that they have little opportunity for regular job transfers which would help them gain managerial and firm-specific knowledge.

Therefore, promotion to higher positions in the management level is highly restricted. Likewise, discriminatory practices in the internal labour market against female production workers start with their being allocated to the simple assembly or processing type of jobs. Female workers are concentrated in sewing, weaving, electric and electronics assembly and shoemaking, all of which are simple assembly and processing types of occupations. The requirements of these occupations are simply precision, speed and no absence from work. The firms' unwillingness to provide female workers with training, as well as the limited promotion opportunities for women, are important elements behind the large wage differentials between male and female workers.

The wage paid by Korean firms includes the cost of living allowance, family support, education allowances and housing allowances. These fringe benefits are normally offered only to male workers. This is an additional factor that creates wage differentials between male and female workers. Se Il Park describes sex discrimination in the Korean labour market as follows:

The employment discrimination in the labour market can be decomposed into occupational segregation and discrimination in the internal labour market. In respect of the former, female workers are driven into low-wage occupations even when they have the same individual characteristics as the male workers such as the same education level and job experiences. As regards the latter, firms' employment policy or practices relating to job assignment and transfer, training, promotion and retirement are disadvantageous to female workers.

Another form of sex discrimination in the labour market is wage discrimination. It refers to the relatively low wages paid to female workers owing to the firms' policy or practices on wage payment, despite the fact that the female workers have the same education level and job experiences and are in the same occupation as the male workers.

Se II Park regarded occupational discrimination and internal labour market discrimination as the major sources of employment discrimination against women. We would argue that there is also discrimination at port of entry, and that this is more important than the other two sources of discrimination. Female workers are over-represented or crowded in low-wage firms and sectors, which constrain their opportunities for on-the-job training and promotions throughout their working lives. This may be a more important factor for explaining the wage differentials by gender, than occupational discrimination, internal labour market discrimination, and innate productivity differences between men and women.

SEGMENTED LABOUR MARKETS AND MALE-FEMALE WAGE DIFFERENTIALS

We have discussed earlier the segmentation of the Korean labour market into high-wage firms and low-wage firms. An important feature of this labour market structure is that workers may not be free to move from low-wage to high-wage firms. While individuals are free to leave their current job, they may not get the desired position in higher wage firms. We notice that there exists a remarkable wage differential between white collar male workers in low-wage and high-wage firms, and that the same is true for blue collar male workers.

The wage differences among women between high- and low-wage firms are much narrower than for men. Thus the wage differential between male workers in the high-wage firms and female workers in the low-wage firms particularly after age 25 constitutes another influential determinant of the wage gap between male and female workers in Korea. Additional work by Bai and Cho (1992b) estimating separate earnings functions for low-wage and high-wage firms suggests that the discrimination coefficients (D1 and D2) are much higher in high-wage firms, and that policy against discrimination should focus on high-wage firms.

POLICY PROPOSALS FOR WOMEN'S EMPLOYMENT AND WAGES

Citing the much-quoted phrase, 'People are poor because the rate of wages paid by the industries of the United States will not permit them to be anything but poor,' Wachtel and Betsey once argued, 'In our society work is invariably prescribed as the path out of poverty. However, for a significant proportion of the poor this remedy falls on deaf ears, since they work but are poor. The working poor earn their poverty.' Does the fact that female workers in Korea are largely employed in low-wage industries and low-wage firms force them to remain in poverty, as Wachtel and Betsey argued? Or is industrialization changing this situation?

One feature that is consistently emphasized throughout this chapter is that women's employment and earnings problems are related to their being employed in low-wage firms. Therefore, government policies that have the purpose of facilitating female employment and its upward mobility must be reorganized in accordance with industrial restructuring. Since the industrial structure in Korea is polarized into high-wage firms and low-wage firms, whilst middle-wage firms have been weak, a government policy promoting sexual equality across all manufacturing sectors would conflict with economic growth and efficiency.

First of all, we review the current legal framework and government policies for women's employment. Then we suggest four major policies to reduce sex differentials which, at the same time, encourage growth. We first discuss macroeconomic and industrial policy as the best policy for reducing pay inequality between high-wage firms and low-wage firms. We then examine micro-level labour market policies relevant to high-wage (or low-wage) firms, and microeconomic policy proposals based on human capital theory are also discussed.

INSTITUTIONS AND GOVERNMENT POLICIES

Korean women's participation in the labour force is affected by various laws, government institutions and policies, and the legal framework has also been changing quite rapidly in the recent past. The Equal Employment Opportunity Law, promulgated on 4 December 1987 and amended on 1 April 1989, has as its purpose to secure equal opportunity and treatment for employees regardless of their gender, as well as to protect the maternal role of women. The law contains a number of provisions regarding discrimination. Employers are required to provide equal opportunity to females and males with regard to recruitment and employment.

Therefore, gender-segregated job advertisements are prohibited, as are restrictions applied only to women, eg. age and/or marital status. The law requires employers to offer equal pay for equal-value work in the same enterprise, where equal value is defined by skill, endeavour, responsibility, working conditions, or other things which are required in the process of work. The law also states that employers shall not discriminate on the basis of gender, with regard to education, placement, and promotion of employees. Lastly, the employer shall not discriminate, on the basis of gender, against employees with regard to retirement age or dismissal, and shall not enter into an employment contract which provides that marriage, pregnancy or child birth of female employees will be cause for retirement.

The Labour Standards Law, promulgated in 1953, had been the only legal protection for female workers before the

Equal Employment Opportunity Law. The Labour Standards Law prohibits night work, or work in a mine for female workers and limits women's overtime working hours. Female workers are not authorized to work between ten p.m. and six a.m. or on public holidays, unless there is both consent from the worker and approval from the Ministry of Labour. The law also allows menstruation and maternity leaves and nursing hours. Female workers are allowed one day's leave with pay for menstruation every month. Pregnant female workers are allowed sixty days leave with pay, thirty days of which shall be reserved for use after child birth, and female workers with infants under one year of age are allowed breaks twice a day for nursing, of not less than thirty minutes each.

The Equal Employment Opportunity Law of 1988 modified the maternity leave provisions, and provided for up to a year's leave following child bearing, including the paid maternity leave (sixty days) before and/or after child birth. The period of leave for child-rearing is to be included in the length of service, which affects promotion and retirement bonuses. Also, employers are required to provide female employees with necessary facilities for nursing infants at the workplace. Enforcement of the law is important. Marriage bars and gender-segregated job advertisements have been common in the past. Therefore, the government, via the Ministry of Labour, has actively publicized the provisions of the Equal Employment Opportunity Law since 1988, via pamphlets, and workshops held jointly with research institutes or women's organizations.

In addition, the government has undertaken regular inspections for the observance of the law. Orders have been issued for the corrections of discrimination in retirement and dismissal in establishments with ten or more workers (in 1988), in some large hospitals and hotels, and in the banking and finance industry (in 1993). Between 1988 and 1992 there were 4,886 such corrections orders of which those for retirement/dismissal formed 40 per cent and another 30 per cent were regarding leave for child-rearing. Other efforts to publicize the law include a government plan to nominate March as The Month of Equal Employment, which includes World Women's Day (8 March).

Central and local governments and other public sector enterprises are being required to take the initiative in abolishing their gender-discriminating personnel and human resource management systems and to develop better programmes for maternity protection. The government is also considering inspecting the employment rules of all establishments with one hundred or more employees. Furthermore, the government is now seriously considering imposing quotas for women's employment for selected industries and/or occupations, where women's employment usually has been restricted. Regarding enforcement of protective legislation concerning women, a survey conducted in August 1991 shows that, out of 520 establishments which have 300 or more female employees, only 317 establishments (61 per cent) allow leave of absence for child-rearing.

The government is therefore considering transferring some of the cost of such leave to social insurances such as medical insurance or an unemployment insurance programme, a change which was made in Japan in 1975. The government is also considering whether some of the protective legislation in the Labour Standards Law is now out of date. The prohibition of women's employment in certain industries and occupations has lost its meaning due to factory automation. Also, restriction of female workers' overtime, night and holiday work tends to be an obstacle to women's employment. In addition, menstruation leave with pay (Indonesia is the only other country allowing such leave) also has a negative effect on women's employment. Therefore, the government is considering amendments to some articles of the Labour Standards Law in the near future.

Limited availability of day care inhibits participation by married women. The existing legislation requires that establishments in which more than 1,000 female workers are employed must provide a child-care facility, and since 1987 the Korean government has been operating eighteen model child-care centers in major public and agricultural production sites. Nonetheless, there is a great shortage of child-care centers. According to an estimate made by Ministry of Health and Social Affairs in 1993, there are 3.95 million children of the age of 0-5 raised by married female workers. Of them only 3.6 per cent received the benefits of public and private child-care centers. The government plans to eliminate current restrictions on the facilities and to provide tax incentives for private facilities.

INDUSTRIAL RESTRUCTURING AND ECONOMIC GROWTH

Women are primarily employed in low-wage industries or low-wage firms. The substantial wage premium paid to workers in high-wage firms have been shown empirically. It appears that the economic status of workers, both male and female, in export-led economic development can be more effectively improved through fostering the knowledge-intensive and technology-intensive firms, and small and medium-sized firms producing parts and raw materials. Thus, industrial policy which aims to transform the industrial structure and encourage small and medium-sized firms may help to increase equity in the labour market as well as further economic efficiency.

Another alternative measure to enhance the economic status of female workers, which is no less important than industrial restructuring, is to maintain continued economic growth and increase the share of the manufacturing sector in GNP. This can enable female workers to move from low-productivity sectors to high-productivity ones, and facilitate the improvement of their wages and employment.

MICRO-LEVEL LABOUR MARKET POLICY

Female workers face disadvantages in being hired for good jobs, and once hired, face discrimination in terms of training, job assignment, job transfer, promotion, dismissal and retirement. Discriminatory action against female workers tends to take the form of industrial and occupational segregation and/or wage discrimination. The Korean government should show a strong commitment to the Equal Employment Opportunity Law to eliminate deep-rooted sex discriminations in the high-wage sector.

For this to be accomplished, detailed criteria should be established to determine whether a discriminatory action has occurred, and the penalty against any violation of Equal Employment Opportunity Law, which is currently minimal, should be increased. The abolition of unjustified discrimination against female workers can be justified both on equity and efficiency grounds.

The government itself has not been in the forefront of equity in hiring. There are 90,000 low-level government officials in Korea ranging from the ninth level to the sixth level, among which 12.5 per cent are female. On the other hand, only 1.2 per cent of 20,000 high-level government officials between the fifth and the first level are female. Sex discrimination in public enterprises can be illustrated by the following figures. While 38.1 per cent of total employees in the private sector are women, female workers account for only 18.0 per cent of employees in public enterprises. The combined annual budget of the public enterprises is 1.7 times that of the central government, and they account for 10.5 per cent of the value-added and 2.5 per cent of employment in Korea's non-agricultural sectors.

Public enterprises definitely belong to the high-wage sector. If we assume that Korea's level of industrialization is about 20-30 years behind the advanced countries, then the seriousness of sex discrimination in the public sector can be detected when the current statistics of female employment in the public enterprises of Korea are compared with those in the developed countries 20-30 years ago. In 1975, the proportions of female employment in public sectors were 53.4 per cent in the UK, 47.5 per cent in the US, 64.4 per cent in Sweden and 29.6 per cent in Japan.

We therefore suggest a quota system be initially implemented in the public sector which should be extended to the private high-wage sectors after a brief period of evaluation of its performance. We also propose that in low-wage firms where more than 500 female workers are employed, occupational segregation must be eliminated so that promotion of female workers to managerial posts can increase. In Korea, female managers are almost non-existent, and it is difficult for women in white collar jobs to be promoted to managerial posts.

HUMAN CAPITAL FORMATION

Opportunities for on-the-job training for workers in the manufacturing sector are rare, and such training is also very poor in its content. This has not changed much for the last fifteen years. The extremely low level of training within manufacturing firms is observed consistently across numerous studies. For example, a recent survey in 1991 by Bai and Cho showed that only 27.3 per cent of manufacturing workers surveyed in Seoul area received on-the-job training. This indicates little improvement over the past fifteen years. On-the-job training for women is even scarcer than that for men. Bai and Cho's survey showed that only 20.7 per cent of female employees have undergone a job training programme compared with 33.7 per cent of men.

The 1990 report of the Ministry of Labour on women's job training through the in-plant training centre reported similar results. As of 1990, only 4,665 women had gone through the in-plant training programme, compared with a figure of 21,025 for men. Employers generally prefer paying for job training levies to conducting an in-plant training programme. They are even more conservative when it comes to providing job training for women. It should also be noted that, as of 1990, 84.4 per cent of in-house training for women was concentrated on the assembly processes in labour intensive industries such as textiles, electronics, footwear, sewing, and so on.

We would therefore argue that in addition to the current public job training system, job training centers exclusively for women should be established and the programme should fully reflect the supply and demand characteristics of the female labour force. At the same time, the Ministry of Labour should consider the establishment of technical colleges or technical high schools for women, especially in such fields as electrical and electronics, communications, information processing, safety management, quality control, environment management, etc. Such vocational education would make a substantial contribution to ensuring long-term industrial competitiveness and to sustaining economic growth, and would broaden women's employment opportunities in high-wage sectors.

An effective way to enhance women's upward mobility in industry is to offer them more educational opportunities aimed at imparting a higher level of skills. The level of higher educational advancement in Korea has already reached that of many developed countries. The problem in higher education in Korea is quality, not quantity.

As of 1990, only 0.3 per cent of girls and 15.6 per cent of boys were in technical high schools, and the numbers of technical high school graduates have been stagnant for the last ten years, while those from academic high schools have been increasing rapidly. In order to upgrade technical training for female workers, it is necessary not only to establish girls' technical high schools to provide training in appropriate types of skills, but also to give special emphasis to vocational education to all high school students, regardless of sex.

As for college students, humanities degrees have been traditionally preferred to science and engineering degrees in Korea, particularly for women. For example, 15.4 per cent of female and 38.7 per cent of male college students are working for science and engineering degrees. The ratio of college graduates studying science and engineering to those studying humanities and social sciences changed from 46.7:53.3 in 1981 to 37.2:62.8 in 1990, reflecting a trend towards emphasis on humanities and social science degrees. In the face of intensified competition from other developing countries in the traditional labour-intensive industries such as textiles and electronics, and in light of the application of computer aided design and manufacturing (CAD/CAM) in the traditional labour-intensive industries in developed countries, the cheap and abundant labour in Korea no longer provides a cost effective substitute for computer aided assembling or factory line work.

Continuous advancement and adjustment of industrial structure, based on changing international comparative advantage, should take place in Korea. Demand for machine and equipment operators, engineers and technicians in microprocessing, micro-electronics, CAD/CAM and robotics, and demand for 'hybrid' managers who possess complex and multiple skills in the fields of engineering, information technology and general management are expected to increase rapidly in the near future. There is an urgent need for linking education and training with changing skill demands, i.e., demand for information- and knowledge-intensive workers. To enhance the upward mobility of female workers in industry, there is a need to increase the intake of women in those courses offered at the certificate, diploma and degree levels by the educational institutions.

Government policy should focus on the qualitative improvement of higher education in science and engineering and develop a close link between the changes in skill requirement and the manpower supply of educational institutions. The aging population of the developed world is likely to be less flexible and hence less amenable to the challenges of knowledge- and information-intensive jobs. The requisite expertise will be in short supply because of the almost stagnant or even declining size of the young college graduated work force in the developed countries. If Korea succeeds in 'factor creation' of the requisite expertise, companies in the developed countries will have an incentive to relocate the information and knowledge-intensive firms and jobs to Korea.

If this occurs, Korea may have a good chance to move out of a labour-intensive, assembly and processing type of industrial structure towards a more knowledge-intensive industrial structure. The most important problem that Korea must resolve is how to make women's higher education more relevant and responsive to the rapidly changing skill requirements of the economy.

In Korea, despite the advances made in women's participation and the changes in their employment, women's employment remains concentrated in low-paying industries. Recent legislation such as the Equal Employment Opportunity Law has been much more favourable to women's employment than was the practice in the past. The labour movement can potentially help efforts to improve women's relative position. In Korea, however, labour movements historically have not been very strong. Also union leaders have been interested mainly in improving the wages and working conditions of male workers, neglecting those of female workers, in a society where men are perceived to be superior to women.

This parallels the case of Germany where the industrial labour unions have strong power, but the wage differences between the sexes which existed in 1913 still remain today. It therefore implies that the strengthening of labour movements should proceed with special attention given to the problems of female workers. We have discussed industrial and economic policies in the previous section. Other long-term social changes may be important. Women should be encouraged to be equally responsible for household income, just as their husbands should be expected to assume some responsibility for housework.

8

Diversity and the Status of Women

'The secondary status of woman is a pan-cultural fact' so argued Sherry Ortner in 1970 in her now famous essay, ' Is female to male as nature is to culture?' At the end of the twentieth century it is impossible to universalise the subordination of the world's women in such a fashion, let alone homogenise the mass of Indian women. Grappling with diversity and difference is central to understanding the position of women in India. Since the heydays of the women's liberation movement in the 1970s, when there was a sense of women's solidarity and sisterhood, feminist theorists have shifted their attention to the study of difference among women. Scholarly analysis used to focus on women's shared oppression and male domination, but more recent research has shown that male domination and female subordination is far from uniform. On the contrary, women's experiences are distinguished by their specific locations within particular ethnic, class and religious groupings.

Thus, no unitary categorisation of Indian women is possible. For example, in India over the past two decades the achievements of urban middle-class women in salaried and professional jobs have been as spectacular as the relentless exploitation and acute deprivation of female agricultural labourers. There are many powerful and influential Indian women in the professions, business, bureaucracy and government who enjoy the privileges and benefits of their class position. Such women have also gained from the anti-colonial struggles of the Indian nationalist movement, which gave them a voice in the political arena.

After independence from British colonial rule in 1947 these women had relatively easy access to the expanding civil service as well as representation in parliament. However, the vast majority of women in India do not belong to this affluent middle class. Their lives are constrained by problems typical of a post-colonial developing economy.

At a discursive level there are also contradictions. On the one hand there are belief systems in India which relegate women to an inferior position in society. On the other, competing views construct women as powerful, life-giving and forceful. Similarly, Indian women face a huge gulf between the constitutional guarantees of formal equality and the every-day reality of inequalities generated by divisions of caste and class. Despite the formulation of specific government policies designed to improve the position of women over the past several decades, the majority of women have seen little real progress. For example, in 1976 the Equal Remuneration Act was introduced, which prohibited gender discrimination in recruitment and required employers to pay equal wages for equal work.

However, this legislation only covered those in government employment. As most women do not work within this arena, only a fraction of women workers have benefited from this act. This chapter shows that the efforts of the women's movement to improve the status of women over the past several decades have been undercut by conflicting sources of community authority flourishing in the diversity that is Indian society. The general indices on the status of women, such as literacy, life expectancy, male/female sex ratio, and labour force participation, indicate the precarious position of Indian women at the end of the twentieth century.

MALE / FEMALE SEX RATIO

One of the startling aspects of gender relations in India is the male/female sex ratio. Despite the biological advantage of the female foetus and globally higher female life expectancy, the situation is reversed in India. Infant mortality rates for girls are higher than boys. The sex ratio has been declining steadily since 1901. The 1991 census shows the number of females per males to be 92.9 to every 100 males. In most countries around the world, regardless of relative wealth and prosperity, the sex ratio is weighted in favour of women (e.g. Colombia 102 females:100 males; France 105:100; Thailand 102:100). Though there was a slight rise in the female numbers in India's sex ratio from 93 to 93.4 during the decade 1971-81, scholars attribute this to better data collection methods rather than an improvement in the status of women.

LITERACY

Between 1971 and 1991 female literacy leapt from 18.7 per cent to 32.6 per cent. Although this indicates an absolute increase in female literacy, there remain wide disparities between male and females rates and between rural and urban areas. Only 20 per cent of rural women are literate compared to 50 per cent of men. Among the urban population 45 per cent of females are illiterate compared to only 20 per cent of men. Primary school enrolment for boys is 99 per cent compared to only 66 per cent for girls.

This is because girls from poorer backgrounds have the heavy burden of domestic chores and child-minding and face a general apathy towards the education of girls. It is assumed that boys require a better education since they will be future earners. In higher education there is a relatively favourable attitude towards education of girls, particularly in the cities among the upper and middle classes. However, university educated women only constitutes 3 per cent of the female population.

LABOUR FORCE PARTICIPATION

Officially, the labour force participation of women is low. In 1971 only 12.06 per cent of the labour force was female compared to 22.3 in 1991. Moreover, only 6 per cent of the female workforce is employed in the relatively well paid, secure, 'formal' organised sector jobs while 94 per cent are found working in the casual and informal sector of the labour market. Here they face adverse conditions of low pay, lack of protection from unscrupulous employers and job uncertainty. The low rate of participation partly reflects the narrow official definition of 'economic activity'.

Large areas of women's work are excluded from official statistics. For example, women in rural households collect edible roots, greens and fruits. In urban areas women prepare fuel from dung cakes and collect half-burnt coals; among artisan communities, they actively participate in the production within the family. Yet, these activities are excluded from official statistics. Another reason for the low participation rate is the real lack of employment opportunities for women-especially in areas where women are displaced in large numbers from their traditional occupations as a result of mechanisation and commercialisation. As will be discussed below, there is also a strong cultural expectation that women will not be employed outside the home on marriage. Cultural practices and expectations relating to status and hierarchy remain strong influences on women's status in India.

DOMINANT BRAHMANICAL VERSUS SUBALTERN FOLK TRADITIONS

One of the major distinguishing aspects of the Indian traditions is the tension between the dominant Brahmanical traditions drawn from élite Hinduism and the subaltern heritages drawn from daily life of the ordinary people. Variously described as the 'great' tradition versus the 'little' tradition or the orthodox versus the popular, the Brahmanical is derived from textual and scriptural sources, while the subaltern is based on fluid localised oral traditions at the village level. These oppositions provide an important conceptual framework that underpins female power and feminine principles in India's cultural traditions. Although the notion of *Shakti* (female power embodied in a mother goddess) is present in both traditions, the Brahmanical cosmology embodies the passive aspects of femininity while the latter often reflects the assertive.

These traditions are expressed with enormous regional variations. Northern India is characterised by patrilineal kinship systems and patriarchal values which rigidly circumscribe the lives of women. The existence of the Dravidian kinship system in southern India and the influences of the matrilineal traditions in northeastern India afford a more positive view of females. These competing cultural constructions are reflected in the demographic outcomes of women's lives. For example, in the southern state of Kerala female life expectancy is 72 years and the female to male sex-ratio is 104 women per hundred men compared to the northern Indian state of Utter Pradesh, where it is 87.9 females per hundred-one of the lowest in the world.

Generally speaking, women in the south live longer, are more valued and are regarded as more critical to their natal kin than are women in north India. Caste is an important principle of social organisation in Indian society, which significantly shapes gender relations. It is a system of hereditary social ranking associated with Hinduism, which governs social relations and the distribution of power in Indian society. It is both a cultural and economic system of stratification. Divided into hierarchically ordered castes, *Brahmins,* (priests) occupy the highest rank, followed by *Khshatriyas* (warriors/noblemen) *Vaishyas* (traders/merchants) and *Sudras* (artisans/labourers). There are numerous sub-castes and outside the caste system are 'untouchables', the lowest strata of society.

In India today, as part of a process of self-affirmation and political mobilisation, the formerly untouchable and other subordinate castes have come to refer to themselves as *dalits* or 'the oppressed'-a term that I use later in the chapter. Classifying society into different groups is not unique to India, but what is characteristic of the Hindu social order is the notion of ritual purity and impurity, which is sanctioned by religious principles. Caste remains a pan-Indian phenomenon despite its religious association with Hinduism. In other words, although ritual purity does not have the same religious connotation in other non-Hindu communities in the Indian subcontinent, caste distinctions based on descent and birth are also found among Muslims and other minority groups. Consequently, low-caste Christians are likely to experience the same level of cultural humiliation as non-Christian untouchables as well as suffer economic hardships.

In contemporary India caste intersects with class inequalities and low caste is frequently synonymous with low socio-economic status and poverty. The relationship between caste and the position of women is particularly evident in the beliefs surrounding female sexuality. Female sexuality is seen to pose a danger to caste purity due to the perceived threat of lower caste men gaining sexual access to upper caste women. Therefore, within higher castes, religious ideologies prescribe a greater control over women to ensure caste purity. Historically Brahmin women have been subjected to greater control over their mobility than have lower caste women. Rules of marriage and inheritance have circumscribed the freedom of upper caste women. We will consider the instances of dowry and sati later in this chapter.

In modern India, the phenomenon known as 'sanskritisation', whereby lower castes emulate the practices of upper castes to gain higher status, have meant that men within such communities have invariably imposed greater restrictions over women's mobility. Traditionally Brahmin men have exerted control over lower caste women's sexuality as a means to demean and humiliate lower caste men. Today many of these upper caste practices continue to have serious consequences for women.

At the beginning of the chapter, among urban upper middle-class, a high caste family, the position of women is quite high due to the legacy of the nationalist movement. The women's movement in 1970s was able to draw upon the positive gains of the anti-colonial struggles. However, more recently feminists have focused on the centrality of gender in reproducing caste inequalities. This is particularly significant when we look at the caste/class nexus and violence against women. As Rege argues Violence against women reveal definite variations by caste; while upper castes are subjected to control and violence within the family, it is the absence of such controls that makes lower caste women vulnerable to rape, sexual harassment and the threat of public violence.

ACTIVITIES OF THE WOMEN'S MOVEMENT

Despite the relatively dismal statistics on women's status in India and the strictures posed by the caste/class system, it would be inaccurate to characterise women in India as passive victims of their circumstances. On the contrary, the Indian women's movement has provided a powerful challenge to continued subordination of women. Legal reforms as well as struggles to maintain a livelihood and guarantee safety from violence have all been part of the Indian women's movement. Clearly, legal improvements in women's status do not necessarily equate to real qualitative improvements in the lives of individuals, especially when broader economic and social contexts remain unaltered.

Nevertheless, it is important to recognise that the emergence of the women's movement in India enabled hundreds of thousands of women to participate in activities significantly empowering them both individually and collectively to enforce changes. For a village woman in a highly stratified community, unaccustomed to interacting with males outside the confines of family and kin, a bus-ride to town without a chaperone and attendance at a rally may be phenomenal achievements. The activities of the women's movement highlight a number of seemingly contradictory and complex factors governing women's lives. The deep class and caste divisions in Indian society have inhibited the emergence of a unified feminist movement.

Nonetheless, the campaigns to address specific women's problems have occasionally brought middle class and poor women together. For the most part, working-class and peasant women confront exploitation through their own specific organisations, but middle-class women with feminist ideals have become involved in these struggles performing roles as lawyers and lobbyists for the working-class and peasant groups. By examining a selection of the campaigns waged by the Indian women's movement concerning the changing nature of women's position in the last two decades.

The experience of colonialism had an important influence on women's activism. During the 19th century women supported the fight against colonial rule and in turn were supported by nationalists in their quest for formal equality as citizens. Yet the nationalist discourse ignored the realm of women's rights within the family. It was within the domain of the home that the colonised subject could remain sovereign. During this period women's innate qualities were utilised as mothers of the nation. After independence, women were guaranteed constitutional equality. However, by the 1970s such legal claims ceased to have any meaning and feminists began to challenge the patriarchal nature of Indian society. Focussing on legal reform feminists utilised state mechanisms to bring about changes, but they were well aware that the state itself was a patriarchal institution.

An important departure for the women's movement was the emergence of 'autonomous' women's groups in the 1970s. Previously women's organisations were affiliated to political parties such as the women's wing of the Communist Party of India. Many of the new women's groups were left oriented but they remained independent by eschewing political party affiliation. There was also a proliferation of scholarly work on women's status, the establishment of research organisations on women's studies such as the Centre for Women's Development Studies in New Delhi and the Research Centre for Women's Studies, SNDT Women's University in Bombay.

In 1975 the appearance of a number of publications gave a boost to the women's movement and highlighted the stark inequalities experienced by women. These included Towards Equality, the report of the National Committee on the Status of Women, and several journals in various Indian languages and especially the bilingual (Hindi and English) magazine *Manushi: A Journal of Women and Society*.

In the 1970s the world-wide recession and the expansion of capitalist relations of production had a serious impact on Indian society. It is not surprising that many of the issues taken up by women during this period related to working-class, peasant and tribal women. These included the right to better working conditions, campaigns against inflationary prices, land rights and so on. Emphasis was placed on issues of basic survival and the articulation of economic transformation with pre-existing patriarchal ideologies and their mutually reinforcing influences, which continued or heightened gender inequalities. Let us now turn to an exploration of some of these struggles.

The vast majority of Indian women live in rural areas. Landlessness is a major problem for the rural poor. The ways in which women have been particularly affected is their diminishing opportunities for subsistence activities and loss of control over land. Felling of forests and clearing land for large development projects such as dams, and large scale capitalist farming posed greater threats to survival needs of the rural poor. During the period 1961-71, many poor peasants were dispossessed of their agricultural land and became dependent on wage work for survival. However, during this period, male agricultural work increased by more than doubles the rate of female wage work. Women were further marginalised into casual and unskilled labour. Traditional access to forest produce particularly among communities that relied on gathering became increasingly scarce.

For women there was also the growing burden of travelling far to collect water and fuel for cooking. For many their working day extended to 14 - 15 hours per day. Against this background the Chipko or tree hugging movement became emblematic of women's struggle for basic survival needs and a safe environment. In the early 1970s in the foothills of the Himalayas spontaneous protests erupted against plans to fell trees by timber contractors.

The form of protest was to protect trees by embracing them in order to prevent logging. By 1975 women in surrounding villages had formed Mahila Mangal Dals (women's welfare organisations) to extend their struggle to general issues on protecting fields and forests (Sharma et 1985). One of their actions included targeting the male dominated *panchayat* (village council). Women were critical of men within their communities who usually moved their grazing cattle through the fields, where women grew their crops. Women's protest resulted in the head of the council filing a case against them. However, the district magistrate dismissed the case when faced with combined protest from the women. Interestingly, Chipko was not regarded as part of the women's movement in the 1970s but gained importance in the 1980s as a manifestation of eco-feminist principles and as a symbol of 'woman centred' feminism.

SELF-EMPLOYED WOMEN'S ASSOCIATION (SEWA)

In 1972 in the western Indian state of Gujarat, women employed in the 'informal' sector of the labour force (street vendors or home-workers engaged in piecework) united to form the Self-Employed Women's Association (SEWA). It was effectively a trade union of self-employed women. This form of organising among women was unique since the vast majority of women in India do not work in large factories or enterprises where they can be protected by labour regulations, government legislation or become unionised. The organisation evolved from India's oldest union the Textile Labour Association (TLA), and was also inspired by Mahatma Gandhi's campaign against the mill owners. Initially the Department of Labour refused to register the union on the grounds that there was no recognised employer. Finally SEWA was granted recognition as the activists argued that its members had the right to 'freedom from exploitation, assurance of regular wages and access to opportunities for advancement'.

According to SEWA's secretary Renana Jhabvala, 'the United Nations decade for women gave a boost to the growth of SEWA, placing it within the women's movement'. She further adds that SEWA's adoption of a unique structure combining the strategies of a trade union and co-operatives enabled it to struggle against the everyday oppression of women. SEWA now claims that it is turning from an organisation into a movement, with a membership of 46 000 across five states. The organisation played an important role in securing credit for low-income women. A further significant outcome for the movement came when its general secretary became a member of the National Planning Commission giving SEWA influence at the national policy level. Moreover, SEWA was instrumental in the formation of the National Commission on Self-Employed Women.

ANTI-DOWRY CAMPAIGN

In the 1980s the campaigns against dowry and dowry harassment became major foci of feminist protest across India. The protests fundamentally challenged the nature of patriarchy within the private domain of family and kinship. More significantly, they echoed an important feminist critique about the effectiveness of legal reform concerning women's property rights. Women's property in India is intimately linked with the custom of dowry. The changes in dowry practices and the pressure of ever increasing demands on the amount paid by the bride's parents to the bride's parents-in-law raise a number of questions about the status of women in India. Upon marriage daughters are given gifts of household goods such as furniture, crockery, electrical appliances (in recent years refrigerators, televisions etc.) as well as personal items of clothing, jewellery and cash.

Additionally gifts are made to the groom and his family. However, dowry is more than a simple economic transaction; it is deeply embedded in the cultural practices of patrilineal kinship systems, the cultural valuation of a 'woman's worth' as well as Brahmanical religious principles. Within the dominant Brahmanical culture the giving away of a bride is a ceremonial 'gifting' of a virgin daughter. In the transfer of this gift the 'wife-givers' accrue merit. Further, the ceremony surrounding the exchange expresses symbolically the responsibility of the bride's father to furnish the household of the newly married couple. Hence the dowry frequently consists of an elaborate array of household goods as well as cash.

The assumption here, of course, is that a wife is not expected to be gainfully employed, and therefore she is an economic liability in her husband's household. As a result, she has to be compensated for in marriage. The gift of the daughter is considered to be the best form of marriage in Brahmanical ideology because of the accumulation of merit and the gain of rank and prestige. The opposite is the practice of accepting a bride price that is categorised as a morally inferior form of marriage.

In most agricultural land-holding upper caste groups the seclusion of women is closely associated with giving elaborate dowries. In contrast, the practice of bride price generally occurs within communities where women actively participate in agricultural production. In 1956 the Hindu Succession Act enabled daughters to inherit land. In a predominantly agrarian society, where land is an important asset, it was hailed as radical legislation since it reversed the traditional practice where women were only eligible to inherit movable property. However, since the implementation of this reform, women have rarely exercised this right. They generally waive their claims in favour of their brothers or are intimidated into relinquishing their rights. While this applied largely to upper caste land-owning families, a new phenomenon was now emerging in communities which previously had no custom of dowry.

They were turning away from customary bride price and were adopting the giving of 'dowry'. For some scholars this change signified 'sanskritisation' while others attributed the rise in demand for dowry partly to the monetisation and commercialisation of the economy. Dowry, far from being a marker of a 'backward' traditional mentality, has emerged as a very modern phenomenon, with educated men demanding more in accordance with their professional status. A number of women's groups brought to public attention increasing cases of women who were being abused emotionally or physically for the amount of dowry they brought into marriage.

In a growing number of cases women were murdered. In the late 1970s a number of feminist organisations in Delhi carried out a sustained campaign of demonstrations, street theatre and exhibitions to highlight the dowry-related crimes which were previously ignored by the media and the general public. Dowry deaths that had been hidden in police reports as suicides were now exposed as murders. In May 1979 a young woman, Tarvinder Kaur, was killed because of her parents' inability to fulfill the demands of her in-laws. It seems that like many women throughout India she was under constant pressure to procure more money from her parents to finance her husband's business. The protests that followed her death drew wide media coverage. 'Within weeks, feminists reversed the indifference of decades, linking death-by fire with dowry harassment, showing that many official suicides were in fact murders.'

The campaigns against dowry harassment have continued in the form of protests, often involving demonstrations in the husband's neighbourhood or workplace. In response to these actions the state has been prompted to adopt legal measures. These include, compulsory investigation and post-mortems of married women who have died within seven years of marriage; changes to criminal laws which encourage prosecution of dowry murders; and the establishment of anti-dowry harassment cells within the police force where women report dowry harassment. Amendments to the Indian penal code made cruelty to a woman by her husband or any relatives a crime punishable by imprisonment. In a significant departure from earlier laws, the definition of cruelty was extended to include mental cruelty.

Whether these actions have resulted in any marked improvement in the status of women remains open to question. Paradoxically, demands by the women's movement to protect women against violence may have the unintended effect of relegating women to the familial sphere. Nevertheless, one of the major gains of the period is the public way violence against women was linked to the cultural dimensions of gender relations in India.

ANTI-RAPE CAMPAIGNS

The print media in India has sympathetically reported the issues of violence against women. In the late 1970s the acquittal of two policemen accused of raping a young woman at a police station provoked national outrage. The anger galvanised a major campaign for the women's movement and subsequently laid the foundation for the emergence of a number of feminist organisations. These include the Bombay based Forum Against Rape (which later changed its name to Forum Against Oppression of Women, to indicate its wider objective), Stri Sangarsh in Delhi, and the Stri Mukti Andolan Sampark Samiti.

The 'Mathura rape case', as it came to be known, sharpened the focus of public discussion about the endemic violation of women's rights in India. Mathura a sixteen year old tribal girl, who had lost both her parents in childhood and who worked as a maid servant, was raped by two policemen within a police compound in Desai Ganj, a small village in Chadrapur District of Maharashtra. She was brought to the police station around 9 pm on 26 March 1972, on a complaint filed by her own brother that she had eloped with her lover. When she along with her relatives, were about to leave the police station around 10.30 pm, she was detained by two constables, Tukaram and Ganpat. She was taken to the rear side and was raped by Ganpat, while Tukaram looked on. He too would have raped her, but was too drunk to do so. So he had to content himself by merely molesting her.

In 1974, the Sessions Court found the two constables 'not guilty' on the grounds that Mathura must have consented since she was an unmarried girl 'habituated to sexual intercourse'. It was also noted that she did not display any visible signs of physical injury. On appeal, the High Court reversed this decision and concluded that passive submission under threat did not imply consent. The accused men, who had been dismissed from the police force, appealed to the Supreme Court, which in turn reversed the High Court's ruling. In 1978 the Supreme Court justices found, 'no reason to doubt that a nice girl-impoverished, powerless and frightened though she might be-would have resisted the orders of two armed police officers' original emphasis.

The Supreme Court's judgement was widely condemned. In particular four eminent law professors (two of who were women) wrote an open letter to the Chief Justice of India. The letter was also circulated widely, revealing the antiquated rape laws, the biased and conservative views of the judiciary and above all the utter failure of the legal system to extend human rights to the protection of women, especially the poor, illiterate and the powerless. Following the circulation of the letter, agitation around rape issues gained momentum, involving not only feminist organisations, but also civil liberties groups, lawyers and political parties.

It generated massive public debate and exposed the systematic sexual assault of women by those in positions of authority such as the police, the armed forces, prison wardens, hospital management and so on. The significance of mass rape in Indian society as a retaliation and assertion of power against groups who are in the process of challenging their subordinate status and the rape of individual women in marginalised communities became the focal points of these debates.

As a result of the mounting pressure the government established the 84th Law Commission and submissions were heard from women's groups throughout India. Consequently, in 1983 the Criminal Law (Amendment) Bill focused almost exclusively on custodial rape. The burden of proof rested on the accused only in cases of custodial rape and there was to be a minimum sentence of 10 years. Although the Law Commission's recommendations included the major demands of the women's organisations-such as the onus of proof being placed on the accused; the women's right to privacy regarding her past sexual history; immediate medical examination of both the accused and victim-in practice these were ignored.

Several women's organisations had argued that custodial rape should not only apply to state officials but should also be extended to include employers, money-lenders, contractors and land lords who routinely terrorize economically vulnerable women into submission either by the threat or actual committal of rape. In other words, a specific category-'economic rape' or 'power rape'-should be included. The emphasis on custodial rape also left unchallenged familial rape, particularly rape within marriage. Women's groups had demanded that there be in camera trials. Instead the government imposed a ban on press reporting of rape cases on the pretext of protecting the identity of the victim.

This was an ironic outcome since it was largely due to the positive role of the media that the campaigns became widely known. The legal changes were a minor victory for women's rights. The most important aspect of the agitation, once again, was the increasing public awareness of violence against women and the breaking of the taboo surrounding rape. Social attitudes towards rape have remained ambiguous; violation of honour and the stigma attached to the victim have not disappeared. Yet it seems more women now have the courage to report it.

COMMUNALISATION OF GENDER IDENTITY

As we have seen through the 1970s and 1980s, violence against women was a rallying point for the women's movement. During this period there was broad ideological unity about the key issues affecting women's status. However, this situation changed in the mid-1980s for two reasons -the emergence and growth of identity politics and the rise in fundamentalist and religious revivalist ideologies. A combination of social forces underpinned these developments including, rapid economic transformation; general feelings of the loss of identity; and reactions against the assertion of new confidence by those inspired by feminist and other egalitarian ideologies. Of particular concern was the confidence of the raising 'backward' castes-the hitherto marginalised groups who were gaining a political voice. On the whole, political actions of the 1980s were characterised by the struggle to control meaning and symbols rather than material resources.

Since independence the government of India has made some attempts to provide affirmative action for historically disadvantaged groups. There are quotas reserved for 'scheduled' castes and tribes in government employment and education. In the Indian Constitution disadvantaged groups are classified under a schedule for taking affirmative action in their favour. This is largely based on the census classification of communities developed during the colonial period. In 1990 the government implemented the recommendations of the Mandal Commission that the quotas should be extended to 'other backward castes' (OBCs). This resulted in a backlash from the dominant castes in many parts of India. If the recommendations are followed this would offer greater opportunities for women from dalit communities (oppressed castes).

The centrality of women in the construction of community identity gained significance during this decade. Previously within the movement issues about the woman's body representing the community had been widely debated in the analysis of rape as assertion of male power- particularly its use as a form of reprisal against women of 'other' communities. This practice entails notions of the violation of male honour, i.e. loss of control over 'their' women. Feminists during the 1970s and early 1980s had spoken out on issues of violence in terms of domestic violence, individual, familial and mass rape. By the end of the 1980s a different threat of violence came from fundamentalism, which, in this case, was largely Hindu.

The rise of fundamentalism is a global phenomenon. It is difficult to identify the exact reasons for its emergence at this particular juncture. It has been argued that resurgence in crises of cultural identity are more pronounced in areas of uneven capitalist development where the advantages of economic development have not benefited people equally. The resulting frustration over the inability to control resources has led some groups to seek self-affirmation through a return to 'traditional' community. Here, women's roles are used as markers of community. We also find that during colonial periods, the status of women was used as a measure of civilisation.

The identity of people centred on women. Currently, as post-colonial states are engaged in a similar process of constructing their identity in a rapidly changing world, women's roles are used to symbolise the cultural essence of communities or even the nation. Whatever the reasons, in the current Indian context it becomes increasingly evident that the state has adopted a communalist posture. When disenchantment grew with the failure of the Indian state to deliver the fruits of development, it cynically utilised the 'communal card' to win electoral support. The impact of communalism seriously jeopardised the questions of gender justice. The following two cases-the Shah Bano controversy and the death of Roop Kanwar-exemplify how demands of communalist forces were utilised to side-step the issue of gender justice.

In India there are no uniform civil laws with regards to the rights of women in matters of family, marriage, child custody and inheritance. This was part of the British legacy, and although it aimed to allow for the maintenance of customary laws of different communities, in practice it had the effect of rigidly codifying practices that were previously fluid and localised. However, uniform criminal laws were developed under colonial rule. After independence, the government was unwilling to confront the question of implementing a uniform civil code due to the devastating communal riots and disunity that followed partition.

The lawmakers, with their emphasis on a secular India-which guaranteed the freedom of all religious communities-were reluctant to interfere in matters of personal law. After all, it was envisaged that personal laws would enable the communities to maintain their distinct identity. By contrast, women's organisations had pressed for a uniform civil code since 1936. Their aim was to formulate common laws that would provide gender justice since the rights of women were secondary within all religious communities. Here we see the contradictory aspects of the Constitution relating to women's rights. On the one hand, it promises equality for women as individual citizens. On the other, women's individual rights conflict with their membership of collective communities.

The following discussion of the Shah Bano case highlights the complex relationship between gender and community identity. A 73 year-old Muslim woman, Shah Bano, petitioned the courts to obtain maintenance from her husband who had divorced her after forty-three years of marriage. She applied under the Criminal Procedure Code Section 125, which entitles destitute, deserted and divorced women to maintenance from their former husbands. The courts ruled in her favour, but her husband Mohammad Ahmed Khan, himself an advocate, appealed to the Supreme Court.

He argued that laws relating to marriage and divorce were outside of the court's jurisdiction, adding that as a Muslim he had abided by Muslim Personal Law which required him to pay maintenance during the initial three months of separation-a period known as *iddat*. However, he was not obliged to pay maintenance from three months after the divorce. In order to arrive at a judgement the Supreme Court consulted the Quran since Shah Bano's counsel had cited verses from the Quran to lend support to the idea that the righteous had a duty to provide a reasonable maintenance. The Supreme Court's ruling in 1985 can be described in the following terms:

First it upheld Shah Bano's right to maintenance and both under Section 125 and under Muslim personal law. Second, it asserted that Section 125 'cut across the barriers of religion', that is, it transcended the personal laws of the religious communities which a given married pair might belong to. Third, it was critical of the way women 'have been traditionally subject to unjust treatment' and urged the government to frame a common civil code.

Although, most of the liberal Muslim intelligentsia along with women's groups and democratic organisations supported the court's decision (whilst remaining critical of the judiciary's attempt to link religious matters to the civil code), this ruling enraged a section of the Muslim community. Fundamentalist Muslims mobilised populist support against the uniform civil code, arguing that such interference with Personal Laws meant an end to a distinct Muslim identity and began a campaign of 'Islam in Danger'. Feminists campaigning for a uniform civil code were joined by the most unlikely of supporters-Hindu communalists. However, Hindu chauvinists did not support the demand for a uniform civil code because they were interested in the rights of Muslim women. Rather they wanted Muslims to conform to the 'national mainstream'. Inflammatory remarks about '*barbaric* Muslims' were made frequently and communal violence was incited across northern India.

Meanwhile a Muslim League MP drafted the Muslim Women's Bill that would exclude divorced Muslim women from section 125. The ruling Congress Party government opportunistically supported the bill, which stated that husbands were not obliged to maintain their wives three months after the divorce. It would be the responsibility of the woman's natal family to support her and those who could not afford to do so could appeal to their local Waqf board (private Islamic charitable organisations). Women's organisations, the progressive Muslim intelligentsia and major political parties opposed the Bill.

The government had previously suffered an electoral backlash as Muslims turned away from the Congress Party, so, in a bid to capture the 'Muslim vote' the government appeased Muslim conservatives and finally passed the Muslim Women's Bill in February 1986. The Shah Bano case was a blow to the demand for a uniform civil code. In 1987 Roop Kanwar, an educated 18-year-old woman committed sati (widow self-immolation), on the funeral pyre of her husband in the northwestern province of Rajasthan. After it had been announced that Roop Kanwar would undergo *sati-daha* (the act of committing sati), the Rajasthan government, under pressure from several groups, prohibited the ceremony.

However, thousands gathered at the ceremony in defiance of a court order. Later the location was accorded the status of a pilgrimage site. In their opposition to this incident feminists were portrayed as a Westernised urban élite with little sympathy or understanding of the deeply held beliefs of 'real' people. For example, Prabhash Joshi wrote in the newspaper *Jansatta* on 18 September 1987,

This incident is one of the innumerable contradictions of our country where millions of people think in a way that is radically different from that of a handful of those who man the courts and the government, and who live among English educated people...sati is not an ordinary occurrence. One out of a million widows takes a vow to commit sati and it is but natural that her Roop Kanwar's supreme sacrifice becomes the centre of people's worship and reverence. Therefore, this cannot be seen either as an issue of women's civil rights or of discrimination between men and women. It is simply a question of a society's social and religious beliefs.

An issue of fundamental women's rights was suddenly framed in terms of a simplistic tradition/modernity dichotomy- a struggle of the religious majority against an irreligious minority. Presented in this way, feminists were ridiculed as agents of evil Western ways. Yet, as a number of observers indicate, this was the re-invention of tradition. Far from being a place of worship, the *sati-sthal* resembled a political rally. Thousands of young men in their 20s and 30s gathered to chant slogans. The sentiments expressed among the supporters of sati were remarkably similar to the Shah Bano case.

As Prof Zoya Hasan, has explained,

The issue is not one of conflict between tradition and modernity, but the organised revival of tradition made worse by the Indian State's compromise with the forces of tradition for the sake of political survival...sati or dowry deaths or the denial of the rights of Muslim women have become contemporary phenomena. 'Sati' as indeed the reactions against the Shah Bano judgement, was not spontaneous responses of people who were steeped in tradition, and therefore determined to protest their religious identity. As a matter of fact, both issues were set off by an organised campaign that involved evoking religious sanction to assert a distinct political identity.

Sati had become a symbol of identity in response to the declining legitimacy of the land owning Rajput community. The Rajput (warrior) and Marwari (money-lending) castes had lost their traditional power as a consequence of the land reforms that took place in Rajasthan in the 1950s.The revival of *sati-daha* was a reassertion of their identity.

In the wake of communal violence the complex nature of identity and difference among women became apparent. What were the implications for those seeking change under a common umbrella of women's interests? First, it was evident that women did not speak with one voice in their efforts to construct identities. Nor did their interests cut across classes and communities. Second, it was incorrect to assume a convergence of their political orientations. For example, in the 1970s and early 1980s women's groups were guided by a broadly left orientation. By the end of the 1980s the presence of women within the religious right had gained prominence.

Third, it seemed that at times women's rights could be at odds with rights of minorities. In the case of Roop Kanwar thousands of women supported *sati-daha,* while the Shah Bano judgement, an apparently just cause for women's rights had turned into a ploy to harass a religious minority. As a consequence, women's rights were sacrificed. In the decade that has passed since the Shah Bano controversy erupted communal tensions have intensified and the prospect of a uniform code seems remote.

COMMUNALISM AND FEMINIST SCHOLARSHIP

The aggressive communalism of Hindu chauvinists has sparked scholarly efforts to trace the roots of the current communal tensions to the emergence of nationalism in the nineteenth century. Studies investigating stereotypes that were created by colonisers as well as the oppositional identities that were constructed by Indian nationalists were examined. Focusing on a majority Hindu identity, this research was devoted to the study of the colonial period and understanding the formation of colonial subjectivities through 'colonial discourses'. These studies emphasise colonial domination and its response to the creation of a nationalist identity and as such overlook much of the pre-colonial origins of caste hierarchies and domination.

In the context of feminist scholarship this uncovered the notion that nationalist discourse categorised the 'Indian woman' as Hindu, urban, Brahmin (upper caste) and middle-class. Over a period of time these specific markers were not mentioned and the interventions of non-Brahmin women were rendered invisible. In post-independence India, particularly in the 1970s and 1980s feminists pursuing women's rights invoked the language of citizenship that implicitly denied caste and community. However, as far as women's rights in the uniform civil code are concerned, some observers in India contend that it is no longer possible to produce feminists concerns in terms of unproblematic 'human rights' or 'citizen's' rights.

Given the evolution of current communal politics women's groups are now completely rethinking issues of gender. There is urgency within the women's movement to 'evolve a new form of politics that will among other things seriously engage with issues of caste and religious community'. In order to mobilise women, the feminist movement in India tried to appropriate symbols from the Indian tradition, such as the use of the goddess imagery, as source for empowerment. This was particularly necessary because they had consciously tried to develop a mode of feminism that was distinct from Western feminism. Madhu Kishwar, the editor of *Manushi* once argued the need to draw from Indian cultural traditions which people hold dear.

It was important to have an understanding of the images that have a powerful force in the hearts and minds of women 'to identify their points of strength and use them creatively'. She claimed this at a time when religious fundamentalism was on the increase. It was especially important that 'anti-women' forces did not seize a monopoly on religious and cultural symbols. However, the search for this kind of gender symbolism today is fraught with problems. At the time the goddess image was an effective and powerful source for the women's movement, but in recent years it has been shown to be alienating for minority women since it derives from the majority Hindu tradition.

Redressing the disparity between formal political equality and the meaningful exercise of political power was one of the major platforms of the women's movement. Bridging the gap between rhetoric and reality is seen as a precondition to the empowerment of women. Two issues that I want to take up now are the conditions surrounding women's economic and political participation. The changes that have taken place in recent years will radically impact on women's lives in the new century. These changes concern the Indian government's efforts to liberalise the economy and the constitutional amendments to statutory reserve quotas for women in local self-government.

An important political innovation since Indian independence has been the creation of *Panchayati Raj*-elected self-governing bodies at the village level. Its architects believed that efforts had to be made to democratise local institutions, without which development would be ineffective. As we have seen, the growth of informal political activity through the women's movement has been widespread. Yet, women's participation in the formal political structure has not improved greatly. During the period 1971-77 women constituted 3.8 per cent of the representatives in the Lok Sabha (the lower house of Parliament). This had only increased to 7.2 per cent by the end of 1992. To expand women's participation in grass roots political institutions-the *Panchayati Raj*-legislation was introduced to reserve 30 per cent of the total seats for women. Within this quota one third of seats are reserved for women from scheduled castes and tribes.

As early as 1959, recommendations were made to secure representation of minorities and especially women in the Panchayati Raj. The underlying reasoning was the recognition of the crucial role of women as active participants in the development process rather than passive recipients of its benefits. However, it was not until 1993 that the 73rd Constitutional Amendment Bill was enacted to reserve one third of the seats for women. Effective implementation of the 73rd Amendment would mean that about a million women would be able to enter national politics. However evidence to date on participation in decision making in decentralised governance shows that in most cases, women's roles have been actually performed by male members of the family.

A recent study by Bhaskar on the social backgrounds of women candidates has also revealed a conventional social pattern of gendered public activity. That is, the overwhelming majority of women members are married (95.2 per cent). They are generally older (aged 35-45), the ideal age when they can combine family and political roles (mostly after completing their reproductive tasks) and only 3 per cent are in full-time paid employment. Their occupational status shows that 55 per cent are non-earning members, dependant on either their spouses or fathers.

ECONOMIC LIBERALISATION AND GLOBAL INTEGRATION

In the late 1980s India reversed earlier policies of protecting domestic industry and began to pursue economic liberalisation. In 1991 this direction was consolidated in the New Economic Policy. In keeping with the requirements of international lending institutions such as the IMF and World Bank, structural adjustment policies have been formulated with the aim of increasing global competitiveness via trade liberalisation and export-led growth. The Indian government's structural adjustment policies have proposed reductions in public sector employment, limitations on agricultural subsidies, de-nationalisation of banks and insurance companies and reductions in public expenditure.

Some social scientists have considered the implications of economic liberalisation and forecast that the dramatic shift in economic policy and especially the rapid opening up to the world market will polarise Indian society as never before. In particular, it has been argued that economic liberalisation and marketisation will reinforce asymmetrical gender relations. While it is clear that marginalised groups will be adversely affected, it is the expansion of the middle class that has influenced the direction of economic policy.

Its growth has already attracted considerable world attention in terms of the size and number of consumers in the global market. To foreign investors and government officials it offers a very attractive market for transnational corporations. Forty million Indians have annual incomes with the purchasing power of US$600 000 per annum and a further 190 million have incomes of US$20 000. The effects of structural adjustment policies on women elsewhere suggest that with growing inequalities the burden will be shifted to women.

Feminists in India are concerned that gender issues will be seriously compromised as liberalisation proceeds. The evidence suggests that 'privatisation of public sector enterprises, reduction in investment in public sector units and lower government expenditure on poverty eradication programs will hurt the interests of women'. Moreover, the proportion of women workers will fall because it is the public sector rather than the private sector that has favoured the recruitment of women. Reduced employment opportunities resulting from the new economic policy have affected women directly and indirectly. The trade liberalisation policies have attempted to integrate women into the global economy, particularly through export processing industries and the expansion of export processing zones.

However, their job securities are threatened by the prohibition on unionisation and decentralisation though subcontracting. A recent study examining the impact of the New Economic Policy on 610 women workers in five industries shows that 'the status of women's employment has moved toward being irregular and casual and the few who had some measure of protection are now facing the threat of losing their jobs'. On the one hand, it is anticipated that the unorganised sector will grow since the absence of labour legislation makes it attractive for employers to recruit women.

On the other, in areas like the agro-processing industry where women work in large numbers, the import of modem technology in industries which are to be taken over by corporations such as Kellog, Pepsi, Nestlé and General Foods will reduce employment in low-skilled jobs. At the same time, because the provision of education is now premised on 'user-pays' principles, the prospects for the retraining of women in technical skills seem limited-particularly for poor women. However, let us be clear that prior to liberalisation women did not fare substantially better. Although the state created jobs for women as rural functionaries and reservation policies allowed *dalit* women to gain education and employment, the development model did not benefit women.

Lip-service was paid to 'socialism', but in reality it did not seriously challenge class interests. For example, the 'green revolution' created a capitalist class in the countryside, while rural landlessness increased. Nevertheless, market reforms are unlikely to offer better solutions to women in changing the sexual division of labour in Indian society. Earlier studies of women producing for the world market show this to be the case. In the 1970s a major study of lace makers in India showed that caste ideology of female seclusion was compatible with the piecework system of lace production. The lace industry rapidly expanded during the 1970s due to international demand. However, the exporters made no efforts to improve conditions and women continued to work on a piece-rate basis from home since the prevailing ideology saw the work of the 'housewife' as supplementary.

At the beginning of the new millennium the major challenges for women in India present a conundrum-the need to forge alliances to fight against the adverse socio-economic conditions of women comes into direct conflict with the reality of differences among women. It is clear that interests of Indian women are not identical. Yet, whether these differences become divisive and a hindrance to gender justice remains to be seen. Women are now caught in a bind. If they speak of common roots, they will not only end up idealising tradition but also risk drawing from symbols that are unacceptable to a cross-section of women. The alternative may be to invoke a secular cosmopolitanism-but neither is this view shared by all women.

In this scenario the existence of a syncretic tradition, removed from both upper caste Brahmanism and ascetic Islam, seems to be forgotten. Until some form of new syncreticism emerges the scope for alliance will be hampered. Thus, at the end of the twentieth century the differences among Indian women are more than an empirical fact of diversity. A complex picture emerges of the ways in which gender, caste and class influence one another. More significantly, despite the need to recognise diversity and difference there are certain homogenising forces at work, namely the normalising process of the nation-state and the increasingly powerful forces of the global economy.

Bibliography

Andrews, B., Brewin, C. R., Rose, S., et al. 2000. "Predicting PTSD Symptoms in Victims of Violent Crime: The Role of Shame, Anger, and Childhood Abuse." *Journal of abnormal psychology* 109: 69-73.

Baldinger, B. G., and Nelson, D. T. 1995. "Crime Victims and Psychological Injuries." *Trial* 31: 56.

Bisson, J. I., and Shepherd, J. P. 1995. "Psychological reactions of victims of violent crime." *The British journal of psychiatry* 167: 718.

Bjerregaard, B. 2000. "An Empirical Study of Stalking Victimization." Violence and Victims 15: 389-406.

Black, J. 1995. "Rethinking the naming of sex crime victims." *Newspaper Research Journal* 16: 96.

Blackburn, S. 1999. "Gender Violence and the Indonesian Political Transition." *Asian Studies Review* 23: 433-448.

Breault, K. D., and Kposowa, A. J. 1997. "The Effects of Marital Status on Adult Female Homicides in the United States." *Journal of Quantitative Criminology* 13: 217-230.

Bubar, Roe, and Pamela Jumper Thurman. 2004. "Violence Against Native Women." *Social justice: a journal of crime, conflict & world order*. 31(4): 70 (17 pages).

Chilton, R., and Jarvis, J. 1999. "Victims and Offenders in Two Crime Statistics Programs: A Comparison of the National Incident-Based Reporting System (NIBRS) and the National Crime Victimization Survey (NCVS)." *Journal of Quantitative Criminology* 15: 193-205.

Cling, B. J., *Sexualized Violence against Women and Children: A Psychology and Law Perspective*. The Guilford Press: 2004.

Davis, K. E., and Frieze, I. H. 2000. "Research on Stalking: What Do We Know and Where Do We Go?" *Violence and Victims* 15: 473-487.

Denkers, A. J .M., and Winkel., F. W. 1998. "Crime victims well being and fear in a prospective and longitudinal study." *Sage Urban Studies Abstracts* 26.

Dunn, J. L. 2001. "Innocence Lost: Accomplishing Victimization in Intimate Stalking Cases." *Symbolic Interaction* 24: 285-313.

Dwyer, D. C. 1995. "Response to the Victims of Domestic Violence: Analysis and Implications of the British Experience." *Crime and Delinquency* 41: 527-541.

Epstein, J. N., Saunders, B. E., and Kilpatrick, D. G. 1997. "Predicting PTSD in Women with a History of Childhood Rape." *Journal of Traumatic Stress* 10: 573-588.

Erez, E., Laster, K. 1999. "Neutralizing Victim Reform: Legal Professionals' Perspectives on Victims and Impact Statements." *Crime & Delinquency* 45: 530-553.

Fenwick, H. 1996. "The rights of victims of crime: Protection from harassment and intimidation?" *The Journal of criminal law* 60: 84-93.

Gartner, R., Dawson, M., and Crawford, M. 1998/1999. "Woman Killing: Intimate Femicide in Ontario, 19741994." *Resources for Feminist Research* 26: 151-173.

Gaumer, C. P. 1995. "Protecting the Innocent: Victim-Witness Rights in Illinois." *Illinois bar journal* 83: 568.

Hart, B. In: Eds. 1996. *Battered Women and the Criminal Justice System.* Thousand Oaks, CA: Sage Publications, pp 98-114.

Herman, S., and Wasserman, C. 2001. "A Role for Victims in Offender Reentry." *Crime & Delinquency* 47:428-445.

Johnson, K. W. 1997. "Professional Help and Crime Victims." *The Social service review* 71: 89-109.

Kalaher, K. 1997. "The Proposed Victim's Rights Amendment: Taking a Bite Out of Crime or a Dog With No Teeth?" *Seton Hall legislative journal* 22: 317.

Kamphuis, J. H., and Emmelkamp, P. M. G. 1998. "Crime-Related Trauma: Psychological Distress in Victims of Bankrobbery." *Journal of anxiety disorders* 12: 199-208.

Katz, J. 1997. "Staying Alive: Women Who Saved Their Own Lives." *Cosmopolitan* 222: 188.

Kenney, J. S. 2002. "Victims of Crime and Labeling Theory: A Parallel Process?" *Deviant behavior* 23: 235-266.

Kumar, G. S. J. 1997. "Victimization of Women: Coping with Violence." *International Journal of Sociology of the Family* 27: 139-155.

Kury , H. Ferdinand., T. 1998. "The Victim's Experience and Fear of Crime." *Sage Urban Studies Abstracts* 26.

Lowenstein, L. F. 2000. "Victims of Violent Crime Leading to Post-Traumatic Stress Disorders." *The Police journal* 73: 256-262.

Lurigio, A. J. 2000. "Are all victims alike? The adverse, generalized and differential impact of crime." *Violence and Abuse Abstracts* 6.

Madriz, E. I. 1997. "Images of Criminals and Victims: A Study on Women's Fear and Social Control." *Gender & Society* 11: 342-356.

Marietta, J. D., and Rowe, G. S. 1999. "Violent Crime, Victims, and Society in Pennsylvania, 1682-1800." *Pennsylvania history* 66.

Martens, P. L. 2002. "Immigrants as victims of crime." *Violence & Abuse Abstracts* 8: 3-84.

McPhail, Beverly A. 2002. "Gender-Bias Hate Crimes: A Review." *Trauma, Violence, & Abuse: A Review Journal* 3: 125-143.

Mesch, G. S. 2000. "Women's Fear of Crime: The Role of Fear for the Well-Being of Significant Others." *Violence and Victims* 15: 323-336.

Nettleton, H., Walklate, S., and Williams, B. 1997. "Three Models of Probation Involvement with Victims of Crime." *The Liverpool law review* 19: 203.

Peltzer, K. 2000. "Risk for traumatization among violent crime victims in an urban community sample in South Africa." *Curationis* 23: 22-27.

Petersilia, J. R. 2001. "Crime Victims With Develo-pmental Disabilities: A Review Essay." *Criminal Justice and Behavior* 28: 655-694.

Pino, N. W., and Meier, R. F. 1999. "Gender Differences in Rape Reporting." *Sex Roles* 40: 979-990.

Ruback, R. B., Menard, K. S., Outlaw, M. C., et al. 1999. "Normative Advice to Campus Crime Victims: Effects of Gender, Age, and Alcohol." *Violence and victims* 14: 381-396.

Sebba, L. 2001. "On the relationship between criminological research and policy: The case of crime victims." *Criminal Justice* 1: 27-58.

Wadham, J., and Arkinstall, J. 2000. "Rights of victims of crime explain how victims' rights will be affected by the Human Rights Act." *The New law journal* 6943: 1023-1024.

Weinrath, M., and Gartrell, J. 1996. "Victimization and Fear of Crime." *Violence and Victims* 11: 187-197.

Weisman, C. S. 1995. "Armed by Fear: Self-Defense Handguns and Women's Health." *Women's Health Issues* 5: 3-7.

Yee, J. L., and Greenberg, M. S. 1998. "Reactions to Crime Victims: Effects of Victims' Emotional State and Type of Relationship." *Journal of Social and Clinical Psychology* 17: 209-226.

Index